age Hospital Grows Up

The Hospital Seal  1938

The General Hospital

# A COTTAGE HOSPITAL GROWS UP

## The Story of the Queen Victoria Hospital
### East Grinstead

E. J. DENNISON

BAXENDALE PRESS

© E. J. DENNISON

UPDATED EDITION BAXENDALE PRESS 1996

FIRST PUBLISHED ANTHONY BLOND 1963

TYPESETTING BY BAVERSTOCK PRESS

PRINTED BY ANTONY ROWE LIMITED

PRODUCED IN GREAT BRITAIN

PUBLISHED AND DISTRIBUTED BY BAXENDALE PRESS

26 ALBION SQUARE LONDON E8 4ES

TEL: 0171 249 0886

ISBN 0 9520 933 91

BRITISH LIBRARY CATALOGUING-IN-PUBLICATION DATA

A CATALOGUE RECORD FOR THIS BOOK IS AVAILABLE FROM

THE BRITISH LIBRARY

To all those who have contributed
in any way whatsoever to
the growth of the Queen Victoria Hospital.

# Contents

# Illustrations

# Introduction

OVER the years there have been many requests for a second edition of this book and I did think about publishing an updated edition of it in 1988 which was the 125th anniversary of the Hospital's foundation. As readers will find, however, the late 1980's was not one of its happiest periods; there was widespread gloom as to our future at that time, even as to whether we would survive at all, and I did not feel inclined to write about it. Today, however, there is a different feeling altogether, and this, coupled with the fact that both the Hospital Librarian and the East Grinstead Public Library told me recently that the book is still in constant demand, has persuaded me to do so. I have kept the first edition intact, so this edition consists of the original first edition, together with two new updating chapters, covering the years 1963 to 1995.

I have deliberately, as far as possible, kept politics out of the text of this second edition. Politicians come and go, and it is a fact that since the Government took over our Medical Services in 1948, there have been no fewer than 21 different Ministers of Health, and they have of course between them been in charge of the Service for very nearly 50 years. Having read through most of the Reports aimed at improving the Service, the three Cogwheel Reports, the Samuel Report, the Royal Commission, the Griffiths Report, and various Working Parties, I have found one constantly recurring theme; almost universally they recommend that there should be more participation in management by the Medical profession. In this connection it is interesting that in 1991 the British Association of Medical Managers was founded, with Sir Roy Griffiths as its first patron, and that it runs special courses to train doctors in Hospital Management.

Some readers will notice that at the end of the first edition, in 1963, we had a total of 316 beds, and that in our application for Independent Trust Status in 1993 we had 206. The explanation

7

of this is of course the closure of the 50 beds at Oakleigh, together with Wagg Ward with its 30 beds having become a Day Centre, and Kelsey Fry and McIndoe Wards with 30 beds each being partially given over to Outpatients. These rearrangements have been fully described in the text, and are of course due to modern improvements in medical and surgical technology, also fully described in the text. The Queen Victoria Hospital can in fact be looked upon as having, over the years, modernised itself.

Altogether, what with new Management, new Independent Trust Status, the new Burns Unit, the projected new Day Theatre scheduled to be functioning by early next year, plus the Management's purchase of the waste land at the rear of the Hospital to make room for further expansion, together with the enormous enthusiasm that I found, on a recent visit to the Hospital, on the part of everybody concerned with it, and with our ever vigilant local press, I feel confident that my successor will in the year 2013 be able to write a third edition of its history to celebrate the 150th anniversary of this thoroughly modern Hospital.

E. J. Dennison 1995

Wray Corner
Reigate

# Acknowledgements to 1st Edition

THE Queen Victoria Hospital is unique whatever way one looks at it, and it was crying out, so it seemed to me, for somebody to write its story. I wondered at first whether there would be sufficient material to make a full-length book, but very soon found there was more than enough. I have tried throughout to show the steady growth of the Hospital, and to mention as many as possible of the literally hundreds of people who over the years have contributed in some way to this growth. If any have been left out I offer them my apologies. The main sources of my information have been the various committee minute books, extending, with one notable gap, from 1888 to the present day.

I have been fortunate all the way through in meeting with willing co-operation on all sides and I particularly would like to acknowledge the help I have received from:—

Mr. T. John Shields, Librarian of the British Medical Association who kindly obtained and lent me the three early books by Dr. Waring, Dr. Horace Swete and Sir Henry Burdett; Mr. Baldock, Chairman of the Cranleigh Village Hospital, Mr. G. A. Gibbs, Secretary of the West Cornwall Hospital Management Committee, Mr. C. G. Tomlinson, Secretary of the Banbury and District Hospitals Management Committee, and Mr. G. R. L. Heasman, Secretary of the Iver, Denham and Langley Cottage Hospital, who kindly sent me the particulars of the early and recent history of these hospitals and permission to mention them.

I am also particularly want to thank Mr. and Mrs. R. G. Andrews for so kindly allowing me to inspect the original Cottage Hospital in Green Hedges Avenue, which is now their home.

I am very grateful to Mr. Wagstaff, Secretary of the Tunbridge Wells Group Management Committee for depositing the old Queen Victoria Hospital Minute Books in our Library here, and to Mr. John Watson, in charge of the Library, for making these books freely available to me: also to Mr. Johns, Secretary of the Queen Victoria Hospital for his co-operation in lending me certain old books including the delightful original casebook written in Dr. Rogers' own hand, and for his help generally; also to Mr. Moore, Assistant Secretary, for making the recent House Committee Minute Books available to me, and most especially to Mr. J. H. Mitchell, Chairman, and members of his House Committee, for their permission to quote from these books. I am also particularly grateful to Dr. Russell M. Davies for several suggestions and much helpful information and advice, and to Mr. Gordon Clemetson for his technical help with the photographs.

I owe a special thank-you to Mrs. Clemetson, Editor of the Kent & Sussex Courier, not only for several quotations from her paper, but also for her co-operation in lending me all the original papers in connection with the Peanut Ward and the Corneal Graft Bill, and for her own story of the Peanut Club.

To Mr. Hollingdale, News Editor of the East Grinstead Observer also a very special thank-you for his co-operation in giving me access to a number of reports of special events and some of the pictures from his paper.

Mrs. Kirkhope comes high on the list and I wish to thank her for the loan of several of her late husband's papers, for his photograph and for her keen support.

I want also to thank Lady McIndoe for the loan of Sir Archibald's photograph, and for her encouragement. The one deep regret I have over this publication is that Archie died on the very day I had set aside to tell him about it; I think had he known of it, he would have approved.

Mr. Burgess also I thank most sincerely for lending me all the Minute Books of the Working Men's Fund and numerous other papers; Lady Kindersley for her interest and a number of otherwise unknown facts and figures; Mr. Alfred Wagg for some personal letters, some research and again general encouragement, and Mr. J. E. Blacksell for much helpful information about the Guinea Pig Club. I am grateful also to Miss Clare Blount for the loan of her father's photograph, to Mr. Tom Rowntree for the reproduction of his father's portrait, and to Mr. John Smith for the photograph of his great-aunt Mrs. Oswald Smith. Mr. Fred Gear has lent me a number of old reports and papers from which I have gathered some useful information and for which I thank him, as also Mr. Michael Leppard for the extracts from the old Parish Magazines. I wish to thank also the heads of the various Hospital Departments for their co-operation in giving me the up-to-date figures and facts about the work going on in the Hospital today, and especially Mr. John Watson for the technical information about the new Laboratories. Last but by no means least my thanks are due to my secretary, Mrs. Audrey Allen, who worked as a Medical Secretary at the Hospital during the war years, for making a number of suggestions and for the endless typing and re-typing.

E. J. Dennison 1963

# Acknowledgements for updated Edition

EVERYBODY whom I have asked for advice or assistance in preparing this second edition of the Queen Victoria Hospital's history has been, as I found when writing the first edition, very helpful and co-operative. I have wanted to do it for some years, and I am grateful to Mr. Park and the Trust Board for their unquestioning acceptance of my wish, and to Mrs. Clifton for having given it her official blessing; to her Executive Assistant Marilyn Davis, and Sheila Averill, for their help generally and for searching the Hospital cellars to try and find certain missing documents, and particularly to the latter for giving me so much of her time showing me all the departmental rearrangements that have taken place since 1963.

I am grateful once again to the Librarians at the British Medical Association who have supplied me with details of the many Committee Reports that have affected us all so much over the years; to Lady McIndoe for her description of Archie's Memorial Service and Chair, and again for her general encouragement; and to Meyrick Emrys-Roberts, from whose book on Cottage Hospitals I have been able to quote the details of the Foundation of the Cottage Hospitals Association. Special thanks go to John Myson who allowed me to see the League of Friends' Minute Books, to John Watson who produced the Annual Reports of the Research Laboratory, to Ann Standen for sharing with me her extensive knowledge of the Guinea Pig Club, and to John Bennett for showing me round, for his general support throughout, and most especially for his final reading of the whole script.

One of the nicest things about my research for this second edition has been that it has put me in touch with many old friends with whom I used to work; I have had long telephone conversations with Percy Jayes, Robin Beare, Peter Stevens, Tom Cochrane, Giles Romanes, Peter Steel, Roger Orcutt, Mike Awty, Charles Palmer, Joan Godfrey, Liz Hodgson, and Edna Storey, all of whom have given me their personal details. And of course my own two ex-partners Graham Carnegie and Richard Dunstan whom I thank for their consistent general support and encouragement. I visited Don Attwater at his home in Smallfield, and gathered information about various events that took place during the time he was Matron and Chief Nursing Officer, for which I am also most grateful.

On a recent visit to the Hospital I met Bryan Christopher and Alan Del Mar, both of whom were very helpful, and have corresponded with Peter Williams, Francis Briggs, Tim Taylor and his partner Andrew Robertson, who gave me particulars of his uncle Douglas, and with Frankie Wilde, to all of whom my best thanks.

A special thank you also to my publisher for his patience during all the longer-than-expected time it has taken me to complete the job, and another big one to my good neighbour Pauline Ainsworth who has made typing sense out of all my rather less than perfect tape recordings, and put the whole thing into its final shape.

E. J. Dennison

Wray Corner, Reigate 1995

# I

# Green Hedges

THE story of the Queen Victoria Hospital begins in the year 1863 when East Grinstead's Cottage Hospital, only the fifth of its kind in the whole country, was established. Prior to this, admission to hospital from this area had meant a journey to London or Brighton, and, since there were no ambulances, the journey had to be made by train or coach, so it is certain that many of the more seriously ill people had to remain in their homes. This was the situation, not only in East Grinstead and its neighbourhood, but generally in the country districts throughout the length and breadth of Britain. The position is well described in Dr. Andrew Wynter's article on Village Hospitals in the 1866 edition of "Good Words":—

> "In large tracts of country there was no refuge to which poor creatures suffering from the terrible accidents on the introduction of steam machinery to agricultural pursuits and the railway, could be taken, but the Union Workhouse. Even in his own home imagine a poor wretch with a fractured leg, or some accident involving the nervous system, shut up in the single sleeping room of his cottage with noisy children and subject to the barbarous, because untutored, nursing of his wife. If taken to the nearest Town hospital, perhaps 20 miles, in a rough cart, the injury was necessarily aggravated. If treated at home, possibly miles from his doctor, or a case requiring hourly attention, he could only get a visit once a day."

In 1859 Dr. Albert Napper, the village surgeon at Cranleigh, in Surrey, set out to alter these conditions. Wynter again describes how Dr. Napper—

> "Bethought him that it was certainly a mistake that the means of administering to the accidents and diseases of poor

13

human nature should be confined to the great cities and populous places and that the intermediate country, sometimes 15-20 miles distant, should be altogether left out of the reckoning."

Dr. Napper was greatly assisted in his project by the Rector of Cranleigh, the Reverend J. H. Sapte, who lent him a cottage rent free, and this cottage, with local help, was furnished and fitted up to receive six patients. The cottage dated from the 14th century and is described as being "a Surrey Cottage and nothing more, with a sound roof and walls, interior is homely, the walls are whitewashed, the ground floor is paved with brick". Sir Henry Burdett in his "Cottage Hospitals", published in 1877, mentions that the cost of adapting Cranleigh Cottage was about £50. He goes on to say—

"The effective manner in which the alterations have been carried out is worthy of all praise and we must particularly mention the ingenuity displayed in the construction of a bathroom with a supply of hot and cold water."

Dr. Napper intended his hospital for the accommodation of the poor, and what he meant by the poor is clearly laid down—

"Not the Parish pauper who in times of illness or accident has a claim on the Union Workhouse, but chiefly that large and deserving class who support their families by honest labour and have no claim upon the Parish for relief".

It was provided in the Rules of the Hospital that patients should be received on the payment of a weekly sum, the amount of which, dependent on their circumstances, was to be fixed by their employer in conjunction with the Manager of the Hospital. Another contemporary writer stresses that the Hospital patient—

"Has the privilege of being able to pay something, however small, according to his means, for the treatment he receives".

These remarks make strange reading to us today, accustomed as we are to the modern Health Service, with its free Hospital treatment.

The Cranleigh Hospital was an immediate success and was

(*above*)  The original Cottage Hospital, Green Hedges 1863.

(*left*)  Mrs. Oswald Smith of Hammerwood House.

(*below*)  The second hospital, Lansdowne House, 1888.

(*left*)  The third hospital,
Queen's Road, 1902.

(*below*)  The fourth hospital
Holtye Road, 1936.

very quickly copied in other villages. An enthusiastic supporter, Dr. Waring, writing in 1867, says—

"With £100 in hand one would be fully justified in at once establishing a Cottage Hospital of six beds."

and he goes on to say—

"Wherever the state of the funds will warrant the expense, the services of a nurse who has received regular training should be secured, but lacking this, choice should be made of some respectable trustworthy woman who has a good character for skill, intelligence and sobriety, who will faithfully carry out the instructions from the Medical Officer."

Regarding the furnishing of the wards, he says—

"Patent commodes which can be removed as required are preferable to a water closet, which in peasants' hands soon gets out of order."

and he adds—

"The general management of the affairs of the Hospital should be conducted by a small committee of which the Clergyman of the Parish and the Medical Officer should be members; amongst the duties which devolve upon the Manager is providing innocent amusement and occupation for the patients, and for this nothing is better than a small library. An Honorary Secretary should be appointed. No difficulty has been experienced in finding competent medical men to take charge; they should be legally qualified and their services should be gratuitous."

So rapidly did the number of Cottage Hospitals multiply throughout the country that by 1888 there were no fewer than 175 of them, and before the end of the century this number had risen to over 300. The original building at Cranleigh is still in use though numerous additions and alterations have been made to it, and today the Cranleigh Hospital, with 14 beds, is administered by the Guildford Hospital Management Committee under the South West Metropolitan Regional Hospital Board.

According to Dr. Horace Swete's "Handybook of Cottage

Hospitals", published in 1870, the village of Fowey in Cornwall had the distinction of establishing the second Cottage Hospital in England, in the year 1860, with 5 beds. This seems also to have flourished at first, for in 1862, according to the same book, it opened a branch in another village nearby, which was run in conjunction with the parent hospital. The fate of these two hospitals is not known for certain, as no continuous record was kept, but it is known that a hospital existed in Fowey in the year 1880 and from then on a continuous record exists to the present day. The Fowey and District Hospital, moved and enlarged in 1889 and again in 1914, today has 14 beds and is administered by the West Cornwall Hospital Management Committee under the South-Western Regional Hospital Board.

The third village to have a Cottage Hospital was Bourton-on-the-Water in Gloucestershire. This Hospital was opened on March 11th, 1861, with 6 beds and, though it is not today housed in the original building, it has had a continuous existence from that date to this. Today there are 16 beds and the Hospital is administered by the Banbury & District Hospital Management Committee under the Oxford Regional Hospital Board. There is an interesting link between the Bourton Hospital and our own East Grinstead Cottage Hospital, for the Curate at Bourton at the time, the Reverend C. W. Payne-Crawfurd, was a member of an East Grinstead family, and it is recorded not only that he rendered very material assistance to Mr. John Moore, the founder of the Bourton Hospital, but also that he played a big part later on in establishing the East Grinstead Hospital.

Mr. Wallace Hills, in his "History of East Grinstead", published in 1906, states that East Grinstead was the fourth place in the British Isles to boast of a Cottage Hospital, and in fact the earliest available evidence, again that of Wynter, would seem to confirm this claim. Writing in 1866, he says "The East Grinstead Hospital was the fourth established in order of date". Dr. Horace Swete, however, writing in 1870, and saying "I have taken some trouble to gain correct information", states that the Iver, Buckinghamshire, Cottage Hospital was opened in March 1863, seven months before East Grinstead, and there are numbered annual reports which place Iver as early as 1863, one of them actually referring to it as "the third oldest Cottage Hospital in the country". On the strength of this evidence it seems likely that Iver was in fact fourth—even Swete accords first three places to Cranleigh, Fowey and Bourton—and East Grinstead therefore takes fifth place.

The Iver Hospital, now the Iver, Denham and Langley Hospital, has 26 beds, and is today part of the Windsor Group of Hospitals administered by the North-West Metropolitan Regional Board.

The idea of establishing a Cottage Hospital at East Grinstead may well have originated in the mind of the Reverend C. W. Payne-Crawfurd, who appears to have returned to his home town shortly after the Bourton Hospital was opened. The main credit, however, must go to Dr. John Henry Rogers, described as physician and surgeon, one of the local general practitioners of the time. Dr. Rogers lived in the house known as Green Hedges, on the south side of Green Hedges Avenue. In addition to his work as a General Practitioner he ran the free Dispensary in the High Street, in the house which now stands immediately behind the War Memorial, and he also acted as Assistant Warden to Sackville College. The house that Dr. Rogers selected for his purpose was one of his own cottages, No. 2 Green Hedges Cottages, and it can still be seen today, situated at the far end of Green Hedges Avenue on the left side of the footpath leading to Wellington Town Road. It is at present occupied by Mr. and Mrs. R. G. Andrews.

We have gained a rough idea of the sort of establishment this hospital must have been, but unfortunately the only precise details of it which are available are the following short extracts:— (a) from Dr. Swete's "Handybook of Cottage Hospitals", from which the illustration is also taken—

"*East Grinstead*. This hospital is one of the brick and tile cottages common in Surrey and was founded by Dr. Rogers, who had considerable uphill work carrying out his intentions. At his own expense he built a large room to the rear of the cottage which is seen in the illustration with a timber bay window. The special feature of this hospital is the garden, which teems with a profusion of flowers, Dr. Rogers being an

17

enthusiastic botanist and florist. The furnishing of the hospital cost, with the surgical instruments, appliances, etc. £167 9s. od. The annual expenditure is on an average about £120, of which nearly £40 is paid by the patients. This Hospital is conducted on the Cranleigh model."

(b) from Wynter's "Good Words":—

"The East Grinstead Hospital has indeed had a great fight for it and had it not been for the determination of Dr. Rogers and his worthy coadjutor, it would probably have fared but badly. It retains all the characteristics of a Surrey cottage of the better class, with the addition of a spacious room at the back of the house amply lighted by two large windows; this addition was made at the expense of its founder, Dr. Rogers. The poor rustic brought here in his hour of trouble must look upon it as a little paradise, surrounded as it is by its well kept little garden, and overlooking a perfect bower of flowers, the culture of which appears to be the hobby of the doctor. This hospital makes up seven beds."

It is recorded that Dr. Rogers was materially helped, not only by the Reverend Payne-Crawfurd, but by other local residents, "one lady supplying the entire furniture of a room, another person giving all the medicinal and surgical appliances, and others helping in various ways." Two rooms were, in fact, added to the cottage, one upstairs and one down, and it is probable that the upstairs room contained 4 beds, for Mr. Andrews recalls that when he moved into the cottage and began stripping the walls of this room for redecoration he found four biblical texts which had been overpainted, but which originally had no doubt appeared one over each bed. Though the hospital is said to have had 7 beds there are, in fact, only two other bedrooms on this floor, one of which could have contained 2 beds, and the other 1 bed probably occupied by the Resident Nurse, so that most probably there were never more than 6 patients accommodated in the Hospital at any one time. One of the local residents who helped Dr. Rogers in his project was a Mr. Charles Hill, who appears later in the story as a member of the Management Committee when the Hospital was re-opened at a later date and in another place. It is recorded also:—

*"At East Grinstead the medicines are supplied at little above cost price by a local druggist."

It appears that at first Dr. Rogers ran the Hospital entirely at his own expense, but that after a time a few local residents subscribed, though we gather that Dr. Rogers continued to bear the major part of the hospital's expenses throughout its life.

There is no record of any opening ceremony, but we know that the first patient was admitted on October 14th, 1863, and we are fortunate in having the following description of this case, taken from Dr. Roger's own casebook and written up in his own hand-writing:—

"*Case* 1. Admitted October 14th. Encysted tumour of scalp. S——P——36, married, husband a stonemason, o children, residing at Turners Hill, Worth. Was a patient at the Dispensary in the summer of '63. Was then suffering from dyspepsia and general debility, from which she got relief. During the time of her attendance at the Dispensary she showed me an encysted tumour on the top of her head about the size of a nutmeg, which she said was very troublesome to her. I advised her to come into the Hospital as soon as it was opened and let me remove it. She did so, being the first patient admitted. On the following day, October 15th, I removed the tumour, running first a sharp bistoury through it and then dissecting out the lateral halves which had adhered firmly to the skin at the upper part. Mr. R. Gullidge assisted me. She appeared to suffer very little pain, scarcely a drop of blood escaped. I put a pledget of lint over the wound and secured it by a six-tailed bandage. Not the slightest unfavourable symptom followed the operation and the patient left the Hospital on the 19th well in health and with the wound healed."

This casebook contains records of 40 cases in all, admitted during the years 1863 and 1864, and it makes fascinating reading. Take for instance the following extracts from the notes on Case 2, a 16-year-old girl suffering from an ingrowing toe-nail. (It should be remembered that chloroform had only been

* "Cottage Hospitals—Their Objects, etc." by Dr. Waring, 1867.

introduced as a general anaesthetic a very short time previously).

> "I brought her gradually under the influence of chloroform, of which ½ a drachm was used. It produced its effect very gradually, more than five minutes elapsed before she became insensible. I divided the nail down the centre and then removed each lateral half. She uttered a slight shriek when I was dividing the nail but manifested no further evidence of sensibility. Water dressing was applied for the first few days; experienced no inconvenience or pain and the foot soon healed up. Left the hospital shortly after quite well."

and this delightfully candid description of another minor operation.

> "Chloroform was administered to the extent of about 10 drachms before the operation was completed, about two-thirds of that amount before it was commenced, with the effect of producing merely a muddled state. At no part of the time was he insensible, said he knew all that was being done. He suffered considerable pain though much less than I imagine he would have done had no chloroform been given."

There are many interesting technical details in these pages which serve to show what tremendous advances have been made in medicine and surgery since Dr. Rogers' time. One of these, for instance, is the radical cure for hydrocele, which he says "has lately been so extensively practised", by painting the inner wall of the sac with fused silver nitrate. This is a method of treatment which would scarcely be considered today.

Dr. Rogers, in one case, permits himself a mild pat on the back when he describes how—

> "One old man with ulcers of his legs came all the way from Bermondsey to see me, having heard there of a man at Forest Row who had been cured by me of the same complaint."

Two other cases of some interest are the following:—

> "*Case No.* 20. A man aged 45. Had come, he said, on foot all the way from Crawley. He said he was quite destitute. As

it seemed to me that the best thing that could be done for him was to take him into the hospital, I offered to do so on condition that he would, when he was able to work, pay at the rate of 7s. per week for his maintenance. This he consented to do, signing a paper to that effect."

This man was admitted and had a minor operation performed on his knee, but alas, when it was nearly healed—

"on Monday asked permission to work a little in the garden. As it would benefit him greatly to use the limb I consented to his doing so. He worked in the garden on the following day and conducted himself with extreme propriety but in the evening he went out, under the pretext of getting shaved, did not return until near ten and was reported by the nurse to have been very drunk. This morning he was up and at work in the garden when his wife came by in a state of drunkenness. There was a row between them and they went off together quarrelling."

and

"*Case No.* 32. Fracture of lower jaw and bruises. W—— N——, aged 20, single man, who was brought to my house by the Police Constable . . . about 7.0 a.m., who told me the young man had applied at the Police Station stating that he had been injured as he thought, by some person kicking him when asleep last evening on the road between Holtye and East Grinstead, to which place he was making his way from the Hop Gardens at Staplehurst, in which he had been at work. He told the policeman he had applied for admission into the Union House but had been refused on the ground that he had three shillings and some pence in his pocket. As he was much grazed and bruised about the face and right thigh, the policeman thought it a case requiring medical treatment, and therefore went with him to the Union House with the intention of endeavouring to secure his admission. Just as they reached the House they met the Relieving Officer who at first refused to give an Order, but in consequence of a remark made by the other Relieving Officer he directed the policeman to go to his house and tell his wife to make out an Order. He did so and obtained the Order and gave it to him and directed him to go with it to the Union House close by. Sometime after N—— again came to the Police Station and said that a great fat man, to whom he gave the Order, jeered at him because he stuttered, said he was not going to be humbugged and finally refused to admit him. On this the policeman brought him here that I might examine him. I did so shortly after at the Hospital and found various grazes and bruises about the face and that the lower jaw was broken across a little to the left of the median line. He complained much of pain in his back and his right thigh I could detect no injury in the back but there were marks across the thigh as if from the pressure of wheels and there is reason to believe that they were so produced. It seems that last night Mr. P. J. P—— the Postmaster came to the Police Station and stated that as he was driving home in the evening in a four-wheeled chaise, he felt that the wheels had passed over some object which he thought was alive, but that he was too frightened to stop and see what it was. As the place where Mr. P—— ran over something is about the spot N—— describes as the place where he lay down and fell asleep, there is no doubt in my mind that the injuries on his person were not produced as he thought from the kick of a man, but by the passage of Mr. P's horse and trap over him. They are injuries which might have been so produced and the marks on the thigh could hardly have been produced in any other manner. I had him stripped and washed and put to bed. He had no shirt and his few clothes were in a very dilapidated condition. As there was but little displacement of the fractured jaw I did nothing to it, but propose tomorrow endeavouring, as the teeth seem sound, to secure the fragments by wires round the teeth. He had some supper, bread and milk."

On page 33 of the Casebook there appears the rather alarming diagnosis of "cholera". On reading the details, however, one is relieved to find that this diagnosis, was, in fact, not correct, for it appears that the patient, a girl aged 12—

"had been allowed to eat a quantity of apples which had no doubt disagreed with her." "I hope", said Dr. Rogers "that the disease will undergo a spontaneous cure"."

Evidently it did so, for on the next page we find—

"Nature has effected a perfect cure, by expelling the offending contents of the alimentary canal. As there were no symptoms to combat I gave no medicine. She has been kept in bed where she has dozed much, and supplied with beef tea thickened with arrowroot, and dry toast."

Although Dr. Rogers ran the Hospital almost entirely at his own expense, there were a few subscribers, and in the year 1865 during which 34 patients were admitted, the following Balance Sheet was issued:—

| | | | | | | | |
|---|---|---|---|---|---|---|---|
| Donations and subscriptions | 75 | 12 | 6 | Food, wine, medicine, fuel, etc. | 86 | 7 | 4 |
| Payments by patients | 33 | 12 | 0 | Nursing Staff | 17 | 0 | 0 |
| Collecting box at Hospital | 2 | 7 | 6 | Rates, insurance, furniture | 12 | 5 | 0 |
| | £111 | 12 | 0 | | £115 | 12 | 4 |

showing a total deficit for the year of £4 0s. 4d.

The first Cottage Hospital was closed in 1874, after 11 years, and we can let Dr. Rogers himself tell us why. Sir Henry Burdett, writing in 1896, gives the following extract from a letter written to him by Dr. Rogers—

"In the completion of its 11th year, after having had over 300 cases under my care I closed the Hospital in October 1874. I did so for the following reasons:—In this district there are many very wealthy residents and landed proprietors but scarcely any volunteered to help me. I got what money I required for furnishing it by writing direct appeals to individuals, and afterwards to meet the current expenditure. I daresay I could have done so up to the present year, but after a time I became wary of making these appeals to people who seemed to consider that, by contributing to the support of the Hospital they were conferring a favour upon me. This was especially annoying as I was not only giving my daily professional services, but was also the greatest pecuniary contributor. In addition to this there were frequent attempts on the part of wealthy people to get their servants or dependents into the Hospital, so as to avoid paying towards their support. At length, after having experienced for some years the meanness of the wealthy, and too often the ingratitude of the poor, I closed the Hospital and by the sale of the furniture raised a sufficient sum to pay off the outstanding debts without any further appeal to the charitable feelings of my wealthy neighbours. I allowed the furniture and fittings to remain in my cottage for upwards of 2 months after I had closed it as a Hospital, and then as no one offered to do anything to resuscitate it I sent for an auctioneer. Some time after a few persons, who had occasionally contributed to the Hospital, met together and passed a vote of censure on me— the founder and chief supporter of the Hospital—for having closed it without obtaining their consent."

During these first 11 years of the Hospital's history there accumulated the fairly considerable sum of some £200 in the banking account. In 1890, some 2 years after the Hospital was reopened on another site, the same Mr. Charles Hill who had so greatly encouraged and helped Dr. Rogers, reported to the new Management Committee—

"The fittings etc. of the old Hospital were sold and the sum added to the Reserve Fund, making up about £200. The amount was further increased by a bazaar at Rowfant, and by careful investment rose to over £300."

There is therefore evidence of continued interest and thought being given to the idea of reopening the Hospital, and in 1881 this very nearly happened. Dr. C. H. Gatty of Felbridge Place became interested and built a house in Moat Road which he proposed to open as a Hospital. He furnished it and equipped it, but, according to Wallace Hills, writing in his "History of East Grinstead"—"because people grew impatient and ventured both publicly and privately to ask him when he proposed to open it, he took offence, removed the equipment, and finally sold the property to Mr. John Betchley". The house, which would have made an excellent small hospital, eventually found its way into the hands of the East Sussex County Council and is known today as The Moat Road Clinic. This affair was described elsewhere by the late Mr. Edward Blount of Imberhorne Manor as having been "due to unfortunate misunder-standings". There appears to be no further evidence of what these misunderstandings may have been and this curious incident in our story therefore remains unexplained.

It was a further seven years before the Hospital was finally reopened. Meanwhile the Reserve Fund was being carefully tended and was steadily growing, and when it was finally paid over to the new Management Committee, it proved most useful, as will presently appear. While, therefore, there was a period of some years during which the Hospital did not actually function, there is evidence that it was very much alive both financially and in the hearts and minds of the local people.

# 2

# Lansdowne House

SOME 13 years after the closing of the first Cottage Hospital a local groom, while out exercising two of his master's horses, met with a serious accident. According to a contemporary description:—

"The poor man was so dreadfully injured that it was thought necessary at once, for the sake of his life, to send him direct to East Grinstead, but on arriving there it was found there was no public place where he could be taken in and it was probable that he might have bled to death in the street, but fortunately Mr. Wallis happened to be at home, and he very nobly took him into his own house, attended to his wounds and watched him for some hours. The Sisters of St. Margaret's then very handsomely sent to say they would take him into their Infirmary, which they did, and under their tender care and able nursing and the surgical skill of Mr. Collins the poor man was in time enabled to return to service. This accident so appealed to the tender feelings of Mr. and Mrs. Oswald Smith of Hammerwood House that they decided at once to open a Cottage Hospital at their own expense. Upon hearing this the medical officers of the town—Messrs. Covey, Collins and Wallis, generously offered their gratuitous services to the Hospital. A suitable house was found, and at considerable expense it was furnished with every comfort that patients could possibly require."

This same incident, and the re-opening of the Hospital, was also described in the following extracts from the East Grinstead Parish Magazine:—

"*January* 1888. *A NEW COTTAGE HOSPITAL.* For several years the need of a Cottage Hospital for this town and neighbourhood has been felt. Recently the terrible accident to a groom of Lord Henry Nevill (who, when recovery was despaired of was nursed in the Infirmary at St. Margaret's) made the need a necessity. Mr. and Mrs Oswald Smith, with their usual liberality, have secured a new house, opposite the Local Board Land, in the London Road. This they are now having fitted up as a Cottage Hospital. The rooms are of good size and airy. Five beds with bathroom and all needful appliances will be provided, and ready for use by the time this number of the Parish Magazine is issued. All parishioners and neighbours must feel grateful to the donors, (who make themselves responsible for the first year's expenses) for a noble Jubilee Gift. Messrs. Covey, Collins and Wallis will have medical charge of the patients, a trained nurse and a servant will be in charge of the Hospital."

"*February* 1888. *THE COTTAGE HOSPITAL.* On January 11th this excellent Institution was opened with a short service of prayer by the Vicar. Mrs. Oswald Smith, prevented by illness from being present was represented by Rev. C. C. Woodland, Vicar of St. Stephen's, Hammerwood. There are now two patients in the Hospital who are in charge of a trained nurse with 5 years' Certificate from Guy's Hospital, London."

The house selected for the purpose was on the corner of Garland Road with the London Road, part of the premises now occupied by Grinstead Motors, and known at the time as Lansdowne House.

The new Hospital was opened on January 11th, 1888, and had accommodation for 5 patients, a male and a female ward with 2 beds each and a third room with 1 bed for emergencies. In addition there were, as a member of the Committee told a public meeting shortly afterwards, "2 good bedrooms, one occupied by the nurse and the other by the servant, and there were also good offices in the way of kitchen, scullery, cellars and larder". It had as well, what must have been something of a rarity for those days—"a good bathroom".

Miss Kate Taylor was appointed Nurse to look after the 5 beds, and so becomes the first of our known Matrons, for while it is certain that the original Cottage Hospital had Resident Nurses, there is unfortunately no record of their names. Miss

Taylor remained in charge for 4½ years, and for more than half of this time carried out the entire nursing duties herself. Her first patient was admitted on January 17th, but there is no record as to the nature of the case.

Mr. and Mrs. Oswald Smith very generously undertook to defray the whole cost of the Hospital for the first year, but it was always their intention that it should, in due course, be self-supporting, and within a short time they asked a number of local residents to form a provisional committee to assist them in the conduct and management of the Hospital and help them to put it on a public footing. This committee had its first meeting at the Hospital on Thursday, May 22nd, 1888, and consisted of the following members:—

| | |
|---|---|
| Mr. W. V. K. Stenning | Dr. P. E. Wallis |
| Chairman | Rev. C. Woodland |
| Dr. C. E. Collins | Mr. W. Young |
| Mr. T. Cramp | Mr. S. Lowdell |
| Mr. H. Jeddere Fisher | Major Margary |
| Mr. G. Head | Mr. Guy Oswald Smith |
| Mr. J. Southey | Dr. G. Covey |

Dr. Collins agreed temporarily to undertake the duties of Honorary Secretary.

One of the first tasks of this Committee was to draw up a set of provisional rules for the Hospital. They decided firstly that the area from which patients might be admitted should include West Hoathly, Felbridge, North Lingfield, Forest Row, Hartfield, Hammerwood and East Grinstead. A proviso was made that patients coming from a distance must first send a certificate from a doctor to the effect that they were suitable and such as were likely to receive benefit. The financial arrangements were precisely laid down, Rule 3 reading as follows:—

"No patient will be received gratuitously. The least payment is 2s. 6d. per week and increases in amount according to the means of the patient. The amount is in all cases except accident to be fixed before admission by the Secretary or the Hospital Committee. Payment to be made at least a week in advance."

and similarly Rule 4—

"Before admission the patient or some friend or friends must sign an agreement for the weekly payments and also get some responsible person to sign the agreement for removal in case of discharge or death."

Cases of infectious, contagious or chronic disease, advanced consumption and "such as may be considered unfit by the medical staff", were specifically excluded, and patients were to be directed to bring in with them "two nightgowns and a brush and comb."

Visiting hours were defined also at this first Committee Meeting, and it is of some interest that these hours, namely "between the hours of 2.0 and 4.0 p.m. on Thursdays and Sundays" remained unchanged for nearly 75 years.

Rule 11 stated:—

"The lady visitors will in rotation undertake the duties of Lady Superintendent. Each lady doing so for a month at a time. These duties will be to collect the payments of the patients, to pay the ordinary expenses, and generally to superintend the domestic management of the Hospital."

The ladies who undertook these onerous duties were Mrs. Oswald Smith herself, assisted by Mrs. Collins, Mrs. Covey and Miss Wallis.

At its next meeting 9 days later the Committee decided that the whole scheme should be laid before the public, and that a Public Meeting should be held at an early date.

The Meeting was in fact held on Saturday, July 21st, at the Public Hall. It appears to have been well attended, and a long account appeared in the following week's edition of the East Grinstead Observer. Mr. H. R. Freshfield, a Governor of the Sussex County Hospital, Brighton, and of other hospitals, was elected Chairman of the Meeting. He opened by giving a talk on the usefulness of Cottage Hospitals generally, and reminded the Meeting that the project was one which would call for a liberal response in the shape of annual subscriptions. The Honorary Secretary then read out a list of subscriptions which had already been promised and it was at this point that Mr. Stenning, the Chairman of the Provisional Committee, mentioned the funds left over from the old Cottage Hospital. He stated that a sum of upwards of £300 was vested in stocks in London and he presumed that this sum would be handed over to the new permanent Committee as soon as it was properly formed. The Secretary read a telegram just received from Mr. W. Pledge, "whose employees were that day holding their annual beanfeast at Uckfield", which said:—

"Though unable to be present at Meeting my employees have just collected £2 8s. 6d. for the Hospital."

Sir Edward Blount's proposal that the provisional Committee which had been running the Hospital for the last two months should be re-appointed for the rest of the year, was carried unanimously, and a short general discussion followed, at the end of which a number of further subscriptions were promised.

The new Hospital was thus firmly established on a public footing with a properly elected Committee of Management and a reasonable financial outlook. The Committee quickly got down to work, meeting at the Hospital the following Thursday. At this meeting they elected Sir Edward Blount and Mr. J. Cotton Powell to join them, and they also appointed Mr. Ranger as Collector to canvass the neighbourhood for subscriptions and to receive as remuneration 5 per cent of whatever he collected. This appointment was evidently a useful one, for there is a report at a meeting a year later that Mr. Ranger had collected £177 and had received in commission the sum of £8 17s. 6d.

The main business of the Committee during the remainder of 1888 was to arrange a meeting of the now fairly numerous subscribers to the Hospital with a view to electing a permanent Committee of Management.

The Subscribers Meeting duly took place on November 3rd in the hall of the new Literary & Scientific Institute, and it is reported that there was a good attendance, "including many influential residents". A resumé of the working of the Hospital during the year was given by the Acting Secretary, Dr. Collins. He reported that the medical officers had done duty for a month at a time, and that the great necessity for the existence of such a hospital in the town had been amply proved. "Several cases of serious accident" he said, "have been successfully treated, and operations have been successfully performed in several cases, which would otherwise have had to go to

London". There had, in fact, been 21 cases admitted during the year. It is worth noting that even at this first meeting it was mentioned in the Committee Report that if the work developed as it promised to do, more appropriate accommodation would become necessary. The Committee estimated from their own experience and from statistics of 174 similar institutions in the country that a sum of about £300 a year would be needed to run the Hospital efficiently, and Mr. Charles Hill brought up the matter of the old Cottage Hospital funds again, mentioning that he thought there should be no difficulty in transferring the money to the new Trustees.

The subscribers were evidently so satisfied with the Committee that had acted temporarily throughout most of 1888 that they unanimously re-elected it to carry on during 1889, though it was given powers to add to its numbers if necessary. On the whole this first Annual General Meeting of subscribers showed that the new Hospital had got off to a reasonably auspicious start.

The permanent Committee now consisted of the original Temporary Committee, plus the addition of Sir Edward Blount and Mr. J. C. Powell, and the following local residents who were elected under the Committee's powers given to them at the Public Meeting:—

| | |
|---|---|
| Mr. J. K. Esdaile | Mr. J. Stewart Oxley |
| Mr. J. McAndrew | Mr. T. Ravenshaw |
| Mr. J. Henderson | |

The new Committee thus properly constituted had its first meeting at the Hospital on January 8th, 1889. This meeting was attended by Mrs. Oswald Smith and was the occasion for the formal handing over of the Hospital. At the same time Mrs. Oswald Smith handed over the sum of £50, which had been subscribed by the late Mr. Bernard Hale, and she expressed the wish that this sum should form the nucleus of a Capital Fund for the Hospital, which suggestion was agreed to by the Committee. She also promised on behalf of herself and her family a generous yearly subscription to the running expenses of the Hospital. The Committee drafted a formal letter of thanks to Mrs. Oswald Smith, thanking her for the handsome manner in which she had re-started the Hospital and for all her kindness in connection with it. Apart from the furnishing and initial expenses of opening the Hospital, Mr. and Mrs. Oswald Smith had spent the sum of £212 13s. od. on the running of the Hospital during its first year. The meeting proceeded then to appoint a Secretary to the Hospital, Mr. Perkins, whose remuneration was fixed at £5 5s. od. per annum, and the meeting also decided that the drugs and medicines required should be ordered for a quarter of the year at a time alternately from Mr. Dixon and Mr. Martin. This meeting also elected Mr. George Head as Treasurer and Mr. H. Jeddere Fisher, Mr. Guy Oswald Smith and Mr. W. V. K. Stenning as Trustees. The Reverend C. C. Woodland, the Reverend D. Y. Blakiston, Mr. W. V. K. Stenning and Mr. J. Southey were appointed members of the House and Finance Committee and a gardener, Mr. Wallis, was appointed at a wage of one shilling per week. The tenancy agreement was formally handed over to the Secretary by Mr. Joseph Turner and a decision was made to insure the Hospital Furniture for a sum of £300. Altogether this was a most fruitful meeting.

The Minute Books of the General Committee and of the House and Finance Committee are available and make most interesting reading; in fact, most of the remainder of this Chapter is extracted from these books. We find that the sum of £50 mentioned above was placed on deposit with Messrs. G. & G. S. Head, Bankers, of East Grinstead, also that the furniture was insured as arranged for £300 with the Sun Fire Office. There is a further note at the first House Committee meeting that in response to an appeal made in the East Grinstead Observer, Mr. George Read gratuitously presented the Hospital with a carrying chair.

The following year passed quietly with the work of the Hospital going steadily ahead, so that in 1890 the number of cases admitted had risen to 42 and it was reported that sometimes all 5 beds were occupied at once; in fact, in November of that year it was found necessary to employ temporarily a probationer nurse to assist in the nursing duties.

There is an entry in the minutes of the General Committee for January, 1890, to the following effect—

"Mr. Cramp suggested the desirability of substituting payment to the Matron and servant instead of supplying them with ale".

This was agreed to, and at a subsequent meeting we read the proposal—

"that in future the Matron be allowed the sum of £1 15s. od. per quarter as an equivalent for ale hitherto supplied by the Committee".

A year later, in 1891, we find the Matron's salary was increased to £35 per annum, plus £10 uniform allowance.

It was early in 1890 that an event of outstanding significance in the Hospital's history took place. In their report for the quarter ended March 25th, the House & Finance Committee report—

"The old Cottage Hospital Fund of £374 6s. 9d. has been transferred to the three new Trustees".

This link with the original Hospital thus makes our history continuous from 1863 to the present day. The money from the old Hospital was invested in 2¾% Consols, and later, as will be seen, was to prove a source of great strength.

It was also mentioned at a meeting in 1890 that the Secretary was instructed to make arrangements with employers of labour in the district to have a box upon their premises so that their workmen might be invited to make a small contribution weekly. This is the first time that the working man, for whom it will be remembered the Hospital was originally intended, is mentioned in connection with its administration, and it is from this very small beginning that the East Grinstead Working Men's Hospital Fund grew, and became, as will be seen later, a source of great benefit, financial and otherwise, to the Hospital.

The annual expenditure crept up from £367 in 1889 to £485 in 1891, but subscriptions had also increased and at the end of 1891 the Committee were able to report that the Hospital had in its Capital Account the comparatively large sum of £703 11s. od.

The year 1892 was an eventful and anxious one. The first blow fell early in the year—the death of Mrs. Oswald Smith, less than four years after she had re-established the Hospital. Very many tributes had been paid to this great and generous lady during the few years following the Hospital's re-opening and there can be no doubt from reading them that she was a person of great humanity and personality and that her name must stand high in the list of those to whom the Hospital owes its great history. The last tribute to her was paid at the Annual Meeting of subscribers held on February 16th, 1892, at the Victoria Hall in the Jubilee Institute, when a motion was passed unanimously:—

"That this General Meeting of Subscribers sincerely deplores the loss of Mrs. Oswald Smith, to whose kindness, energy and liberality they are so greatly indebted for the re-establishment of the Cottage Hospital".

Only a week later, on February 24th, disaster struck not only the Hospital, but numerous individuals and organisations in the Town, in consequence of the failure of Head's Bank, a local Bank which had done business in the Town for some 90 years. It will be remembered that Mr. George Head was appointed the original Treasurer to the Hospital in 1889, and that the Hospital funds had been deposited with his Bank. George Head had died in the meantime but his son, Mr. G. S. Head, had taken over the treasurership of the Hospital. It appears that at the time of the failure the Hospital had £325 on deposit with the Bank and some £150 in the Current Account, so that they faced an initial loss of about £475. But this was not all. Following the failure of the Bank, the owner of the Hospital building also went bankrupt, and put the property up for sale! It is a great tribute to those who were running the Hospital at the time that it survived this severe double blow. The old Cottage Hospital Fund, invested in Consols, was redeemed, a special subscription list was opened, and on May 31st a special Meeting of the Committee authorised Mr. Southey to attend the auction sale and to offer up to £700 for the freehold. Fortunately this sum was enough to cover the purchase price of £675, plus the legal expenses, and thus the situation was saved. For the first time the Hospital now owned its own premises and had left itself with a debt of only £49 11s. 6d. still owing. It is of some interest that the special subscription list was again headed by Mr. Oswald Smith with a donation of £100.

In the meantime, following this unfortunate affair, on April 5th Mr. Perkins, the Hospital Secretary, was directed to write to Mr. G. S. Head asking him to be good enough to resign his position as Treasurer to the Hospital. This he did, his resignation was accepted, and he was subsequently succeeded in this office by Mr. F. B. Whitfield. It is only fair to add that subsequently the Bank paid a dividend which amounted to about a quarter of the Hospital's initial loss.

The next blow came in June of the same year, when the Matron, Miss Taylor, resigned. Her resignation was accepted, the appointment was advertised, and no fewer than 63 applications for the position were received. Out of these the Committee in due course appointed Miss Oxtoby as the next Matron. It is recorded that, on leaving, Miss Taylor was presented with a cheque for £11 12s. 6d., and an address ornamentally engrossed upon vellum, by the Committee.

After all these upheavals the rest of the year passed uneventfully and in 1893 the Hospital settled down again to a steady routine. A probationer nurse was appointed to help with the increasing work, and it is recorded that she was to receive only her keep and no remuneration for the first year, but, if satisfactory, she was to be paid £10 for the second year. There was a mild flutter of indignation in the Committee, caused by Dr. Covey having brought a local lady in to watch him perform an operation, while at the same time he appeared to exceed his share of the 5 beds by having no less than 4 patients in at the same time. This caused the Reverend D. Y. Blakiston, the Vicar of East Grinstead and a member of the Committee, to write complaining that:—

"It violated the equitable arrangements which the Committee agreed should exist among the Medical Officers, and ought not to be allowed to recur, since the other doctors had cases awaiting admission".

He thought also that the admission of an outsider to the operating theatre was "unseemly and against surgical rule". To what extent this disapproval influenced Dr. Covey's resignation early the following year does not appear, but at least it is pleasing to find that on his retirement the Committee were able to send him their "best thanks for his services in the past". It is, of course, possible that the two incidents were unrelated. In this connection, however, it is interesting to note that while the Annual Report for 1893 had mentioned that the accommodation of the Hospital had proved inadequate for all the cases needing admission, the same Report for 1894 says that pressure for admission had not been so great. One cannot avoid having the feeling that Dr. Covey's resignation may have had something to do with this, and that his successor, Dr. James Harrison, appointed in February, 1894, may perhaps have been less keen on taking his patients into hospital.

The reports for 1894 are of great interest. First comes a very curious entry in the Management Committee Report for January 2nd, recording the receipt of a letter from Mr. Isley, forwarding a cheque for £40 1s. 6d., "the proceeds of a smoking concert held at Bellaggio by friends interested in the prosperity and growth of the Hospital". What was the connection between the East Grinstead Hospital and this Italian holiday resort? The clue was discovered accidentally recently while reading a report in the East Grinstead Courier describing the auction sale of Hatton Court, a large house in Dormans Park nearby. The report stated that Hatton Court was built by Mr. Arthur Burr "whose original intention was to construct a private estate of 40 bungalows on the style of the Italian lakeside town of Bellaggio", and in fact Hatton Court was originally called "Bellaggio". The Smoking Concert was therefore no doubt held in Dormans Park and not in Italy at all!

Another item of interest in 1894 was the increasing dissatisfaction of the lady visitors. Their duties had originally included the household management, but this had evidently now been taken over by the Matron, and it appears there was little left for the ladies to do but visit the patients. A suggestion was made that ladies might be elected to the Committee, but it does not appear to have been popular, as a decision was shelved until the 1895 Annual Meeting, and even this Meeting got no further than to agree that "as soon as a vacancy occurred on the Committee the question of appointing a lady would be considered". When, however, in the following year the Reverend A. J. Swainson resigned, the Committee lost no time in pointing out their regret that "owing to Rule 11 confining the number of the members of the Committee to 12, they cannot appoint another member". In fact it was more than a quarter of a century later, at the Annual General Meeting held in February 1921, that the first lady members were appointed to the Committee.

Also in 1894, after only two years as Matron, Miss Oxtoby broke down in health, and, after two prolonged periods of absence on sick leave, was finally, in March 1895, given a formal three months notice of termination of her engagement. Following this her health did in fact improve, and the Medical Officers recommended that her services should be retained, but she finally resigned in August 1895. The Hospital was fortunate during this very difficult period to have as probationer Nurse Smith, who willingly accepted the extra work and responsibility involved by the Matron's absences. These services were recognised by the House and Finance Committee, who on 25th March, recommended that Nurse Smith be granted a gratuity of £1, together with the sum of £4 5s. od., being the balance of a special appeal made on behalf of Miss Oxtoby, this to be "in recognition of the large amount of extra work efficiently and cheerfully performed by her during the last six months". She was also to have her salary raised to £15 per year.

In due course Miss M. E. Turner was appointed to succeed Miss Oxtoby as Matron, and took up her duties in September 1895. When Probationer Smith left in 1896, having spent nearly four years at the Hospital, it proved impossible to replace her on the same terms, and a new Probationer was eventually engaged at a salary of £5 for the first year, £10 for the second and £15 for the third.

In 1896 there was a further movement to enlarge the Hospital, and in fact the Annual Meeting of Subscribers instructed the Committee to take steps to do this, but the Committee at this stage found themselves unable to make any recommendation to enlarge the present building. In this year also comes the first reference to the Hospital's funds being deposited with "Messrs. Barclay & Company". Following the failure of Head's Bank, the Hospital funds had been transferred to Messrs. Smith, Bankers of Lombard Street, and Messrs. Molineux, of London. They were now transferred to Barclays Bank, who remained the Hospital's bankers for the next half century.

The report of the Subscribers Annual General Meeting held in February 1897, throws a most interesting light on what was evidently one of the current medical problems. During the previous few months there had been correspondence in the East Grinstead Observer concerning three cases of diphtheria which had been admitted to the Hospital. The complainants, led by Mr. T. Isley, maintained that this violated Rule I of the Hospital, which specifically stated that infectious cases should not be admitted. This complaint brought Dr. Collins to his feet and, in spite of the Chairman's effort to keep the peace, an acrimonious discussion followed. Dr. Collins pointed out that the only reason for admitting these cases was to perform tracheotomy on them and thereby save their lives, and he stated that in fact two lives had been saved. The Meeting then wanted to know what was the general medical feeling on this matter in the country at the time, and in response to this Dr. Collins disclosed that he had, in fact, written letters to all the 270 cottage hospitals in the country, inviting their views, and had also consulted several leading Consultants in London, including the late President of the Royal College of Surgeons, and the outcome of his investigations was that current medical opinion held that, where there was not an Isolation Hospital available, it was right and proper to admit diphtheria cases to General Hospitals for the purpose of doing a life-saving tracheotomy. This weighty argument swayed the Meeting and eventually satisfied Mr. Isley and his friends. It is of some interest to note that the East Grinstead Isolation Hospital was opened only a year or two later.

In July, 1897, the London, Brighton & South Coast Railway Company wrote to ask whether, since their workmen made regular weekly subscriptions to the Hospital, they would, in the event of needing Hospital treatment, also be asked to make a weekly payment? The Committee replied that they were prepared to make a free bed available for the Railway employees for one year but could not bind themselves to do so for longer.

The year 1898 saw two changes of Matron, Miss Turner leaving in January and being succeeded by Miss Morton, who in her turn left to take up private nursing at the end of the year. She was succeeded by Miss Blanche Sleap from Guy's Hospital.

In the meantime the demands being made upon the Hospital were increasing. At the end of 1897 Dr. C. Wright-Edwards was elected to the Medical Staff, so that the Hospital now had four doctors, but still only 5 beds, and the population of East Grinstead alone was about 6,000. No wonder many people felt that the accommodation should be increased. In their Annual Report for 1898 the Medical Officers stated firmly "the Hospital is not now large enough for the demands made upon it".

At the Annual General Meeting of Subscribers early in 1899, Dr. Wright-Edwards moved the following resolution:—

"That this Meeting recommends the Committee to take steps to consider the advisability of making improvements and alterations in the Hospital accommodation."

This resolution was passed and a sub-committee was set up to seek an available site for a new Hospital. This sub-committee quickly got to work and on their recommendation the Management Committee in due course purchased a site in Imberhorne Lane, opposite Copyhold Farm, and "very accessible to the railway", for the sum of £275.

Dr. Wright-Edwards, having set the ball rolling, and having been on the staff for only two years, left the neighbourhood towards the end of 1899. He was replaced on the staff by Dr. F. C. Poynder early in 1900.

During 1900 the Committee issued a special Building Appeal, and they made it known that unless there was a liberal response to this Appeal they would not be able to proceed with their building plans. The response, headed by a large donation of £250 from Mr. Buckley, was evidently forthcoming, for they went ahead with their plans, and an architect was engaged to design a new Hospital which, they were told, would cost not less than £4,200. The matter was rapidly becoming more urgent, for at the end of 1900 the Medical Officers stated in their Annual Report that there were no fewer than 4 patients actually waiting for their turn to be admitted for operations.

The Annual Report for 1900 is notable for giving us one further item of interest, for in it the name of Mr. Edward Blount appears for the first time as a member of the Management Committee. Mr. Blount's name will appear frequently in the

39

following pages, for his association with the Hospital was to last for the next 50 years.

On January 8th, 1901, another appeal for Building Funds was launched, as it was still intended to use the Imberhorne building site. Only 8 days later, however, on January 16th, Mr. Perkins, the Hospital Secretary, heard by chance that the Holiday Home in Queen's Road was about to come into the market. This building, owned at the time by Mr. Oswald Smith, and used today as offices by the Eurogauge Company, had originally been used as a coffee tavern, called the Elephant's Head, after, it is said, Mr. Oswald Smith's family crest. On ceasing to be used for this purpose the building had been leased to the Ragged School Union, and opened by them as a Holiday Home on September 2nd, 1885. Fifteen years later, to the great good fortune of the Hospital, it happened that the Union no longer required the building for this purpose, and so it became free at this most critical moment in the Hospital's history. Mr. Perkins got into touch with Mr. Oswald Smith who offered to present the building outright, free of all expenses, to the Committee for their new Hospital. This offer was, of course, too good to refuse and it was gratefully accepted. Thus it was that the Oswald Smith family was once again responsible for a further great step forward in the Hospital's history. The Committee forthwith abandoned their original plan to build in Imberhorne Lane and proceeded to organise their move to the new site in Queen's Road. This was to be quite a formidable undertaking and would require public financial support, so they decided to hold a Public Meeting in the town. This meeting gave the necessary encouragement and a temporary Sub-committee was elected to make all the arrangements.

It happened that at the time there was a country-wide movement to erect memorials to the late Queen Victoria, and the Public Meeting held to discuss the new Hospital unanimously decided that the Town's memorial to the Queen should be associated with the new Hospital, hoping in this way to ensure that ample funds would be subscribed. It was thus, at this important moment in its history, that our Hospital became known as the Queen Victoria Cottage Hospital.

Plans for altering the building were prepared by Mr. H. E. Matthews, and in September 1901, Mr. H. Young's tender for

40

the work having been accepted, the alterations were begun. At the beginning of 1902 the Committee were able to announce that it was hoped to open the new Hospital soon after midsummer, and the Medical Officers in their Annual Report stated "this is the last Report which we expect to make from the present building." In fact, the new Hospital was opened on October 15th, 1902.

At the opening ceremony some interesting figures concerning the old Hospital were given. The yearly average of inpatients over the 12 complete years 1889-1901 inclusive, had been 44 per year. The yearly average expenditure £306 11s. 5d. (It will be recalled that the original estimate given to the public meeting that inaugurated Lansdowne House had been £300), and the yearly average receipts £351 7s. 9d. There had, in fact, been a slight surplus of receipts over expenditure for every one of these years.

# 3

# Queen's Road

So well had the Committee done its work during the 14 years at Lansdowne House that, after purchasing the freehold of that building for £675 and, in addition, the now superfluous building site in Imberhorne Lane, there was still the comfortable sum of £325 invested in the names of the Trustees. This was no mean achievement, taking into consideration also the loss sustained in the 1892 financial disaster.

The Imberhorne site was now sold at a small profit to Mr. Alan Stenning; Lansdowne House was sold to Mr. Wallace H. Hills (the author in 1906 of the 'History of East Grinstead'), and the money thus acquired, together with a magnificent gift of £1,000 from Mr. (later Sir) Abe Bailey, in memory of his wife, headed the new Building Fund. Many other smaller subscriptions brought the total available to well over £3,000 and, when the expenditure of some £3,200 on the new building had been paid off, the Hospital still had £233 standing to its credit.

At the same time the Chairman of the Management Committee, the Rev. C. C. Woodland, who presided at the opening ceremony, warned his audience that they could not have a larger Hospital without increased yearly expenses, and that it was more than ever necessary for local people to subscribe generously to the Hospital. The more was this so because unfortunately, in the time that had elapsed between his gift of the building and its official opening, their great benefactor Mr. Oswald Smith had died, and they would thus lose his yearly subscription of £50.

The new Hospital had a Men's Ward and a Women's Ward, with 6 beds each and one room for Private Patients. There was no separate Children's Ward, but when required cots were put up in the main wards.

Mr. Abe Bailey's large contribution to the new Hospital was

recognised by the calling of one of the wards after his late wife, the Kate Bailey Ward, while Mr. Oswald Smith's gift of the building was commemorated by a plaque in the entrance hall. Many gifts of various kinds were received and were acknowledged in the annual reports, including the gift by Mr. A. E. N. Ward of a Rontgen Ray apparatus. This machine, the very earliest form of X-ray diagnostic apparatus, would have enabled only very primitive X-ray photographs to be taken, and, since the process had only been discovered some 6 or 7 years previously it must have been almost unique to find such an ultramodern machine in so small a country hospital at that time. To what practical use this early machine was put it is difficult to say, since there is no mention of the number of X-ray pictures taken at the Hospital until 1926. During these years the science of radiology was advancing very rapidly and since there is no mention in the annual reports of its use or replacement, we must regretfully conclude that this original piece of apparatus was probably little used, but nevertheless its possession by the Hospital at so early a date is of some interest.

The Management Committee of the new Hospital in 1903 was constituted as follows:—

| | |
|---|---|
| *Trustees:* | Mr. H. Jeddere Fisher, Mr. B. G. Oswald Smith, Mr. W. V. K. Stenning. |
| *Life Members:* | Mr. Abe Bailey, Mr. J. P. Baker, Mr. J. Henderson, Mr. S. P. Lowdell. |
| *Medical Officers:* | Mr. C. E. Collins, Mr. J. Harrison, Mr. F. C. Poynder, Mr. P. E. Wallis. |
| *Hon. Treasurer:* | Mr. F. B. Whitfield. |
| *Hon. Secretary:* | Mr. H. A. Perkins. |
| *Subscribers:* | Rev. D. Y. Blakiston, Sir E. C. Blount, K.C.B., Mr. E. Blount, Mr. G. H. Broadley, Mr. T. H. W. Buckley, Mr. E. M. Crookshank, Mr. C. H. Everard, Mr. J. Southey Hall, Mr. E. Martin, Mr. W. Milburn, Mr. J. S. Oxley, Mr. J. C. Powell, Mr. T. E. Ravenshaw, Mr. F. A. White, Rev. C. C. Woodland, Mr. W. Young. |

*Working Men's Hospital Committee Representatives:*
Messrs. Gallard and Hobson.
*Matron:*        Miss Blanche Sleap.

and it is important to notice here the first mention of the East Grinstead Working Men's Hospital Fund, which had recently been founded by Mr. H. M. Hobson. This Fund did an immense amount of good for the Hospital during the next 45 years, and more details of its history and organisation will be given in subsequent pages.

The Nursing Staff at this time consisted of the Matron and two nurses, Miss Archbold and Miss Pelly, and between them during 1903 they looked after a total of 87 inpatients and 61 outpatients. It is worth noting that this is the first mention of any outpatients being treated at the Hospital; there may well have been outpatients at Lansdowne House, but if there were, there is no mention of them in the records.

The expenditure during the first complete year in the new and bigger building was nearly £550, but the receipts unfortunately were some £43 less. However, in the following year, 1904, Mr. Alfred Bridgland, who had served the Hospital in the capacity of Honorary Auditor ever since its reopening in 1888, was able to report that this £43 had been paid off and, receipts having soared to the large sum of £708 8s. 2d., the Committee were left with a credit balance of £2 17s. 8d.

In 1905, 114 inpatients and 92 outpatients were treated. The Committee's report for this year states "had it not been for the noble contributions received from the Working Men's Organisations, they would have had to report a large deficit balance". In this year, also, a legacy of £100 was received from the estate of the late Miss Elizabeth Brown of The Larches, this sum being added to the Capital Account. Incidentally, the fees for the Private Ward at this time were 2 guineas per week.

In 1906, 223 cases in all were treated and this necessitated the employment of another nurse, making 4 in all, while the annual report of the Medical Staff, whose numbers had been augmented in 1904 by the appointment of Mr. W. H. Hillyer, mentioned "the number of patients seeking admission whom it has been impossible to receive for lack of room". The receipts this year at just over £900 left a credit balance of some £50 when all expenses had been paid.

Early in 1907 it is reported that the Annual Meeting of Subscribers:—

"record their heartfelt sorrow at the loss of their valued Chairman, the Rev. C. C. Woodland, who for 18 years as member of the Committee of Management and for the last 6 as its Chairman, has been so closely identified with the progress of the Hospital and so largely instrumental thereto. They gratefully call to mind the kindly courtesy, sound judgment, and entire sincerity of heart by which he gained the respect and affection of all who knew him."

Two other longstanding members of the Committee had also died recently, Mr. Alfred Bridgland and Mr. W. Young, but to take their places on the Committee Mr. H. Lucas and Mr. H. Partridge were added, and as additional members Dr. E. Stewart, (later Sir Edward Stewart) and Mr. Edward Young. About this time also Mr. H. E. Matthews was appointed Honorary Architect and Mr. E. A. Head became Honorary Auditor. In this year also a legacy of £500 was received from the estate of the late Mr. E. L. Hannam.

In 1908 the Committee suffered a further serious loss in the death of Mr. Jeddere Fisher, who had been one of the Trustees since 1888. Mr. Edward Blount was appointed to succeed him. There also occurred, after a short and acute illness during which he was nursed in the Hospital, the death of Dr. J. Harrison, who had been a member of the Medical Staff for 14 years. He was succeeded by Dr. S. L. Walker, while in 1909 a further addition to the Medical Staff was made in the person of Dr. R. A. Fegan of Forest Row. Also in 1909 the Reverend D. Y. Blakiston left the district and was succeeded on the Committee by the new Vicar of East Grinstead, the Reverend W. W. Youard.

Further mention of Forest Row occurs in the report for 1909, when we find that Mrs. Hyde made a donation of £500 to the Hospital in memory of her husband, this gift to be specifically used for the purpose of making additions to the two general wards of 2 beds each, the 4 beds being known as the "Hyde"

45

beds and left as far as possible for the use of patients from Forest Row.

In 1910 there began one of the most successful associations the Hospital has ever had, in the person of Miss Leonora Garlett, who succeeded Miss Sleap as Matron. Miss Garlett reigned as Matron for some 27 years and even today, more than 25 years after her retirement, is still held in affectionate memory by many local residents who knew her.

In 1911 Mr. W. V. K. Stenning died. He had held the position of Trustee since 1888. His place was taken by Dr. Nathaniel S. Lucas, while at the same time Mr. E. P. Whitley Hughes and Mr. Frank Hill were added to the Committee. Mr. Guy Oswald Smith resigned from the position of Trustee, his place being taken by Mr. F. S. White. This seems finally to end the long association of the Oswald Smith family with the Hospital.

For the first time, in 1913, the total receipts for the year exceeded £1,000, although the Committee reported "several subscribers have ceased their support through the passing into law of the National Insurance Act, but we trust they will reconsider the matter and again help us, as the Act certainly does not meet the serious medical and surgical cases requiring in-treatment in the Hospital". The average cost of food per head per week this year was 6s. 5¼d. and the average total cost of each inpatient per week, including drugs, was 19s.

It is curious that the annual reports for the following years make no mention of any repercussions of the 1914-18 War, either of wounded being admitted or of staff members leaving for military service. In fact, we know that other houses in the district, among them Norton House and Stildon House, both in the London Road, were used for the reception of war wounded, but there is no evidence that the first World War made any impact upon the Hospital at all.

In 1916 Dr. C. E. Collins died, having been on the Staff for 28 years, and Mr. H. A. Perkins, the Manager of Barclays Bank, who had acted as Honorary Secretary to the Hospital for nearly 30 years, retired, being succeeded in this office by the new Manager of Barclays, Mr. E. J. Miller.

In 1917 a new and long association began, with the appointment of Mr. Cecil William Rowntree to the new post of

Consulting Surgeon. Cecil Rowntree, son of a doctor, had qualified at the Middlesex Hospital at the early age of 22. He had served with distinction in the Royal Army Medical Corps during the war and, having first acted as Medical Officer to the Queen's Westminster Rifles and attained the rank of Major, had been appointed Consulting Surgeon to the American Red Cross. Rowntree did most of the major surgery at the Hospital for the next 26 years and remained on the Staff until his death at Little Warren, Lewes Road, East Grinstead, in October 1943. The high standard of his work and his beneficial influence on the Hospital generally, especially with reference to the surgical planning and equipment of the new Holtye Road Hospital, are still remembered today, but what is not so generally realised is that during the intervening years he achieved an international reputation in the realm of cancer surgery and research. In July 1928 he was appointed Chairman of the International Cancer Conference and also became Vice-President of the Union Internationale Contre le Cancer; he was also made a Chevalier of the French Legion D'Honneur and an Officier of the Belgian Ordre de Leopold, both of these honours being earned by his international services to cancer research. With all this activity it is perhaps not surprising to hear that he suffered in his last few years from cardiovascular illness and died at the early age of 63. His long and successful connection with the Hospital has been commemorated by a plaque fixed to the wall just inside the main entrance of the Hospital, and by the calling of the main operating theatre after him.

In 1920 Drs. P. E. Wallis and R. A. Fegan left the Medical Staff and were succeeded by Dr. W. Evershed Wallis, nephew of Dr. P. E. Wallis, and Dr. W. Geoffrey Watson.

1921 is mainly notable for the fact that ladies were at last admitted to the Committee of Management. At the Annual Meeting of Subscribers held at the Hospital on February 23rd of that year "it was unanimously decided that Mrs. Blount and Mrs. Cooper should be added to the Committee".

The work of the Hospital appears to have gone steadily ahead during these years, so much so that no fewer than 334 patients were treated during 1921. Both income and expenditure were by this time well over the £2,000 mark and the

47

Trustees had acquired, mostly through gifts and legacies, over £5,000 in the Capital Account, most of which was invested in Government and local gilt-edged securities. In 1921 Mr. H. Joyce succeeded Mr. E. J. Miller as Honorary Secretary, and the Committee now consisted of the following:—

| | |
|---|---|
| Mrs. Blount | Mr. Ewan Frazer |
| Mr. E. H. Beadnell | Mr. E. P. Whitley Hughes |
| Mr. G. H. Broadley | Col. E. Lloyd Williams |
| Sir R. Hanbury Brown | Mr. E. Martin |
| Mr. T. H. W. Buckley | Col. C. Needham |
| Mrs. Cooper | Mr. L. Penny |
| Mr. E. M. Crookshank | Mr. H. A. Perkins |
| Mr. C. H. Everard | Rev. W. W. Youard |
| Mr. A. Faber | Mr. E. W. Young |

with Messrs. M. W. T. Ridley, F. W. Mighall, and E. Edwards as representatives of the Working Men's Hospital Fund.

In 1922 Dr. W. H. Marshall and Dr. J. E. Passmore were added to the Medical Staff, while Dr. Watson resigned. In this year too, electric light was installed for the first time and the Hospital was connected to the main drainage system.

Most of the Annual Reports for these years pay tribute to the Working Men's Fund, and it is appropriate at this point to consider for a moment the history of this organisation. The East Grinstead Working Men's Hospital Fund, to give it its full name, was founded in February 1903 by Mr. H. M. Hobson, who remained its Secretary for a number of years. There is some evidence that this Fund was one of the earliest, if not in fact the first, organisation of its kind in the country. Its objects were very simply stated, namely "to assist the East Grinstead Cottage Hospital and to pay the expenses either as inpatients or outpatients of any of its members either at the East Grinstead Hospital or at any other Hospital". Certain other benefits were allowed, such as travelling expenses, including an attendant, and sometimes the provision of special surgical appliances. In order to meet all these commitments the Fund raised money by charging its members, if over the age of 16, the sum of 2d. per week, for which it would include benefits for wives and children under 14. Children from the ages 14-16 were admitted to the Fund at 1d. per week. Members were required to pay subscriptions for three months before they became eligible for benefits except in the case of accidents, and it was specifically laid down that injuries received whilst intoxicated or through misconduct, would not receive benefit. A typical appreciation of the Fund was made in the Hospital's Annual Report for the year 1923—

"It is again to the Working Men's Organisation that we are primarily indebted for the strong financial position of our Hospital. It will be seen from the Statement of Accounts that no less a sum than £295 3s. 5d. has been paid over by them to our Hospital; and this is only the balance of sums collected by them in subscriptions of 2d. per week, after paying the full fees for their patients both in our own Hospital and in hospitals in London, Tunbridge Wells, and elsewhere, and all expenses of conveyance. To this contribution should be added a sum of £115 12s. od. resulting from the Hospital Saturday collections, which is entirely organised and managed by the Working Men's Committee. A glance at the Balance Sheet will show that without this assistance our income would not suffice to meet our requirements. Our working men may therefore claim to have found the solution of the financial difficulties that confront the management committees of our hospitals throughout the country; and it is very gratifying to know that the plan is being widely taken up and schemes on very similar lines are being adopted in our own County, and indeed generally throughout England. Nor should the value of the Working Men's Organisation be measured only by the money contributed; by enlisting upwards of 1,000 men and women as voluntary contributors, its effect in spreading a feeling of pride in 'our Hospital' and real sympathy with its work, is quite invaluable."

and again in 1924—

"it is needless to insist on the value of such support, quite as much from the social and moral point of view as from the strictly financial. As long as our Hospital receives such hearty support from all classes in our town, we can confidently resist any interference from well-meaning but misguided politicians."

This statement by Mr. C. H. Everard, Chairman of the

Management Committee, would appear to be the first straw in the wind heralding the approach of the National Health Service some 24 years later. When this came into being in 1948, the financial state of the East Grinstead Hospital, in common with many other similar institutions throughout the country, was far from being as healthy as it was in 1924, and it was totally unable to resist the politicians. Mr. Everard, who died in 1926, would have been disappointed had he known that the "interference of the well-meaning but misguided politicians" eventually was overwhelming.

The Working Men's Fund had its own Committee and conducted its affairs quite independently of the Hospital and, in fact, did not forbear to criticise the Hospital when this seemed necessary, as, for instance, in March 1930 when it appears a member of the Fund was refused admission although it was stated there was a vacant bed available. This incident was apparently smoothed over satisfactorily, but on another occasion when the Hospital Chairman came to address the Working Men's Meeting and suggested that they increase the weekly subscriptions of their members, the Committee sent him about his business in no mean fashion and continued the old subscription rates. One gathers that there were occasional causes for friction between the two committees, Hospital and Fund, but on the whole the relationship was a very happy one, no doubt largely due to the fact that the Working Men's Committee was well represented on the Hospital Committee. In 1931, in addition to their numerous other regular payments to the Hospital, the Working Men's Committee gave £200 to the new Hospital Building Fund and again in 1933 they gave a further £300 for the same purpose. These two donations were duly recognised by the calling of one of the beds in the new Kindersley Ward "the East Grinstead Working Men's Hospital Fund Bed".

When it first began in 1903 the Fund paid 10s. 6d. per week for every patient treated as an inpatient, but in 1933 this sum was raised to £1. 1s. 0d. In 1934 the Fund was elected a Life Governor of the Charing Cross Hospital in return for its many benefactions to that Hospital, and it was laid down that the current Secretary of the Fund would represent it in that capacity. In 1936 the Fund made itself responsible for the complete wireless installation at the new Holtye Road Hospital, and every one of the 42 beds was equipped with headphones. The subscription was raised to 3d. per week in 1936, but the Fund, in spite of this, had to withdraw some of the benefits which it had previously allowed, amongst them physiotherapy and treatment in Maternity Hospitals. In 1947 the subscription was increased again to 4d. per week, as by then the cost of inpatient treatment and the claims on the Fund were growing appreciably.

The extent of the benefits paid out by this Fund can be illustrated by the fact that in the year 1941 alone its income was over £1,500, so that the Fund, having had a total life of 45 years from 1903 to 1948, must during this time have distributed in benefits to various hospitals throughout the area, but particularly to the Queen Victoria Cottage Hospital, well over £50,000, all of which had been collected in weekly amounts of 2d. to 4d. per week. When the Fund finally ceased to function on the taking over of the Hospital by the National Health Service in 1948, it had only a comparatively small surplus in hand and, after a number of presents had been distributed to the chief collectors and officers of the Fund, the final £20 was spent on an oak seat for the East Court Garden of Remembrance, the war memorial garden in East Grinstead.

It is impossible to mention individually all the workers for this Fund over the years but it can be said that the Fund was exceptionally fortunate in its secretaries, of whom in the whole 45 years of its existence there were only 4, Mr. H. M. Hobson deserving special mention as having founded the Fund in 1903. He was succeeded in 1909 by Mr. M. W. T. Ridley who remained secretary until forced to give up by ill health in 1930, thus having given 21 years of devoted service to the Fund. When Mr. Ridley retired he was succeeded by Mr. W. E. Elphick, who remained in this office from 1931 until 1936, and he in his turn was succeeded by Mr. R. J. Holding, who guided the Fund through the difficult war years and to its final inevitable termination, from 1937 until 1949.

There were many Chairmen during the years, of whom the following served for sufficiently long periods to deserve special mention:—

Mr. W. G. Goddard; Mr. E. Green; Mr. F. Hemsley, who served on and off over a very long period on the committee and had several periods as chairman; Mr. G. H. Payne; Mr. J. Wren; Mr. F. Jones; Mr. J. Pattenden; Mr. A. Berry; and more recently we note the names of Mr. R. C. Burgess; Mr. David Catt; Mr. Albert Draper; Mr. A. K. Pelling; Mr. E. Gates; Mr. P. V. Grinstead and Mr. F. G. Gear. Of them all perhaps it is fair to mention especially Mr. R. C. Burgess as having given outstanding service to the Fund. First elected to the committee in 1934, he acted as its Chairman for most of the time until 1949 when the Fund finally wound up. In addition for very many years he represented the Fund on the Hospital Management Committee, and in due course, when the Fund came to an end, Mr. Burgess was elected in his own right as a member of the House Committee to serve under the National Health Service. He still remains, in 1963, an active member of this committee, and his service to the Hospital therefore extends over a period of 29 years; a truly remarkable record.

In 1924 the Hospital was fortunate in receiving one of the largest single gifts which ever came its way, the sum of £5,000 bequeathed by Mr. Sidney Larnach.

In 1925 Drs. Hillyer and Walker left the medical staff and Dr. J. Graham was added to it. The report for this year pays tribute to "the help given to our Staff by Red Cross Nurses, who are always ready to lend a hand when required, especially when some of the Staff are absent on holiday". It goes on to say— "as long as our Hospital receives such spontaneous and loyal support we at least need not fear any tampering with the voluntary principle which we believe to be vital to the healthy working of the English Hospitals". It is right and proper that the strength of this feeling of local pride and of service to the community, which permeated the hospital system throughout the country prior to 1948, should receive mention in this history, for it is constantly in evidence as one reads through the reports for these inter-war years.

In 1925 no fewer than 200 operations were performed in the Hospital, 47 of them being major ones. In this year also the Capital Account passed the £11,000 mark.

In 1925 Dr. S. A. R. Chadwick joined the Medical Staff, having been taken into partnership by Dr. W. H. Marshall. He lived and worked at Wilmington House on the corner of High Street and Portland Road. Dr. Marshall at the time lived at

Dorset House, which is now the annexe to the Dorset Arms Hotel. Though the Hospital had no X-ray apparatus of its own (what had happened to the Rontgen Ray apparatus presented in 1902?), arrangements were made during 1926 by which "any patients whose condition may demand radiography at the Hospital may have the necessary pictures taken on our premises by Dr. Anstey Chave". Since Dr. Chave lived at Redhill, this arrangement cannot have been a very easy one, although we find in 1927 that 68 patients were X-rayed; it is not suprising therefore to hear in 1929 that the Hospital installed its own X-ray apparatus.

On the death of Mr. Everard in 1926, Mr. Edward Blount took over the Chairmanship of the Management Committee and, except for the years 1936-1941, he remained in this office continuously until the advent of the National Health Service in 1948, when he became Chairman of the new House Committee, from which he only retired in 1950.

In 1926 Dr. Poynder and Dr. Passmore appear to have retired from the Staff and Drs. F. C. Lapage and Dr. L. A. Key were added to it, followed shortly after by Dr. H. B. Shaw and Dr. G. K. Thornton, thus increasing the medical staff to eight. In 1927 Mr. H. Joyce was still Honorary Secretary but Mr. F. B. Whitfield had been replaced as Honorary Treasurer by Messrs. Barclays Bank, Ltd. Lady Kindersley joined the Committee in 1927, another event which was to be of tremendous importance to the Hospital during the coming years. Lady Kindersley's work for, and influence upon, the Hospital were inestimable and there will be many mentions of her name in the coming chapters. Suffice it to say at this point that it was not long before she began to make her presence felt on the Committee.

In 1927 the first small financial cloud appears on the horizon. The report says "the Statement of Accounts does not disclose so satisfactory a financial situation as has been the case in former years"—and in fact the sum of £300 had to be withdrawn from the Deposit Account in order to keep the Current Account solvent. However, a special appeal was made during this year for further subscribers, and in 1928 the Committee were able to report a slight improvement in their finances.

The Annual Report for 1929 draws the attention of sub-

53

scribers to the satisfactory financial position which, it says, "is entirely due to the donation of £500 received from the Ashdown Forest Pageant". This pageant must have been the outstanding local event of 1929. It was staged in Kidbrooke Park in July, and was organised by a Committee consisting of Mr. and Mrs. Olaf Hambro of Kidbrooke Park, Lady Edward Gleichen, Miss Needham and Miss Parsons, with Lord Edward Gleichen, also the author of the pageant, as Chairman. The executive committee was assisted by a representative committee drawn from a very large surrounding area, and a special Horse Committee was set up, since so many of the scenes required the use of horses. The Pageant was produced by Miss Gwen Lally and consisted of eight episodes with a leading cast of 150 people and in addition large numbers of villagers and children. The Pageant was honoured by a visit from the Duke and Duchess of York.

The year 1929 also sees special thanks given to Dr. Shaw and Dr. Graham for their services in connection with the new X-ray apparatus. This apparatus had cost the Hospital £500, in those days a vast sum of money, but, the report says "it greatly enhances the sphere of usefulness of our Hospital".

At the Annual Meeting of Subscribers in 1929 the question of enlarging the Hospital was discussed. The Chairman said that some £8,500 would be needed to alter the present building, and the Committee did not feel they would get for this sum anything commensurate with the amount spent. The Medical Staff were in favour of building a new Hospital, but the Chairman pointed out that this would involve expenditure of some £30,000. The Meeting came to the conclusion that this was not the time to try and raise so large an amount, though one opinion was expressed that it would be forthcoming if there was a crying need for it. Mr. Alan Huggett spoke of the possibility of smaller hospitals being nationalised, and it was eventually decided that the matter should be deferred.

In 1930, 411 patients were treated, and 300 cases X-rayed. The Radiographer stated that her Department was much appreciated not only by the medical profession, but also by dental and veterinary surgeons. This same year also saw the beginning of another long and profitable association, Mr Guthrie Kirkhope being elected to the Committee. Mr. Kirkhope had lived for some years in China, where he had been in business and where he had been a member of the Board of Governors of the Central China Hospital, and he had been awarded the Chao Medal by the Chinese Government for his work on famine relief. He had to retire from this work in 1928 on account of ill health and came to live in East Grinstead, but it was only a short time before he became interested in the East Grinstead Hospital and was elected a member of its Management Committee. A great deal more will be heard of Mr. Kirkhope in this story, for it was not until 26 years later that his association with the Hospital ended. Here it may simply be said that Mr. Kirkhope and Lady Kindersley together put all their efforts into running the Hospital, and it is noticeably from this moment that its speed of development quickened.

In December, 1930, a petition was received by the Hospital Committee from the East Grinstead Chamber of Commerce "urging them to make a serious effort to provide further accommodation to meet the needs of the Town and agreeing to support such efforts with their moral and financial assistance". This was a difficult time financially for the whole country, and the Committee did not feel able to take any action in the matter, but contented themselves in 1931 with "venturing to hope that subscriptions and donations on which the Hospital depends for its very existence, may suffer no reduction". Unfortunately, this hope was not realised, for in the following year subscriptions and donations, in spite of the Committee's appeal, were somewhat reduced, and the Committee felt bound to view "with some apprehension" this shrinking in the income of the Hospital.

In April 1931, a Meeting was held at which the building of a new Hospital was, for the first time, seriously discussed; Sir Robert Kindersley estimated that the new building and land would cost some £25,000 and a special committee was set up, about which more will be heard in the next chapter, to try and raise this sum. It was in August of the same year, however, that Sir Robert generously offered free to the Hospital Management Committee the building site in the Holtye Road. This offer was most gratefully accepted and the first step was thus taken towards the provision of a new Hospital.

In the 1932 Annual Report the Management Committee "note with pleasure the progress that has been made by the

Committee set up to provide and equip a new and larger Hospital, and venture to express the hope that the efforts made in that direction may meet with the success which they deserve". In this year Drs. Lapage and Key left the Medical Staff, followed shortly after by Dr. J. Graham, while Drs. A. Orr-Ewing, R. Stanley and H. Stewart joined it and Dr. T. Izod Bennett was appointed to the new position of Honorary Consulting Physician.

In 1933 the Committee are pleased to report that "the efforts of the Representative Committee appointed to collect funds for the provision of a new Hospital have met with most gratifying success and it has now been decided to commence building some time this summer".

In 1935 the Committee issued its last Annual Report from the Queen's Road premises and they remarked that they desired to place on record their high appreciation of the excellent if unobtrusive work which was carried on there for 33 years.

This phrase "excellent but unobtrusive" is indeed a very appropriate way in which to describe the Queen's Road period of the Hospital's history. No records exist of any specially interesting events during this time, but after reading through the succeeding Annual Reports, one is left with an outstanding impression of the generally very high standard consistently achieved both by the Management and by the Staff, and of the highest devotion and loyalty both by the public and by all those who had anything to do with the working of the Hospital. It is difficult to convey this impression adequately in writing, but some of the following figures will illustrate it. (It must be remembered that at no time were more than 17 beds available in the Hospital).

In 1903, the first full year at the new premises, 148 cases were treated; this grew steadily until by 1930 there were 411 inpatients and 100 outpatients. While at first there were no X-ray facilities, by the end of the period the number of cases X-rayed in one year rose as high as 300. While receipts in 1903 were £505 and expenditure £549, the corresponding figures in the last full year at Queen's Road were—receipts £2,013, expenditure £1,804. It will be remembered that the Hospital began its life at Queen's Road with some £230 in the

56

bank; when it left there the Trustees held securities valued at £16,569. These figures alone pay tribute to the steady hard work and expansion that went on during this period.

Apart from the bare figures, however, some names are outstanding during the period. The three Chairmen, the Reverend C. C. Woodland, Mr. C. H. Everard and Mr. Edward Blount, must have carried the main weight of responsibility, while the three Honorary Secretaries, Mr. A. J. Perkins, Mr. E. J. Miller and Mr. H. Joyce, no doubt carried out most of the hard administrative work that was necessary. The two Matrons, Miss Blanche Sleap and Miss Leonora Garlett, received constant praise from the Committee, as did also the Medical Staff year after year, particularly generous tributes being paid to Mr. Cecil Rowntree from all sides.

Mr. F. B. Whitfield served the Queen's Road Hospital as Treasurer from its beginning up to the year 1926, when the increasingly onerous duties were taken over by Barclays Bank. The financial affairs of the Hospital were mainly looked after by three Trustees, and during the years only six names appear in this capacity; Mr. H. Jeddere Fisher, Mr. B. G. Oswald Smith, Mr. W. V. K. Stenning, Mr. E. C. Blount, Mr. F. S. White and Dr. N. S. Lucas.

The following, by virtue of outstanding services to the Hospital in various ways, qualified during the period and in this order of appointment, as Life Members of the Hospital:—

| | |
|---|---|
| Sir Abe Bailey | Mr. A. D. Cochrane |
| Mr. J. P. Baker | Mr. J. Gow |
| Mr. J. Henderson | Mr. F. A. White |
| Mr. S. P. Lowdell | Mr. H. W. Rudd |
| Mr. E. W. B. Holt | Mr. Frank Hill |
| Mr. W. M. Campbell | Rev. C. L. Norris |

In addition to the above-mentioned who served the Hospital in some special way, mention must be made also of the following who were elected at the Annual Subscribers Meetings to represent the subscribers, i.e. the public, on the Hospital Management Committee. Many who read this book will know very well what membership of the Management Committee meant— many long hours spent in the Hospital's service, not only in committee but out of it, in many and various ways. To every

57

one of the following subscribers, therefore, the Hospital owes a great debt of gratitude for their devoted service. They are listed in order of appointment:—

| | |
|---|---|
| Rev. D. Y. Blakiston | Sir R. Hanbury Brown |
| Mr. T. H. W. Buckley | Col. C. Needham |
| Mr. E. M. Crookshank | Mr. E. P. Whitley Hughes |
| Mr. W. Milburn | Mr. C. H. Beadnell |
| Mr. J. S. Oxley | Mr. Ewan Frazer |
| Mr. J. C. Powell | Mrs. Blount |
| Mr. T. E. Ravenshaw | Col. E. Lloyd Williams |
| Rev. C. C. Woodland | Mrs. Cooper |
| Mr. W. Young | Mr. H. Machin |
| Mr. G. H. Broadley | Miss R. F. Poynder |
| Mr. J. Southey Hall | Mr. F. E. Richards |
| Mr. E. Martin | Mr. M. W. T. Ridley |
| Mr. H. Lucas | Rev. Martin Austin |
| Mr. H. Partridge | Rev. Dr. G. Golding-Bird |
| Sir E. Stewart | Mrs. Nevill |
| Mr. E. Young | Miss Lucas |
| Mr. A. Faber | Miss Wagg |
| Mr. L. Penny | Mrs. Hambro |
| Rev. W. W. Youard | Mr. J. Viall |

Mention must be made also of the loyal devotion given by the following members of the Working Men's Hospital Fund, who over these years, in turn, served two or three at a time on the Hospital Committee:—

| | |
|---|---|
| Mr. Gallard | Mr. F. Jones |
| Mr. H. M. Hobson | Mr. E. Edwards |
| Mr. J. Brown | Mr. J. Pattenden |
| Mr. G. Payne | Mr. F. W. Mighall |
| Mr. M. W. T. Ridley | Mr. G. Baker |
| Mr. J. Tyler | Mr. H. Baker |
| Mr. W. G. Goddard | Mr. R. Slator |
| Mr. W. H. Sinden | Mr. Martin |
| Mr. G. Tizzard | Mr. G. H. Payne |
| Mr. E. Green | Mr. J. Wren |
| Mr. F. Hemsley | Mr. W. E. Elphick |
| Mr. W. P. Luxford | Mr. A. Berry |

Mr. T. Pentecost

Mr. P. R. Hann

Mr. W. Langridge

Mr. H. G. Payne

Mr. R. C. Burgess

Mr. D. Catt

Mr. E. Pattenden

# 4

# Holtye Road

I⊤ was largely as the result of two petitions received by the Cottage Hospital Committee towards the end of 1930, urging them to provide increased hospital accommodation for the Town, that a small sub-committee was set up to enquire into the possibilities. One of these petitions, with 31 signatures, came from the East Grinstead Chamber of Commerce; the other, presented by Mr. Joseph Rice, contained 65 signatures of local interested people. The Sub-committee, comprising Lady Kindersley, Miss R. F. Poynder, Miss E. M. Wagg and Mr. W. H. Giles, decided that it would be wise in the first place to call a public meeting to find out how much support would be forthcoming from the public for such a proposal.

This meeting took place in the Parish Hall on April 21st, 1931, and was well attended. General A. D. Musgrave, D.S.O. was in the Chair, and he was supported on the platform by Sir Robert Kindersley, G.B.E., and Mr. Cecil Rowntree. It was soon evident that plenty of support would be forthcoming, and the meeting, recognising that a new hospital was needed, proceeded to elect a General Organising Committee. The proposed scheme, it was estimated, would cost some £25,000.

This General Committee soon got to work under the Chairmanship of General Musgrave, and since it was rather a large and unwieldy committee consisting of 60 members (later it was expanded to as many as 198 members) it was immediately obvious that it would be best to divide into Sub-committees, and it was decided to set up an Executive Committee, a Sites Committee, a Building and Finance Committee, an Appeals Committee and a Pay-bed Committee. Captain J. P. Price was elected Honorary Secretary of the new scheme and an office for his use was opened at No. 3 Queens Road, East Grinstead, on August 11th, 1931. This office remained in continual use until December 31st, 1935, on which date all records were transferred to the new Hospital building. Mr. W. Guthrie Kirkhope was elected Honorary Treasurer, Mr. E. P. Whitley Hughes, Solicitor, and Mr. H. Osborne, Accountant; Messrs. Barclays Bank were appointed Bankers.

The Sites Committee quickly went into action and, having inspected a number of alternative sites, finally chose a field consisting of 4⅓ acres in the Holtye Road with a south aspect and over 400 ft. above sea-level. Lady Kindersley has been known to tell a story of how when she went with her husband and Mr. Kirkhope to inspect this site, they were unable to gain access to it and had to force their way through a gap in the hedge in order to view the land. Apart from its lack of access, however, the site was eminently suitable and it was purchased by Sir Robert Kindersley, and in August of the same year most generously presented to the Trustees, with the proviso that building must commence within 3 years.

Apart from this outstanding achievement, the first year for the New Hospital Scheme was not a happy one. In September, the General Committee suffered a severe loss by the untimely death of its Chairman, General Musgrave. The project also ran into further trouble at this early stage owing to the general financial state of the country at the time. The Appeals Committee, under the Chairmanship of Lt. Gen. Sir George MacMunn, had drafted an appeal to the public, but the General Committee decided, in view of the financial crisis, that the moment was not propitious, and so the issuing of this appeal had to be postponed. By the end of 1931, therefore, apart from the acquisition of the site, there was only £489 collected towards the building of the new Hospital. Not a very auspicious start, but a lot of hard work behind the scenes had been done, and the stage was set for renewed efforts in 1932.

The Building & Finance Committee, consisting of 26 members, had Lady Kindersley as its Chairman and Mr. F. E. Richards of Coombe Hall as its Vice-Chairman. It had the duty of selecting an architect, receiving plans, estimates, contracts, etc., controlling the funds and buying the equipment for the new Hospital. This Committee split itself into a number of groups; (1) Visiting Committee, whose task was to visit and inspect other hospitals; (2) Plans Committee; (3) Grounds Committee; (4) Economies Committee; (5) Equipment Committee and (6) Furnishing Committee. Mr. F. G. Troup, F.R.I.B.A. and Col. A. C. Denny were appointed Architects for the New Hospital.

The Appeals Committee, having had its main public appeal postponed, set to work to organise various money-raising schemes. One of these was the distribution in January of 1,300 Collecting Boxes, which were to prove a steady source of income. The main event, however, organised by them during 1932 was a Hospital Week from July 11th-18th. Numerous events were arranged during this week—amongst others a Fête held in the Vicarage Garden by permission of Dr. and Mrs. Golding-Bird, which raised the sum of £183 2s. 1d. Mr. Fawell presented an Austin car for auction, and the sale of 1s. tickets for this produced the magnificent sum of £239 12s. od. Concerts, bridge and whist tournaments, donations, a flag day and various other efforts, brought the total for the week to the fine sum of £619 4s. 9d. However, this was not good enough for Mrs. Munn, the Vice-Chairman of the Appeals Committee, who "hoped that a similar week to be held the following year would produce even more". By the end of 1932 the sum collected had only risen to £1,688, still not very far towards the required £25,000.

However, by October 1932, the country's financial state had improved and it was decided that the main Appeal could be launched. Early in 1933 over 8,000 copies of this Appeal were issued, the cost of postage of which, incidentally, amounting to some £50, was given by an anonymous donor.

The Appeal was immediately successful and, largely because of it, 1933 was a much better year in every way—in August the Treasurer was able to report the following financial position—

| | | | | | |
|---|---|---|---|---|---|
| Cash in the Bank | .. | .. | .. | 5,798 | 0 0 |
| Money invested .. | .. | .. | .. | 2,475 | 0 0 |
| Money promised.. | .. | .. | .. | 614 | 0 0 |
| Already paid for land .. | .. | .. | 1,600 | 0 0 |
| Estimate for sale of old Hospital building | | | 1,500 | 0 0 |
| | | | | £11,987 | 0 0 |

Meanwhile the Building & Finance Committee proceeded

with the preparation of specifications for the plans, which had now been approved and in December 1933 another Public Meeting was called at which the plans were exhibited and the general financial position explained.

The Appeals Committee was kept hard at work under its new Chairman, Sir Charles Madden, who took Sir George Mac-Munn's place when the latter went to India in 1933. The joint Honorary Secretaries, Mrs. Dempster and Miss Iris Wallis, together carried on this arduous task throughout the whole period of the Committee's activity, some 14 years in all. It met frequently and in various places, first of all in the Oak Room at the Whitehall and later at Hurst-an-Clays, Stoneleigh, and The Hermitage, in each case through the kindness of the respective owners, Mrs. Musgrave, Mrs. Spalding and Miss Wagg.

A particularly interesting note appears in the Minutes of the Appeals Committee Meeting dated September 4th, 1933:—

"Mrs. Dempster was asked if she could find out about the Peanut Scheme for Children which is run with such success for the Tunbridge Wells Hospital."

Another minute for this same meeting is also worth recording; Mr. Kirkhope had announced that the total funds collected now amounted to nearly £12,500 and the Secretary, somewhat carried away by excitement, added her own words:—

"As the appeal is for £25,000 we are halfway there! Cheers!"

At the following meeting Miss Wagg "undertook to find out if the East Grinstead Branch of the Courier would run the Peanut Scheme here", and again in December the Committee instructed its Chairman to seek a meeting with the Chairman of the Tunbridge Wells Hospital, to discuss the possibility of the two Hospitals joining together for the Peanut Scheme. Actually it was some years before this suggestion bore fruit, in fact not until 1939, but when it did, as will be seen later, it was to prove of tremendous benefit to the Hospital.

Early in 1934 the Architects were instructed to prepare for the commencement of the building of the new Hospital as soon as possible. It will be remembered that Sir Robert Kindersley had presented the land in August 1931 on the understanding that building would commence within 3 years—and time was running short. Sir Robert pointed out to the General Committee that the cost of building was going up. Although they had originally said they must have £15,000 in hand before beginning the building, and they still had under £13,000, nevertheless he thought that building should begin as soon as possible and he believed that starting the building operations would bring in a lot more money.

In May, 1934, the Appeal was registered as a Charity so that it could benefit both from the sale of "Help Yourself" Annuals, and from the Seven Year Covenant Scheme of Income Tax remission. Later the same year a Fête held at Plawhatch, by permission of Sir Robert and Lady Kindersley, made the record sum of £900.

In all, 13 offers were received from different building firms for the work, and in August the contract was given to the lowest bidder, Messrs. Chapman, Lowry and Puttick of Haslemere, whose estimate was for the sum of £25,936—with a stipulation in the contract that an average of 50% of local labour should be employed on the work. Even this estimate, however, was much higher than had been anticipated, and the Economies Committee had now to set to work to see what economies could be effected. In fact, their efforts were most successful and when building operations actually began in November, the estimated cost had been reduced to £20,126, of which by the end of 1934 just over £16,000 had been collected. Early in 1935 it was estimated that the building would be completed by October of that year and that for completion and equipment of the new Hospital only a further £8,000 was required.

Saturday, April 6th 1935 was an important and happy day in the life of the Hospital, for it was on this day that the foundation stone of the new building was officially laid by The Rt. Hon. Lord Horder, K.C.V.O., M.D., F.R.C.S. Reporting the event the following week, the East Grinstead Observer described how Mr. Joseph Rice had, nearly 4 years previously, given the first £100 towards what had at the time seemed "a fantastic dream".

The proceedings were presided over by Mr. Edward Blount, Chairman of the existing Cottage Hospital, who said how

Mr. Cecil Rowntree, from a
Portrait by T. C. Dugdale.

Mr. Edward Blount

Lady Kindersley, from a portrait by Oswald Birley

Mr. W. G. Kirkhope

Mr. Neville Blond

Mrs. Elaine Blond

pleased he was to be asked, "thus effecting" he said, "a link between the old Hospital and the new". He went on to pay tribute to "the courage, determination and generosity of people like Sir Robert and Lady Kindersley", which had made the whole thing possible, and then introduced Lord Horder.

Lord Horder expressed the opinion that the decentralisation of hospital work was a very sound principle. "The dissemination of advances in surgery and medicine is so rapid these days", he said, "that nearly as much is known in East Grinstead as in London, and of course the advantages of treatment in the country are obvious." He could not remember a country hospital as well situated or so admirably conceived; "I am" he said, "an advocate of the voluntary principle, and I hope when we do pass to some other system, that the change will be gradual. It is a great advantage to the people to own their hospital, for they can administer, control and complain about it."

Mr Cecil Rowntree then spoke and, after describing Lord Horder as the most distinguished physician of his generation, said that he hoped the traditions and spirit of the old Hospital would be maintained in the new. The foundation stone was then laid, and when it had been blessed by the Vicar of St. Swithuns, the Reverend Dr. G. Golding-Bird, the hymn "Thou to Whom the Sick and Dying" was sung.

In his speech of thanks Sir Robert Kindersley said that that very afternoon their outstanding debt on the Hospital had been reduced from £5,500 to £4,500 by the generous gift of £1,000 by Mr. John Dewar. He paid tribute to Mr. Rowntree, whose influence, he said, had led him originally to support the scheme, and said he had always had faith in the generosity of the East Grinstead people. Mr. Burt, Chairman of the Urban District Council, seconding the vote of thanks, said that he spoke on behalf of the 8,000 people in the district, who were devoutly thankful for what had been done.

During the remainder of 1935, with work actually progressing on the new building, excitement mounted. A large thermometer was erected in the Town to show how the collection of funds was progressing, and in fact by the end of the year a total of £21,398 was available, not allowing for the value of the old Hospital which was estimated to be £1,500.

65

A provisional Committee with Mr. Guthrie Kirkhope as its Chairman was elected, to make all the arrangements for the opening of the new Hospital. Numerous sub-committees were set up to deal with such matters as Rules and Regulations, Nursing Staff, Medical Staff, and maintenance of the new Hospital which it had been estimated would be in the region of £3,500 per annum. (It will be remembered that when the Queen's Road Hospital opened in 1902 the annual maintenance funds required had been fairly accurately estimated at £300). In addition to all this a further Sub-committee was set up to suggest names of 40 subscribers to either the old or new Hospitals who might be nominated for election to the proposed Board of Management of the new Hospital; and finally another Public Meeting was held in the Parish Hall on November 26th, under the presidency of Sir Robert Kindersley, at which the whole position was again put before the subscribers, and at which the 25 members of the new Board of Management were chosen.

By the end of 1935 all was ready, and it was decided that the Opening Ceremony should take place during the Christmas holidays, when it was hoped that school children would be available to present purses. Incidentally, when the question of a party to celebrate the opening of the Hospital was discussed there was a move to make it a sherry party but finally, so it is recorded, the majority vote was in favour of a teaparty instead, as a matter of principle!

The Opening Ceremony was performed on Wednesday, January 8th, 1936, by Her Highness Princess Helena Victoria. The President of the new Hospital, Sir Robert Kindersley, presented to the Princess the Lord Bishop of Chichester, Lord Leconfield the Lord Lieutenant of Sussex, Mr. W. H. Abbey the High Sheriff of Sussex and his wife, Sir Henry Cautley, M.P. and his wife, Lady Kindersley, Lord and Lady Horder, Lady Madden, Colonel Powell Edwards the Chairman of the East Sussex County Council, Lt. Colonel G. M. Ormerod, D.S.O., Chief Constable of East Sussex, Mr. Edward Blount, President of the old Hospital, and Mrs. Blount, Mr. J. H. Griffin, Chairman of the East Grinstead Urban District Council, Mr. and Mrs. John Dewar, Mr. Cecil Rowntree, Miss Garlett the Matron, the Rev. Dr. G. Golding-Bird D.D., Vicar and Rural

Dean of East Grinstead, and a number of other local people. The National Anthem was sung and, a bouquet having been presented to the Princess by Master Hugo Kindersley, Sir Robert then gave an account of the Hospital and its requirements. After this Lord Leconfield thanked Her Highness for coming, the Sackville Choir sang the hymn "Thou to Whom the Sick and Dying" and the Lord Bishop dedicated the Hospital. Her Highness then proceeded to open the Hospital, Captain F. Gordon Troup, F.R.I.B.A. and Lt. Colonel A. C. Denny the Architects having first been presented to her, along with a number of Senior Officials who had had a hand in the building. On opening the Hospital, the Medical Staff and various members of the Hospital Committees were presented to her. The Princess then proceeded to the Parish Hall, where the presentation of purses by more than 150 school children took place, and the Hospital was opened for viewing by the public immediately she had left; it is recorded that many local people toured the building.

By far the greater part of the £25,000 which had been collected came from individual subscribers, of whom a list was published giving the amount each had subscribed. The list, headed by Sir Robert and Lady Kindersley, contained over 500 names and the amounts varied from over £2,000 given by Sir Robert and Lady Kindersley and Mr. and Mrs John Dewar, down to 2s. 6d. Lord Glendyne gave £1,500 and Mrs. Hotblack £1,100, and there were in addition 3 donations, as well as that from the Working Men's Fund, of £500 or over, the grand total in all being £18,500. The remainder—about £6,500—was raised by a really quite remarkable diversity of special efforts, of which the 1934 Plawhatch Fête produced £900 and the 1933 Bank Holiday Fête over £600. The children's purses produced £271, a dance at the Café de Paris at which various articles were auctioned by Mr. Nelson Keys produced £256, the motorcar draw £247, the Vicarage Garden Fête in 1932 £246, the Plawhatch dance £235 and there were many others, too numerous to mention individually.

There is an impressive list of the various functions which were held. They included public dances, dramatic society performances, bridge and whist tournaments, the collecting of money by Mrs. Fawell's dog in the Town with a tin strapped to its

67

back, the selling of puppies and kittens, a lawn tennis exhibition at Plawhatch at which Mr. Fred Perry and Miss Kay Stammers appeared, a motor Treasure Hunt, a golf tournament, an art exhibition, various articles which were given for raffling—including a grandfather clock and a tea service—the "Help Yourself" Annuals, a gym display by pupils of Miss Newby, a bowling competition, and special church collections. There was scarcely an organisation in the neighbourhood which did not lend its aid in some form or other, amongst them The East Grinstead Urban District Council, the Rotary Club, the Chamber of Commerce, the British Legion, the Cricket Club, the Swimming Club, the Boy Scouts and Girl Guides, the Women's Institute, the Red Cross, Toc H., the Town Band, various dance bands, Mr. Herring's Orchestra, the Police Athletic Club, the Post Office staff, the Operatic Society, the Cycling Club, the Bowling Club and many others, and it is recorded that "The Committee are indebted to almost every business and profession in the neighbourhood for assistance". This had indeed been an outstanding example of how effective a combined voluntary effort could be and, though we must remember that this was the kind of way in which most of the Hospitals in the country were built and maintained in the days before nationalisation, nevertheless the organisers of this particular venture, and the people of East Grinstead who had so loyally supported them, had every right to be proud of their achievement.

On the 14th January, 6 days after the official opening, 6 patients were transferred from the old Hospital to the new.

The new Hospital had two main wards, each of 12 beds, one for men and one for women, a Children's Ward with 6 cots, and 6 rooms for private patients. It had also an operating theatre, anaesthetic room, sterilising room, X-ray department, isolation and waiting rooms, casualty and outpatient departments, kitchens, dining and sitting rooms, etc. and a mortuary, all on the ground floor, with accommodation for the Matron, Sisters, nursing and domestic staff on the first floor. The two main wards were named after the two chief donors to the subscription list, Kindersley Ward and Dewar Ward. Between them, all facing south, lay the Children's Ward (now the Evershed-Wallis Ward), the X-ray Department (now the Edward Blount

Ward), and the Matron's Office (the small room situated between these two Wards). Outpatients were seen in the small room on the opposite side of the main corridor, now used as a Linen Store, and the adjacent cupboards were the outpatients' dressing rooms! A telephone with two extensions was installed in the new building.

It is difficult these days to visualise the entire activities of the Hospital being carried on within this comparatively small area, but it must be remembered that with 37 beds the new Hospital was more than double the size of the old, and it was, in fact, quite adequate for the population, some 10,000, which it served at that time.

The Committee of Management of the new Hospital when it was opened was constituted as follows:—

*President:* Sir Robert Kindersley, G.B.E.
*Vice-Presidents:* Lord Glendyne, Edward Blount Esq. J.P. J. A. Dewar, Esq.
*Trustees:* Edward Blount, Esq., J.P.; W. Guthrie Kirkhope, Esq.; Dr. N. S. Lucas; F. E. Richards, Esq.; P. L. Kindersley, Esq.

*Board of Management:*
*Chairman:* Mrs. R. G. Munn
*Vice-Chairman:* Miss H. M. Beale, O.B.E.

| | |
|---|---|
| Miss Margaret Black | H. Joyce, Esq. |
| Mrs. Edward Blount, J.P., O.B.E. | Lady Kindersley |
| | J. H. Mitchell, Esq. |
| Mrs. Dempster | Miss M. A. Paxton |
| Mrs. J. A. Dewar | Capt. J. P. Price |
| Mrs. Devitt | Mrs. F. E. Richards |
| S. H. Fawell, Esq. | Miss M. Spalding |
| Miss F. H. Hanbury | John Viall, Esq. |
| Miss M. A. Hadden | Miss E. M. Wagg, M.B.E. |
| Mrs. Hotblack | Miss I. P. Wallis |
| A. Huggett, Esq. | A. Willmer, Esq. |
| E. P. Whitley Hughes, Esq. | |

with the President, the Trustees and the Honorary Auditor as ex-officio members, Dr. R. Stanley representing the Medical Committee and Mr. R. C. Burgess and Mr. R. J. Holding the Working Men's Fund.

| | |
|---|---|
| *Honorary Treasurer:* | Arthur Tyler, Esq., A.C.A. |
| *Honorary Auditor:* | Harold Osborne, Esq., A.C.A. |
| *Honorary Solicitors:* | Messrs. Whitley Hughes & |
| | Luscombe. |
| *Matron:* | Miss Leonora Garlett. |

At the same time the Honorary Medical Staff had been very considerably augmented and the following appointments made:—

| | |
|---|---|
| *Hon. Consulting Physicians:* | Dr. H. Gardiner-Hill, M.D., F.R.C.P. |
| | Dr. Donald Paterson, M.D., F.R.C.P. (Children) |
| *Hon. Consulting Surgeons:* | Cecil Rowntree, Esq., F.R.C.S. |
| | W. G. Scott-Brown, Esq., F.R.C.S. (Ear, Nose and Throat) |
| *Hon. Dermatologist:* | Dr. John Franklin, M.D., M.R.C.P. |

*Hon Medical Staff:*

| | |
|---|---|
| Dr. W. Evershed Wallis | Dr. P. L. Blaber |
| Dr. W. H. Marshall | Dr. R. Stanley |
| Dr. H. B. Shaw | Dr. J. H. M. Frobisher |
| Dr. G. K. Thornton | Dr. H. Stewart |
| Dr. A. Orr-Ewing | Dr. C. R. Steel |

Rules for the new Hospital were drawn up, amongst which the following are worth noting:—

*Rule II. Object.* The Hospital is intended for the accommodation of Patients suffering from disease or accident, who cannot be properly treated at home. The following cases are, however, inadmissible: Mental Disorders: Infectious Diseases, including Phthisis: Incurable Cases; Epilepsy and Maternity Cases, or Verminous Cases.

*Rule III. Area.* Patients may be admitted from the Civil Parishes of Cowden, East Grinstead (including Ashurst Wood and Kingscote), Forest Row (including Hammerwood), Hartfield (including Holtye and Colemans Hatch), Lingfield (including Dormans Park and Dormansland), West Hoathly (including Sharpthorne), Worth (including Crawley Down, Turners Hill and Copthorne), and the district of Felbridge.

*Rule IV. Trustees.* The site of the Hospital and the endowments thereof are vested in the Official Trustee of Charitable Lands and the Official Trustee of Charitable Funds in accordance with the terms of a Scheme dated the 24th March, 1936.

*Rule VII. Board of Management.* The Hospital shall be under the direction of a Board of Management (hereinafter called "the Board") consisting of the President, Edward Charles Blount, William Guthrie Kirkhope, Frank Ernest Richards, Nathaniel Sampson Lucas and Philip Leyland Kindersley (the Trustees of the Hospital), the Honorary Treasurer, a representative of the Medical Staff, the Chairman and Secretary for the time being of the East Grinstead Working Men's Hospital Committee, and 25 members of the Hospital, 5 of whom shall retire annually, but will be eligible for re-election.

*Rule VIII. Standing Committees.* The Standing Committees of the Board shall be:—

The House Committee.
The Finance and Building Committee.
The Appeals Committee, and
The Medical Committee.

*Rule XVII. Payments.* Each patient shall pay such weekly contribution as the House Committee may fix, the minimum rate being 3s. per day for Adults and 2s. per day for Children. The House Committee in all cases, shall have the power of fixing a higher or, if thought desirable, a lower rate and the Committee shall have power to remit the whole or part of such payment at its discretion. Accidents and Casualties will receive "First Aid" at the Hospital on payment of a fee based on treatment received, with a minimum of 2s. 6d.

*Rule XX. Length of Treatment.* No patient may remain in the Hospital longer than six weeks except under special circumstances to be reported by the Medical Officer in charge of the case, and with the approval of the House Committee.

*Rule XXIII. Private Patients.* The fees for the Private Wards shall be £6 6s. od. or £7 7s. od. weekly according to whether the Patients live within or outside the Hospital area.

The Board of Management had recommended the employment of staff, with appropriate salaries, as follows:—

Matron, £160 per annum: 2 Sisters, £85 per annum: 2 Staff Nurses, £70 per annum: 2 Assistant Staff Nurses, £60 per annum: 3 Probationers, £30 per annum: 1 Cook, £60 per annum: 1 Kitchen Maid, £40 per annum: 1 House/parlour-maid £45 per annum: 2 Housemaids, £30 per annum: Between Maid, £35 per annum; and a Gardener and Porter, 50s. per week.

When, in April, the final balance sheet was drawn up, the Board were able to announce that—including receipts from the old Hospital Fund and the sale of the old Hospital building—the new Hospital and its equipment "have been cleared of debt which is an extremely satisfactory achievement". The total cost of the new building had been £23,256 12s. 2d. and the Hospital had a cash balance of £214 7s. 7d.

After the tremendous effort of launching the new Hospital, which had taken some 5 years from its first beginning to its final completion, the next 3 years were to be comparatively easy ones—a period of settling in and stabilisation.

There were, of course, various minor difficulties at first, and in retrospect one of the most amusing concerns the serpent and staff which had been erected over the main entrance of the building. Within a few days of the opening the Matron became ill, and there were one or two unforeseen deaths within the Hospital. On the strength of these misfortunes a rumour was spread by some of the more superstitious that the serpent was bringing bad luck to the Hospital, and in fact this belief became so widespread, attracting even the notice of the National Press, that the House Committee, meeting on January 27th, only a fortnight after the opening, "felt bound to draw the Finance and Building Committee's attention to the urgency for taking down the serpent from the tower"! However, fortunately a saner view was taken by the Finance and Building Committee, who, when they discovered its removal would cost £63, replied that "they did not feel justified in incurring this expense at present".

The Medical Committee had recommended that a Pathologist and a Radiologist should be appointed and that their services should be remunerated. They had at the same time drawn attention to the need to provide a new X-ray plant "as the existing plant is limited to the photography of fractures". As a result of these recommendations Dr. Selous from Tunbridge Wells was appointed Pathologist on a "payment for service" basis. Dr. Long, also from Tunbridge Wells, who was appointed Radiologist about the same time, reported that while the X-ray plant was efficient as a portable machine, it was in fact dangerous owing to the connections not being shock-proof. He thought it would cost at least £50 to make it safe, and he therefore recommended the purchase of a new machine which would cost up to £1,000. He also recommended that as he could come from Tunbridge Wells only comparatively infrequently, there would need to be a nurse in the Hospital trained in radiography. This request was later modified and Dr. Long agreed to engage and pay a Radiographer on the condition that the Hospital fed and housed her. This new suggestion being accepted Miss Helen Davies was appointed and managed the department singlehanded for the next 10 years. Within a short time an anonymous donation of £1,000 was received for the specific purpose of equipping the X-ray Department, and an up-to-date all-purpose apparatus was installed.

There was, at this stage, no Physiotherapy Department and any physiotherapy which was required was given by Miss Budgen and Miss Buckpitt, private physiotherapists in the Town. Miss Hadden was appointed official Librarian, a position which she held for some 2 years, and the arrangement whereby Messrs. Martin's and Dixon's supplied drugs and dressings to the Hospital for alternate months, was continued.

The new Hospital quickly justified all the efforts spent upon it, for it is recorded that in the first 5 weeks there was an average of 27 inpatients, and Matron was soon complaining that she had insufficient staff for the theatre and night work.

The Management Committee decided that they could now afford to pay a full-time Secretary, though his salary to begin with was to be only £130 per annum, the same as had been recommended for the gardener and porter! In due course,

Captain Wilfred Banham was appointed to this not very lucrative post and, though his salary was increased the following year to £175 and he was later provided with a house, it is to his eternal credit that he worked so willingly and so well for the Hospital during the next 10 years. He was the first full-time paid Secretary that the Hospital ever had and he set a high standard of administrative ability during the trying years that were to come.

Soon after its opening, the Hospital joined the Sussex Provident Scheme, thus enabling a higher payment to be received for any patients who were members of the Scheme. In June it was decided to name a bed after the East Grinstead Tradesmen and also, at the same time, a cot was named in memory of Admiral Madden, who had given much of his time towards the building of the new Hospital but who unfortunately had died before its completion. A Staff Sports Club was formed, and Matron asked for a grant to build a lawn tennis court.

The Appeals Committee continued to function and in August a most successful fête was held at Saint Hill by kind permission of Mr. and Mrs. Longuet Higgins, which realised the large sum of £578 17s. 11d., while in December of the same year a most successful dance at Whitehall organised by Miss Margaret Munn (now Lady Dudley Gordon) brought in £157 7s. 0d. Subscriptions by October amounted to £772, donations £18, collecting boxes £114, a mile of pennies had produced £70, and fees from the general wards had amassed the sum of £1,054, while the private wards had produced £82; but in spite of all this it was estimated in October that there would be a deficit of between £300-£500 on the first year's running of the Hospital.

Towards the end of 1936 the Medical Staff was increased by the appointments of Dr. E. G. Sibley of Forest Row, Dr. A. C. Sommerville of East Grinstead, and Dr. H. F. Wilson from Dormansland, but apparently their appointments were by no means to be taken for granted as they would be now under The National Health Service, for it is recorded that in each case they were asked before appointment "to furnish the Board with their qualifications"!

At the end of the year Miss Garlett resigned her position as Matron which she had held for 27 years. A fund was opened and in due course she was presented with a testimonial to mark her outstanding term of office as Matron. She was succeeded by Miss Caroline Hall, who had been one of the original sisters when the new Hospital opened, and who had in fact acted as Deputy Matron when Miss Garlett took her summer holiday. This appointment also was a very happy one, for Miss Hall served the Hospital with great devotion throughout the difficult war years, and only in 1947, and then unfortunately for family reasons, did she have to resign the post herself.

It is worthwhile pausing here at the end of 1936 to consider some of the big advances and changes that had taken place as a result of the new Hospital being opened at the beginning of the year. In the first place there had been 712 inpatients as against 279 the previous year at the old Hospital. The X-ray Department had made 547 examinations. New opportunities had also arisen for various services from local people and in the Annual Report for the year 1936, there is mention for the first time of nursing assistance being given by the Voluntary Aid Detachments from East Grinstead and Crawley Down, which was very much appreciated. Here also comes the first mention of the British Red Cross Society and its Blood Transfusion Service, and also of another local effort of considerable help—the formation of a Linen League under the Chairmanship of the Hon. Mrs. Longuet-Higgins, which proved itself extremely useful. The total expenditure during the year was £5,033 14s. 11d. but the total income exceeded this amount by £205 8s. od. Outpatient attendances were 271 and Pathology examinations 58. There had been an average number of patients resident throughout the year of just over 30 per day, at an average total cost of £3 3s. 4d. per week.

Early in 1937 Captain Price resigned his position as Honorary Secretary and, at a ceremony which took place at the Annual General Meeting held in the Parish Hall on March 17th, was presented with an illuminated address and a £75 cheque, as a token of appreciation of his services. In April a further important step in the development of the Hospital was taken, by the purchase for £128 of a plot of woodland behind the Hospital, 100 ft. in depth, which subsequently was to prove most useful. Also in April 1937 it is recorded that a plaque was placed over the doors of the Children's Ward in memory of Dr. P. E. Wallis; one wonders what eventually happened to this plaque, for it is certainly not there now, and there is no record anywhere of its removal.

An interesting note in July, 1937, is that the House Committee decided "that the maternity case admitted as an emergency was not to be taken as a precedent and that the Medical Committee be informed to this effect". The case in question was apparently one of Caesarean Section. In this month also Dr. B. C. Morton-Palmer of Copthorne was appointed to the Medical Staff, while at the same time the Nursing Staff was increased; there were now 3 Sisters, 4 Staff Nurses and 6 Probationers, and the Board had to consider providing additional quarters for Nurses.

During 1937 the Appeals Committee remained very active and amongst others on this Committee, Miss Lindsey Smith was in great evidence at this time, among her many activities being the organisation of the Collecting Boxes which during this year made £231 for the Hospital. An "Egg Week" was organised and this produced 200 dozen eggs, contributed from local sources. During the year a permanent flagstaff was erected and negotiations were entered into with the Urban District Council regarding the rates to be paid by the Hospital. The Hospital Authorities felt that they should be relieved of rates, but as this was not legally possible at the time, they wrote and asked the Urban District Council if they would be good enough to make a subscription to the Hospital Funds equalling the amount of the rates paid; this request, however, was subsequently withdrawn. At the end of 1937 Sir Robert Kindersley purchased Tudor Cottage, next door to the Hospital, in the Holtye Road, and presented it as a free residence for the Secretary, who up to this time had been living in Dormansland. At the same time Captain Banham's extremely meagre salary was adjusted so that by 1940, after several increments, he would be receiving £300 per annum.

In 1937, the first full year in the new building, there was again a slight surplus of income, of £59 3s. 5d., over the total expenditure which had amounted to £6,638 16s. 11d.—rather more than the £3,500 running expenses which had originally been estimated! During this year the work of the Hospital had again increased, 883 inpatients and 448 outpatients being treated, while the number of cases examined by the X-ray Department increased to 833. Mr. Harold Brown and Mrs.

Longuet Higgins had joined the Board in place of Captain Price and Mrs. Dewar.

By the beginning of 1938, after 2 whole years in the new building, things were running smoothly and this year was to prove a period of steady consolidation, perhaps one of the most peaceful periods of the Hospital's whole existence. It was in fact settling down after the recent expansion, and there was as yet no hint of what was to come in the tempestuous years ahead.

Early in the year the whole Hospital mourned the death of Captain Price, who had acted as Honorary Secretary from 1931 until his retirement the previous year. Tributes were paid to him by the various Committees and the Annual Report comments on "the passing of Captain J. P. Price who so willingly gave his services as Honorary Secretary to the new Hospital Committee for so many years. The Board take this opportunity of testifying to the many valuable services rendered by him and to his untiring devotion to the cause of the Hospital which to the end was one of his chief interests."

Among other events of interest during the year, in February a long-lasting appointment was made when Miss Ethel Truby took over the duties of Librarian from Miss Haddon; she continued in this position for the next 21 years. In May an anonymous gift of £250 was received for the specific purpose of building a Nurses Recreation Room and permission was given by the Finance & Building Committee to proceed with this building. On completion later in the year it was named in memory of Maud Barclay, a resident of Forest Row, who, it is now known, left this sum in her will in gratitude for treatment she received at the Hospital. Another legacy also was received of £500 from the estate of Mr. James Henry Stevens, and it was agreed to name a bed after him. The Annual Egg Appeal this year produced the magnificent total of 456 dozen eggs; 3¼ cwts. of tinfoil were collected and sold at 32s. per cwt., and £19 worth of used stamps were collected. Miss Lindsey Smith resigned from the Appeals Committee and Miss Harvey and Mr. Tolley took over the Collecting Boxes. Among other minor problems during 1938, it is recorded in the House Committee Minutes that "X-ray patients must bring their fee with them, or, if they are not an emergency, they are liable to be sent home to fetch the money". It was further laid down that "patients

77

on the black list for non-payment should not be re-admitted".
In the autumn, Doctors P. L. Blaber and H. Stewart left the
Medical Staff and were replaced by Dr. E. J. Dennison and Dr.
J. O. Collin. It was about this time also that an innovation was
made in allowing local dentists direct access to the X-ray
Department, whereas previously they had had to send their
patients first to a member of the Medical Staff, who in turn had
recommended them for X-ray. It may have been partly because
of this that the number of X-ray examinations increased to 964
this year. During 1938 Lady Kindersley presented 2 cups to be
competed for in a Darts Competition open to all Clubs within
a 5 mile radius of the Hospital; this was in addition to the
Kindersley Bowls Cup she had previously presented, which had
already brought in considerable funds. At the same time Mrs.
F. E. Richards presented a handsome trophy, to be called 'The
Richards Hospital Cup', to be competed for by Sussex Football
Clubs.

The main event however during 1938 was the Incorporation
of the Hospital under Royal Charter, which took place on
October 19th and by which the Hospital became a Company,
limited by guarantee and with no share capital. Previously to
this the Board of Management had been liable as individuals
for any losses suffered by the Hospital, but now they could only
be sued as a Corporation with an individual liability limited to
£1. The Hospital became entitled to affix a seal to its official
documents, to hold property in its own name under license from
the Board of Trade, and to act as Trustee for the various funds
entrusted to it. Briefly, the act of incorporation established the
hospital authority as a separate legal entity, with an individual-
ity apart from that of the members comprising it, and it was
considered that by doing this the Hospital acquired increased
dignity and stature. The Board of Management of the unin-
corporated Queen Victoria Cottage Hospital met at the
Hospital at 6.0 p.m. on December 20th and after some formal
business concluded their meeting. They immediately reconvened
themselves at 6.15 p.m. as the Board of Management of the
new Incorporated Hospital, whereupon Captain Banham
produced a copy of the Articles of Incorporation as registered
at Somerset House, a copy of the Board of Trade's Licence
enabling the Hospital to be incorporated as a Company without

the word 'Limited', and also the Certificate of Incorporation, the Board of Trade's Licence to hold lands and the Lord Chancellor's consent for the Hospital to act as a Trustee Corporation. The Honorary Solicitors, Messrs. Whitley Hughes & Luscombe, and the Bankers, Messrs. Barclays, were formally re-appointed to the new body.

At the end of the year Messrs. Richard Place & Co., ceased to be Treasurers to the hospital but Mr. A. Tyler, who had worked with them, continued this job as a private individual, with the assistance now of Mr. C. E. Tolley.

The Annual Report for 1938 records a special tribute to Captain W. J. Banham, with the words—"It was indeed a happy day for all when he joined the Staff". Unfortunately it had also to report that there was this year an excess of expenditure over income of £46 1s. 6d., the total expenditure being £7,143 6s. 3d. In this report also we find that Mr. Colin Darby and Mrs. E. F. Scott had joined the Board, Mr. Joyce, Miss Paxton and Mr. Willmer having left it. At the end of 1938 the Board might have been excused for thinking that they now had a period of stability in front of them. Indeed the early part of 1939 proceeded very much as the previous year had done.

Another small but significant step forward in the development of the Hospital took place in April, when a House Committee minute mentions the introduction of an Almoner's Form—though it was to be some time yet before a full-time Almoner was appointed.

A Variety Entertainment arranged early in the year by the Appeals Committee brought in £160, a fête held in July was most successful, and Egg Week this year produced 526 dozen eggs.

The year 1939 is further notable for the appointment in March of Dr. Douglas Robertson as Honorary Cardiologist, and in July of Dr. J. E. H. Cogan of Tunbridge Wells as Ophthalmologist. In August it is recorded that Miss Garlett, the ex-matron, was admitted as a patient with two special nurses to attend her.

The main item of importance in 1939, however, was the introduction of the Peanut Scheme. The first real step towards this was taken on April 17th, when the Chairman of the Appeals Committee at a special meeting introduced Mrs. Clemetson, known as Aunt Agatha, of the Kent & Sussex Courier, to his Committee. This meeting had been called as the result of an offer by Mrs. Clemetson to expand the Peanut Club in this district for the benefit of our Hospital, and it is recorded that "Aunt Agatha gave a delightful account of how the Scheme was started in aid of the Tunbridge Wells Hospital". In May, 1931, in connection with a special appeal which was being held in Tunbridge Wells to raise money for the new Kent & Sussex Hospital a comic newspaper called "Glad Rag" was produced by local journalists. Mrs. Clemetson wrote in this paper an intended parody on a children's feature, called the Peanut Club, offering a bag of peanuts to anyone who gave twelve 1931 pennies to the Hospital funds, and signed it "Your adoring Aunt Agatha". To everyone's astonishment a little girl, Dorothy Jolley, produced the twelve pennies, and Mr. W. R. Murray, Managing Director of the Kent & Sussex Courier, quickly realised that if one child had taken the suggestion seriously, no doubt many more would do the same and that here was a wonderful way of helping the hospital. It was from this small beginning that the Club had grown, and the membership in 1939 was some 35,000 of whom about 500 came from East Grinstead. The greater part of their success was due to help from the Kent & Sussex Courier, which paid all the expenses of the Scheme, and during the last 7 years the Peanut Club had given £14,000 to the Tunbridge Wells Hospital. The Scheme not only paid the full fees for any of its members who might be treated in Hospital but in addition gave any surplus money collected to hospitals.

There was at first some doubt as to the advisability of introducing the Peanut Scheme to East Grinstead, since it was a contributory scheme and might well overlap the functions of the East Grinstead Working Men's Hospital Fund, and it was decided therefore that the Committee of this Fund should be consulted before anything further was done. However, evidently the consultations were satisfactory, for in July the Board of Management recommended the adoption of the Peanut Scheme. It was immediately successful, and by the middle of October the number of local members had increased from 500 to about 900. Later of course the Scheme brought immense benefit to the Hospital, as will be seen in subsequent chapters.

Sir Archibald McIndoe, an early photograph

(*above*) Mr. Clark Minor, President of the British War Relief Society of Americ[...] hands Mr. Kirkhope the cheque for the completion of the American Surgical Bloc[...]
(*below*) Her Majesty the Queen Mother (then Her Majesty the Queen) with Lo[...] Kindersley and Matron Hall at the opening of the American Wing.

At this time there was no possibility of foreseeing the enormous expansion which was shortly to take place. The Board and various Committees, justifiably pleased with the fine Hospital they had created, could not know that they had merely built the foundation upon which very soon an even bigger structure was to be based.

# 5

# The War 1939-1942

"Mr McIndoe has arrived to take over the Hospital"—thus simply is recorded, in the Minutes of a Meeting of the Board of Management dated September 4th, 1939, what subsequently turned out to be one of the most important events, if not the most important of all, in the long history of the Hospital. The full Minute reads—"Mr. McIndoe has arrived to take over the Hospital on behalf of the Ministry of Health as a Maxillo-facial Hospital, although he had no written instructions".

The Board had however had warning that something of the kind might happen when in the middle of March that year, they had been informed by the Ministry that the Hospital was to be included in its emergency plans, and they had been advised that it might be necessary for them to evacuate a number of patients on the development of an emergency and to make accommodation for 48 additional beds. In May the Ministry had asked permission to erect huts to accommodate 100 extra beds and the Board had purchased additional land at the rear of the Hospital in order to make room for these huts. In July plans had been approved and work on them had already begun.

Meanwhile other steps had been taken to prepare for the emergency, the approach of which had been becoming more and more obvious as the months went by. As early as the end of January the House Committee had written to the East Sussex County Council, in answer to a query, informing them that 17 extra nurses and 7 domestic staff would be required, and in March, in common with the rest of the country, the staff had been fitted with gas masks. In April 5,000 sandbags were ordered from the County Council, and arrangements were made for blackout material, cellophane to cover the windows, shutters for the ward windows, and for a month's emergency food supply to be bought. Towards the end of August an offer had been received from Mr. J. A. Dewar to open his nearby home, Dutton Homestall, as an Auxiliary Hospital with 50 beds in the event of war. This very generous offer had been accepted by the Board and £300 worth of bed and bedding ordered. Three members of the Medical Staff who had previous commitments with the R.A.M.C., Drs. Thornton, Frobisher and Sibley of Forest Row, had left to join their Units, and the Board of Management, whose full strength consisted of some 35 members, on September 1st had set up a small Sub-committee consisting of Mrs. Munn as Chairman, with Lady Kindersley, Miss Helen Beale, Miss Spalding, Mr. Kirkhope, Mr. Harold Brown and Mr. F. E. Richards, to deal with the details of the emergency. Such was the situation when war was declared on September 3rd.

The picture during the first week of the war was a somewhat confused one and the Board's sub-committee met daily in order to try and sort it out. Nobody, including probably the Ministry, had any precise idea of how things would work. Mr. McIndoe, who arrived on September 4th, told the Sub-committee that day that he would accept full responsibility for the Hospital, that the Ministry would accept full financial responsibility, and that the Board would be expected to pay the Ministry for any Civilian patients accommodated in the Hospital. Mr. Kirkhope, however, as Chairman of the Finance & Building Committee, appears to have had some doubts as to the position as set out by Mr. McIndoe, for he advised the Board "to try and retain full control of the Hospital, rather than allow the Ministry to take charge". On September 8th Mr. McIndoe made a plea "for time to be given for things to straighten themselves out", and on September 14th the Board were told that the new huts, when completed, would be leased to the Ministry who would pay rent to the Board for them!

Meanwhile arrangements for opening Dutton Homestall were going ahead and Sister Kennett was appointed its Matron. Mr. Dewar undertook to finance it to the extent of £4,500 per annum and the Secretary was instructed to evacuate all possible patients from the Hospital to Dutton Homestall, only acute surgical cases being admitted to the Main Hospital. Mr. Dewar also offered the Hospital the loan of equipment from the Gordon Hospital in London, of which he was President, and which was closing down for the duration of the war, together with its stores of food, drugs and dressings, at cost price.

Then on the 18th came the news that the Ministry would not recognise the use of Dutton Homestall, but that they intended to increase the beds at the Main Hospital up to 210. Early in October therefore the question of whether to evacuate Dutton Homestall had to be faced. Mr. McIndoe was in favour of keeping it open, but the matter was settled when on October 12th Mr. Dewar withdrew his offer and asked for the patients to be evacuated. On receiving this request the Board considered other large houses in the neighbourhood as alternatives, among them Barton St. Mary, The Beeches, Ashurst Wood, and Gotwick Manor. None of these however appeared to be quite suitable and after further discussion Mr. Dewar was persuaded to allow the patients to remain at Dutton Homestall temporarily.

The Ministry had originally said that the Private Wards, the Children's Ward and the Operating Theatre were to remain in the sole charge of the Board, but they subsequently decided that they wanted the Children's Ward as an operating theatre. This move was strongly opposed by the Board, but they lost the argument and in fact the ward was used for this purpose for the rest of the war. Towards the end of October the confusion became even worse, when it was discovered that the Ministry wanted to send civilian plastic surgery cases from other areas and it was feared that this must mean the exclusion of local cases from the Hospital. The House Committee rather understandably asked the Board if they could "clarify the position regarding the arrangements with the Ministry as to the occupation of beds in the Hospital in the future".

The position was made clear at a special meeting of the Board on October 30th attended by Mr. John Hunter, who was in charge of Sector 9 of the Emergency Scheme, with Sir Harold Gillies and Mr. Kelsey Fry attending as Advisers to the Ministry of Health, and Mr. McIndoe, who by now was officially designated Medical Superintendent. Mr. Hunter explained that the London Hospitals had very largely been evacuated in order to be ready for the reception of large numbers of air raid casualties which were expected; that it was desired to send Maxillo-facial cases to this and three other similar specialist units; that the patients would remain here only for a short time and then go elsewhere for convalescence, and he stressed that there was no wish on the Ministry's part to interfere with the admission of local cases. He said that if the Board wished to open an Auxiliary Hospital they were within their rights in doing so, but the Ministry would not undertake any responsibility for it; and he added that the Ministry would pay the Board for all patients admitted under the Emergency Scheme. In regard to the financing of the Scheme he pointed out that the Board could put in a special claim if they found themselves out of pocket, a clause which had been specially inserted in the Ministry's Agreement in order to make it clear that Hospitals would not be expected to incur overdrafts on its behalf. Sir Harold Gillies spoke for the Ministry, saying that he hoped that they would all pull together, and Mr. Whitley Hughes, on behalf of the Board, expressed the opinion that they should do all in their power to help the Ministry and proposed that the above suggestions be accepted.

In the middle of all this uncertainty there had occurred on September 7th the death in the Hospital of Miss Garlett, the ex-matron. Mrs. Munn, Chairman of the Board, expressed the feelings of all connected with the Hospital by saying—"It is impossible to put into words the services Miss Garlett has rendered to the Queen Victoria Cottage Hospital and to the residents of East Grinstead". Meanwhile the Board had voted the sum of £1,500 to be spent on certain necessary work including a new Nurses' Dining Room, enlargements to the kitchen, and the building of a new combined Mortuary, Post-mortem room and Chapel.

When Mr. McIndoe arrived at the Hospital he was aged 39; a New Zealander, qualified in his own country and having worked for some years in America, notably at the Mayo Clinic, little was known of him when he arrived in this country in 1930. He was a Fellow of the Royal College of Surgeons of England and a Master of Surgery, and had worked for some years with Sir Harold Gillies, whom he had recently succeeded as Consultant in Plastic Surgery to the Royal Air Force. Of his character and outstanding qualities the Board knew nothing, and neither he nor they could have foreseen at this stage how fruitful their association was to prove.

By the end of the year only 74 Emergency Medical Scheme cases had been admitted. The expected large numbers of casualties had not materialised, and more or less normal activities were resumed, the arrangement for an Emergency Hospital at Dutton Homestall being terminated.

The Annual Report for 1939 speaks of the Maxillo-facial Unit "which is situated in the Hospital grounds and consists of three wards of 40 beds each, a Dental Hut, and an auxiliary Kitchen". It also mentions that the Hospital had an excess of income over expenditure for the year of £27 8s. 5d. During the year Miss Hadden, Mrs. Longuet Higgins and Mr. Viall had been replaced on the Board by Mrs. D. L. McIver, Mr. J. B. Roberts and Mr. C. E. Tolley. Miss Harvey took charge of the Linen League while Miss Hilda Truby took on the job of part-time Dispenser.

1940 was inevitably a confused and difficult time. Early in the New Year problems of accommodation arose, one of the main ones being where to put the children whose Ward had been taken over as a Theatre; this was solved by accommodating them temporarily in the balconies of the main wards and in the Casualty Ward. The Nurses' Recreation Room was being used temporarily as a Dental Hut with 2 mechanics working in it, and part of Kindersley Ward had been curtained off for Officers. The position was slightly eased by the opening of Ward I, the first of the new hutted wards to be brought into use, on 2nd March, and by the opening about the same time, of Dutton Homestall as a Convalescent Home for Officers. The administrative position was still far from clear, and while there is no doubt that the advent of the Maxillo-facial Unit had thrown the previous easy running of the Hospital out of gear, there is frequent evidence that everybody was doing their best to make things work smoothly. Nevertheless the Board found it necessary in August to state that "they will not in future accept any financial responsibility for any action taken by the Medical Superintendent without their previous sanction!" With McIndoe's tremendous enthusiasm and only £27 in the Bank one can well understand that relations may have been strained from time to time.

Meanwhile a number of important developments were going on. First amongst these was the provision of further accommodation for nurses; after inspecting a number of houses the Board finally decided on Warrenside in College Lane and agreed to rent it as a Home for 20 nurses with Miss C. Griffin engaged as Superintendent, a position which she held continuously for the next 12 years, while the Ministry of Health agreed to pay for its equipment. The Dental Department quickly outgrew the Nurses' Recreation Room and soon occupied their own spacious hut close by the wards, the hut which today is used partly as a Staff Recreation room and partly as a Nurses' changing room. The Ministry also agreed to erect a hut for the accommodation of the Resident Medical Officer, the hut which today bears the name of Percy Lodge, named after its first occupant, Mr. Percy Jayes. The centre of the main building, which until now had been open, was roofed over and used as a Waiting Room and Medical Staff Room, the latter being furnished by a special fund organised by Mrs. F. H. Fraser. The Waiting Room remains in use to this day but the other room has never served any useful purpose for very long, and its use is still one of the minor problems of the Hospital. Accommodation was becoming so strained that it was found necessary to erect a special building for the storage of food and equipment!

In the spring more of the local General Practitioner Staff, Drs. Morton Palmer, Collin and Dennison, were called up for Military Service, followed soon after by Dr. H. F. Wilson, and Dr. Montague was appointed to the Staff in Dr. Morton Palmer's place.

At the Annual General Meeting in May the Chairman, Sir Robert Kindersley, remarked that though at the moment we were able to deal with local work, we must realise that with a war in full swing there was a possibility that we might not be able to meet the needs of the locality in the future. We must realise, however, that the Hospital with its added beds was rendering a considerable service to our country and its fighting efficiency. Sir Robert had recently been elected Chairman of the National Savings Campaign, a post which he filled with distinction for the rest of the war. At this same meeting Mr. Osborne, who had been Honorary Auditor to the Hospital for so many years, was appointed Auditor, while Mr. P. J. Gripton and Dr. Haldin-Davis were elected to the Board. Captain Banham meanwhile had been promoted to the status of Secretary-

Superintendent and it was laid down that in addition to his ordinary work he should carry out "the duties usually performed by an Almoner". Other appointments made at this time included an Assistant Matron, two Shorthand-typists and a Night Porter. Among the Night Porter's duties was the supervision of the blackout, which hitherto had been the responsibility of the Matron. In March a new telephone switchboard with 25 extensions was installed.

During the summer local residents began to come to the aid of the overstrained accommodation at the Hospital. Mrs. Broderick, Mrs. Fawell and Mrs. Hotblack all offered to take convalescent patients into their homes, while Mr. Brown offered to have convalescent Officers at his house, Hurst-an-Clays, and Mr. Mountain offered his house, Twyford Lodge, as a Convalescent Home. Mrs. Clemetson attended a meeting of the Appeals Committee in July and reported that the Peanut Club during its first year's operation in East Grinstead had acquired 1,046 members and collected £335 towards the Peanut Cot. As an interesting commentary on the voluntary hospital system, it is on record that during this month a man on the list for admission who had a record as a bad payer, was told that he would have to pay for his accommodation in advance.

Mention is made here of Miss Hall, sister of the Matron, as being in charge of the Operating Theatre, though in fact "Cherry" as she is familiarly remembered by all who were at the Hospital in those days, had acted in this capacity for some years, in addition to her main job as Sister in charge of Kindersley Ward. In August Dr. Long retired from his appointment as Radiologist and was succeeded by his partner Dr. Addey.

In the Report of the Board of Management's Meeting for September 9th there is the entry "Enemy aircraft overhead having caused a diversion of thought, the meeting adjourned to watch a formation of 25 enemy aircraft pass over the Hospital." This was of course the time of the Battle of Britain, when such sights were commonplace. During this time bombs were dropped within 200 yards of the Hospital, but fortunately the Hospital building escaped serious damage. Air raid shelters had been provided and, arising out of the constant danger from raids, a request was received from the East Grinstead Medical Officer of Health to base a Mobile First Aid Unit at the Hospital, to consist of a single decker bus with one Medical Officer, one State Registered Nurse and 6 V.A.D.s. For some reason this suggestion caused considerable discussion in the various Committees, but it was eventually decided to accept it on the understanding that it did not involve the Hospital in any extra expense. The Unit functioned for 2½ years until April 1943, when the Council terminated their agreement to staff it. While on this same subject it is recorded that an unexploded bomb exhibited at the Radio Centre Cinema brought in the sum of £78 collected from people who came to view it.

The Annual Report for 1940 lists the available number of beds as 146 and it is interesting to note that during the year 700 local patients had been treated and 728 E.M.S. patients. In payment for the accommodation of these latter the Emergency Medical Service had contributed over £15,000 towards the £17,990 expenditure for the year, and in fact this year the Board found themselves nicely in pocket to the tune of nearly £6,000. Mr. Alfred Wagg and Mrs. F. H. Fraser joined the Board, while Miss Wagg, Mr. Colin Darby and Mr. Tolley left it. Mr. Wagg was shortly after elected to the Finance & Building Committee, and Mrs. Fraser to the House Committee.

By the end of this year the Maxillo-facial Unit was firmly established and published its own report; it contains so much interesting information that it is worth our taking a fairly long look at it. The Staff of the Unit is listed as follows:—

A. H. McIndoe, Esq., M.Sc., M.S., F.R.C.S., F.A.C.S.,
Surgeon-in-Charge

N. L. Eckhoff, Esq., M.S., F.R.C.S.

D. N. Matthews, Esq., M.Ch., F.R.C.S. (Serving in R.A.F.)

R.A.F. Registrar:  Sqdr./Ldr. G. Morley, F.R.C.S.
Resident Surgeon:  P. H. Jayes, Esq., M.B., B.S.
Dental Surgeons:  W. Kelsey Fry, Esq., M.C., M.R.C.S., L.R.C.P., P.L.D.S., Consultant to the Ministry of Health.
D. G. Walker, Esq., M.A., M.B., B.Ch., M.D.S.
A. C. McLeod, Esq., D.D.S., (Pen), B.Sc. (Toronto), L.D.S., R.C.S. (England)

|                          | P. Rae Shepherd, Esq., L.D.S., R.C.S. (England) |
|--------------------------|-------------------------------------------------|
|                          | A. H. Clarkson, Esq.                            |
| *Anaesthetists:*         | J. Truscott Hunter, Esq., M.R.C.S., L.R.C.P., D.A. |
|                          | Russell M. Davies, Esq., M.R.C.S., L.R.C.P., D.A. |
| *Consulting Ophthalmologist:* | Frederick Ridley, Esq., M.B., B.S., F.R.C.S. |
| *Photographer:*          | Miss Lehmann                                    |

It then continues:—"The Maxillo-facial Unit was built under the E.M.S. Scheme as one of 3 main centres devoted to the care of wartime injuries of the face and to reconstructive surgery in general, situated geographically to deal with certain areas of dense population liable to bombing attack and adjacent ports where battle casualties from abroad might be received. This Unit was attached to the Queen Victoria Hospital on the advice of Sir Harold Gillies and Mr. Kelsey Fry, Advisers to the Ministry of Health, intended to deal with injuries of the above type from the south-eastern corner of England and from the south coast reception ports. Many difficulties have been experienced due to the extremely diverse nature of the casualties received and the impossibility of segregating patients into different categories: thus Officers and ranks of the 3 Services, members of the Auxiliary Fire Service and Air Raid Precautions Organisations, and civilians of all types have had to be accommodated in the 3 wards, and it is entirely due to the admirable spirit displayed by the patients that it has been possible to accomplish this successfully. Among the many to whom we are greatly indebted for help are Mr. and Mrs. F. H. Fraser who presented an Ambulance and a Mobile Car to the Hospital, Mrs. Hotblack who was responsible for the erection of a Recreation Hut for the Officers, Lady Kindersley who has added much to the comforts of the Wards, and Major and Mrs. Mappin who have taken a deep and most helpful interest in the welfare of the patients between their periods of treatment. Mrs. Dewar's Ward Shop bringing comforts to the bedside has proved a great success and we are indebted to Lady Glendyne for the gift of wheelchairs for the Wards. During the year

NAAFI Concerts have been held regularly in the Wards and proved a great success. Many friends of the Hospital have generously placed their homes and gardens at the disposal of the patients, among them the Lady Violet Astor, Lord and Lady Kindersley, Mrs. Norman Laski, and Mrs. Fraser, and this has greatly helped in the difficult matter of maintaining the patients' morale during their stay at the Hospital. It would be impossible to name individually all the people who have helped us but we should like to pay a tribute to the self-sacrifice and sterling work of Mrs. F. H. Fraser to whom the entire Unit is indebted for innumerable acts of kindness. There are few patients who have passed through the Unit who will not remember her with gratitude. The first experimental Saline Bath Unit in the country was installed in a corner of Ward III but a new building is now being erected which will house two baths to which there will be easy access from any of the Wards. Representatives of the three Services are always to be found in the Wards of the Hospital. In addition a number of Czechs, Poles, Free Frenchmen and Netherlanders have been treated during the past 12 months. From time to time patients have been admitted who have earned high decorations in the course of duty; a Polish Squadron Leader was decorated by General Zigorsky with the highest award of his country while he was still under treatment in the Hospital; an Officer who commanded one of the cruisers in the Battle of the River Plate, and a famous British Fighter Pilot who has won both the D.S.O. and D.F.C. with bars, were among other patients with outstanding records. Air Raid casualties have been received from a wide area of the country, including members of the Civil Defence Organisations.

In the Dental Department as fitted at present there is room for 4 Dental Surgeons and 5 Dental Mechanics, but the accommodation could be extended to take 2 more Dental Surgeons if necessary. The reason for the size and importance of the Dental Department lies in the fact that large numbers of fractures of the jaw are treated here. At the present time the Department is considered to be the most important Jaw Centre in the country and from time to time the Dental Staff have dealt with patients in other Hospitals who could not be moved. For the purpose of these visits a Mobile Travelling Workshop has been presented to the E.M.S. Maxillo-facial Service by the American Dental Profession so that the benefits of this special Jaw Centre can be transported to any part of our area. During the year a great deal of teaching work has been undertaken in both the surgical and dental departments. Groups of naval, army and air force surgeons have visited us for training and in addition, surgeons from Canada, Australia, South Africa and New Zealand. Good clinical photographs are a necessity for the Plastic and Dental Surgeons and one room in the Dental Department is being used as a Photographic Department. Some 600 photographs are being taken per month on average. This work is done by voluntary helpers whose high standard has been commented upon time and again. We are deeply indebted in particular to Miss Lehmann and Miss Woolland for the excellent results they have obtained. In conclusion the Maxillo-facial Unit would like to pay a tribute to the happy relations which are maintained with the Board of Management and administrative staff of the Hospital, and in particular to Matron Hall, the Secretary-Superintendent Captain Banham, and Mr. W. Guthrie Kirkhope for their efficient and sympathetic handling of the various problems which have arisen during the course of the year."

On January 1st, 1941 the Hospital Staff were delighted to hear that their President, Sir Robert Kindersley, had received a Barony in the New Year Honours, in recognition of his work for the National Savings Movement. Shortly after this the Hospital was honoured by a visit from the Duke of Kent, who wrote a letter of thanks after his visit, in which he praised the magnificent work being done at the Hospital.

One of the most pressing needs early in 1941 was a Physiotherapy Department. Dr. Sommerville, representing the Medical Committee, first raised the matter with the Board early in January. There was no money to build a Department nor was there a full-time Physiotherapist on the staff, but these difficulties were quickly overcome by the Ministry providing some equipment and making two appointments, Miss O. Johnson and Miss W. N. Stevenson, the first of whom arrived on February 10th. Part-time accommodation was found for their work in the Officers' Recreation Room and it is recorded that "a special cupboard is being built to accommodate the equipment"! In March an appeal was made for special funds for a new department and one of the first subscriptions to the fund was the proceeds from a Variety Show organised by Mrs. Fraser at the Whitehall Theatre; the money came in so well that by May plans for the building of the new Department were being discussed.

X-ray work also was increasing and Dr. Addey asked for an assistant for Miss Davies who, in the meantime, had been officially appointed to the Staff of the Hospital. At the same time the question of appointing an Almoner arose and the Board went so far as to advertise this post and received several applications. They decided, however, not to proceed with a permanent full-time appointment, but instead appointed Mrs. Kershaw as part-time Almoner. It was not until October of the same year that the Hospital's first full-time Almoner was appointed.

Early in the year a large unexploded bomb was discovered in the vicinity of the Hospital and the wards and staffrooms in the front of the Hospital had to be evacuated while it was dealt with. As a result of this incident it was decided to build blast-proof walls in front of the windows of the main wards. The front lawn was dug and planted with potatoes, and sand bins were placed on the roof, an extra Night Porter being enrolled for the special duties of Fire Spotter. Mr. W. Harvey Gervis of Tunbridge Wells was appointed Orthopaedic Consultant, and in April the Hospital's first Dietician was appointed. Mr. Kirkhope was given the post of Bursar with a salary of £600 per annum, while the Secretary-Superintendent's salary, which had been increased to £500 on the outbreak of war, was raised again, this time to £750 per annum. Mr. Tyler retired after many years as Honorary Treasurer and was succeeded by Mr. C. E. Tolley who was to receive an Honorarium of £250 per annum. Mr. Rowntree had moved from London and was living at Little Warren in the Lewes Road.

The whole Hospital was by now beginning to burst at the seams. Warrenside was not big enough to accommodate all the nurses and steps had to be taken to find a second Nurses' Home. At the same time the Ministry decided to take over nearby St. Margaret's Convent School, and it was opened as a Convalescent Annexe on June 16th, 1941, with Sister Stroud in charge of 53 beds.

All this expansion of course needed more money, but fortunately it was forthcoming. By May enough money for the first Peanut Cot had been collected and Mrs. Clemetson was able to report not only that there were 1,163 members in East Grinstead, but that the Fund was beginning to become more widely known. Other sums of money received were £400 from the Working Men's Fund, £100 from a Flying Officer patient, £62 from the East Grinstead farmers, £600 from the Claud Johnson estate, and many others; but, most significant of all, the British War Relief Society of America started sending bed-linen, clothing, instruments and other gifts, a small beginning which was to lead to immense results a few years later.

At the Annual General Meeting in August, Lord Kindersley referred to the manner in which Mr. McIndoe's work had concentrated public interest in the Hospital "as nothing else could have done", while at the same time Mrs. Munn emphasised how much the Hospital owed to its old subscribers, and appealed to them to continue their interest. It was at this meeting that Mrs. Munn resigned the Chairmanship of the Board of Management, and the Board recorded its grateful thanks "for the manifold services she has rendered to the Hospital over whose interests she has so carefully and consistently watched during her period of Chairmanship"—which had extended from the opening of the new Hospital in 1936. Mr. Edward Blount was elected Chairman in her place, with Mr. Alfred Wagg as Vice-chairman. At the same time an Emergency Committee was set up consisting of Mr. Blount, Mr. Wagg, Mr. Kirkhope, Lady Kindersley and Mr. Brown, with a quorum of two only. Shortly after this Mr. McIndoe was empowered to set up a Welfare Committee under his own Chairmanship, the members of which were Mrs. Dewar, Mrs. Fraser, Mrs. Laski, Mrs. Mappin and Mr. Wagg. This Committee was empowered to spend up to £100 without further reference, but questions regarding future policy were to be brought to the notice of the Board for approval. Mr. McIndoe was also invited to attend all Board Meetings, though he was not at this stage a full member of the Board.

Meanwhile plans for the new Physiotherapy Department

94

were going ahead. The Board authorised the sum of £1,000 to be spent on it and a further £1,500 had been promised from "a fund in London", while the equipment was to be provided through the generosity of Mrs. Waterson, wife of the High Commissioner for South Africa. At the same time there were plans for building a Dispensary and also an Almoner's Office; the British Red Cross Society announced its intention of building two new Recreation Rooms, one for men and one for women, while the Ministry proposed a grandiose plan to build a Nurses' Home to accommodate 85 nurses, a plan which eventually came to nothing.

The increasing difficulty of obtaining domestic workers is reflected in the decision to award them each a Ministry of Health badge and to call them Hospital Workers. Efforts were also being made to find them living accommodation, for some of them were sleeping at Warrenside which, of course, reduced the room available there for nurses.

Names familiar to us today begin to appear in increasing numbers on the Staff at this time and amongst them should be noted Mr. R. H. J. Millar and Mr. Searle,* both of whom are still serving the Hospital at the present time; also Mr. Cyril Jones, who joined the Staff in 1940 as general assistant to Captain Banham, but who turned his hand to any job that came along, until he finally found his niche as Theatre Technician and graduated to become the familiar figure who now presides in this capacity over the American Theatres; there are also Nurse Batchelor who joined the Staff before the outbreak of war and only left some 20 years later, Nurse Padgham who came in 1940 and who still, as Mrs. Weekes, continues to nurse the patients in Kindersley Ward so efficiently and cheerfully, and Nurse Taylor also with over 20 years continuous service.

One of the minor mysteries encountered by the author in the course of his researches—namely the almost complete absence of any records referring to the Queens Road period (in fact only the bare Annual Reports survive), is explained as follows in the Minutes of a meeting of the Finance & Building Committee held on November 18th, 1941—"it was decided that all the Minute Books of the old Hospital, except the oldest, should be given for War Salvage". While waste paper was indeed in great

* Mr. Searle retired at the end of 1962.

demand at the time, the destruction of these irreplaceable and no doubt extremely interesting records, does seem to be a very great pity. Let us hope that all present and future records will be preserved for the use of some future historian.

In September there occurred the death of Mr. Whitley Hughes, recorded in the following words—"The Board, deeply grieved at the death of their friend and colleague, desire to express their sincere and grateful appreciation of the manifold services which over a period of many years he rendered to the Hospital, both in his private capacity and as Honorary Legal Adviser". Mr. Whitley Hughes' partner, Mr. Oliver Luscombe, was elected to take his place, both on the Board and as Legal Adviser. Whitley Hughes left £100 to the Hospital that he had served so well.

At the end of the year Mr. McIndoe was able to tell the Board that in the two years his Unit had been functioning, up to September 1941, 1,036 Service cases had passed through his hands and only one had finished up by being referred to the Ministry of Pensions. The total expenditure of the Hospital for this year reached the very large sum of £32,436 7s. 10d. but with a contribution of over £24,000 from the Emergency Hospital Scheme, the total income for the year exceeded this by 15s. 11d.! The average cost per inpatient per week is recorded at the low figure of £4 12s. 2d. In this Annual Report the Board also paid special tribute to the Matron, Miss Caroline Hall, "whose duties and responsibilities are so heavy and whose urbanity and unruffled kindness are a source of deep appreciation to all who come in contact with her".

In the Annual Report of the Maxillo-Facial Unit published at the end of the year we read that the Ministry of Health had requested that the Maxillo-Facial Unit change its name to 'Plastic and Jaw Injuries Centre' on account of the great diversity of cases now passing through the Unit; "in fact", says the report, "only 547 of the last 1,000 cases have been facial, while the other 453 have been injuries to other parts of the body which required collaboration with general surgical, orthopaedic and neurological colleagues." It records also that the new Convalescent Annexe at St. Margaret's School had enabled a very rapid turnover to take place; that Mr. and Mrs. Douglas Stern had equipped the Hospital with headphones for every bed; and that Mrs. Norman Laski had presented a system of amplifiers by means of which concerts and special announcements could be relayed throughout the wards.

It mentions also Sister Harrington as being in charge of Ward I and Sister Walker and Sister Mullins in the Theatres,— and another matter of some interest:—

"Probably as a direct result of the excellent spirit which was fostered in the Hospital during and after the Battle of Britain, the patients themselves formed a Club which they called the Maxillonian Club, its object being to promote good fellowship and to cement the many friendships which were formed not only between the patients themselves, but with the Medical Staff. As its secondary object it has in mind the preservation of the spirit of mutual helpfulness which will be valuable and necessary after the War. During the year a most successful reunion Dinner was held at the Whitehall by some 60 Members, some of whom came from stations in the North of England and in Scotland, and the guest of honour was the Commander-in-Chief, Air Chief Marshal Sir Sholto Douglas. It is an excellent commentary on the splendid spirit which exists in the Hospital that such a function could take place".

This Maxillonian Club is of course the forerunner of the now famous Guinea Pig Club, of which more will be heard later. The report goes on also to mention the many kindnesses of Mr. Bill Gardner, Mr. Louis Roney, and Major George Mappin.

The keynote of 1942 is expansion in every direction, made possible by the fact that money was now flowing in in ever increasing amounts. In January the Medical Committee, with the full approval of Mr. Rowntree, recommended that a second Honorary Consulting Surgeon be appointed, since the general surgery had increased so much, and Mr. Nils Eckhoff—already surgeon to the Plastic Unit—was appointed. A new Dental Lecture Hut, financed largely by Mr. Kelsey Fry and his friends, was in course of erection behind the Nurses' Recreation Room. The Welfare Committee was working hard arranging concerts, dances, private hospitality, and also courses of Lectures in such things as French, German, bookkeeping, accountancy, carpentry, sewing and many other subjects. The

97

Occupational Therapy Department presided over by Miss Pick, began to play an increasing part in the rehabilitation of the patients, and later in the year an interesting experiment took place in this Department. With the approval of the Ministry of Aircraft Production and the Ministry of Labour a unit for the production of aircraft instruments was set up, fully equipped with machinery to enable precision assembly work to be undertaken. This unit was the first of its kind in the country. The new Recreation Huts, presented by the Joint Council of the British Red Cross and St. John Organisations, were officially opened by Field Marshall Sir Philip Chetwode on April 10th, and in a letter he wrote after the opening, Sir Philip said what a deep impression the whole visit had made upon him and how pleased he was as Chairman of the Joint Council to see "what we have been able to do to help in the great work that is being done there".

In May the Medical Committee was "viewing with great concern the shortage of civilian beds; the increase in the size of the population coupled with the loss of the Children's Ward was responsible, and while they realised all the difficulties before the Board in this matter, they felt they would be neglecting their duty if they failed to reiterate their request for more bed accommodation". The Board's answer to this was that everything possible would be done to alleviate the position but no decision could be arrived at at present. Children had for some time been accommodated either at the Isolation Hospital or at the Emergency Children's Hospital which the County Council had opened at "Cuttens" in the Lewes Road.

On June 29th the new Physiotherapy Department was officially opened by Mrs. Waterson, wife of the High Commissioner for South Africa. The Board recommended that the new Department should be called the Springbok Building, in recognition of the great contribution of South Africa to its opening, but this name, though it may have been used at first, has not survived. It was decided initially that the new Department should be available only to E.M.S. patients and not to local residents, and it was not until the following January that the Ministry agreed that it might be used by civilian patients on the payment of 2s. per treatment. Since the Recreation Hut given by Mrs. Hotblack was now no longer to be used for physiotherapy, she asked if it could be given to the E.M.S. Surgical Staff as a Mess. This was agreed to and with certain additions it remained the Surgeons' Mess for some years; today it is still in use as a Linen Store. In June Miss Carter, who had succeeded Miss Hilda Truby and for some time had been doing the dispensing on a part-time voluntary basis, was appointed to the staff as Dispenser.

Another achievement which should be mentioned at this point was that of Mrs. F. E. Richards, who had organised the Hospital's group of the National Savings Movement. By the middle of 1942 this group had saved the large sum of £5,478 towards the Nation's War Effort, a truly remarkable achievement, for which Mrs. Richards was formally thanked and congratulated by Lord Kindersley at the Annual General Meeting in July. During the summer Dr. Douglas Robertson was called up for service in the Royal Air Force and Dr. R. Stanley into the Navy. In August the Hospital was visited by Mr. Ernest Brown, the Minister of Health.

In September it became necessary to engage 10 more nurses, and the Larches Cottage, in the Holtye Road, was rented in order to house 7 of them. It was in this month also that the Hospital acquired for the first time its own Laboratory, which was established by the Ministry at the Annexe. Dr. Selous, who previously had travelled from Tunbridge Wells to do the Pathology work, had retired from the Staff owing to pressure of work the previous December, and since then all pathology had been undertaken by the Ministry of Health Laboratory at Cuckfield. It must therefore have been a tremendous boon for the Hospital to have its own Laboratory. The Dental Lecture Hut meanwhile was opened and functioning, and the Board decided to use it for their meetings instead of meeting, as they had done previously, in the Nurses' Recreation Room.

During 1942 the Peanuts were more active than ever. Early in the year they decided to raise the sum of £700 in order to buy a piece of land adjacent to the Hospital, and a meeting of local members was held in the Whitehall on April 18th to launch a special appeal. Money soon began to pour in; the Irish Guards gave a special performance of their pantomime 'Cinderella' which produced £88; through the medium of Mr. J. H. Mitchell the local farmers gave a further £196 and on the strength of this it was decided to name a bed 'The Farmers' Bed'; the Fête held in August raised £255. Many other sources contributed and at a meeting of the Appeals Committee held on September 24th it was announced that well over the £700 asked for had been raised—in fact the final figure was £1,250, and Mrs. Clemetson, who by this time had become a regular attender at all meetings of this Committee, was asking "What can we appeal for next? It seems a pity to sit back when enthusiasm is so high." It was not long before Mr. Kirkhope produced an answer to this question, as we shall see.

About the same time Mr. Wagg purchased 3 acres of the Stone Quarry Wood adjacent to the boundary of the Hospital, fenced it in, and presented it to the Hospital to be developed as a Recreation Ground and Garden for the use of staff and patients. Both this piece of ground, known as 'Waggland' and the new 'Peanut Land' were the subject of tithes which had to be redeemed. Together they raised another problem; the Board of Trade's Certificate allowed the Hospital to own only 10 acres of ground; this figure was of course by now considerably exceeded, and application had to be made for permission to own up to 20 acres.

Amongst the many activities of the Welfare Committee, education was becoming steadily more important, and it was found necessary to employ, with the co-operation of Flt./Lieutenant Wheeler of the R.A.F. Education Service, a full-time airman schoolmaster. Another appointment about the same time was that of Flt./Sgt. Blacksell as Resident N.C.O. Welfare Officer, whose duties were to co-ordinate all the various education services, supervise organised games and be responsible generally for the distribution of comforts and welfare.

At the end of 1942 the Maxillonians, or, as they were now known, the 'Guinea Pigs', held their second annual meeting, which was attended by 130 members from all parts of the country. It is recorded "The Club now seems to be firmly established and will do much to cement the many friendships established between patients and staff alike".

In his Annual Report for the year, Mr. McIndoe, after giving thanks for the co-operation and support that he had received from the Board of Management, wrote—

"It would be difficult to predict the future of this Hospital beyond the war years but it may well be said that with such able direction the steady story of progress which is herein recorded will undoubtedly be maintained, and possibly extended. Changing concepts in national health and hospital administration demand a progressive spirit and an intelligent anticipation of future requirements. It can be said that the Queen Victoria Cottage Hospital will remain in the forefront of this movement."

In presenting this report at the Annual General Meeting, Mr. McIndoe added that they "had not only managed to keep the pace going, but also to expand".

And the main expansion was still to come.

# 6

# The War 1943-1945

THE year 1943 is one of the most important in the whole
history of the Hospital, for no less than 3 major expansion
schemes were taking shape at the same time.

Firstly, arising out of the highly successful 1942 Peanut
Appeal, and Mrs. Clemetson's query "What shall we collect
for next?", there comes a minute of the Appeals Committee
dated February 4th, which reads as follows:—

> "Mr. Kirkhope suggested that as Peanuts normally spell
> children (though grown-ups think it a privilege to join) our
> next goal should be a Children's Ward, or rather Unit, to be
> built at the end of the War at the approximate cost of
> £10,000. This proposal was unanimously accepted and a
> recommendation passed to the Board to that effect."

The Board at their next meeting approved the scheme, and
a Public Meeting was held at the Whitehall in order to launch
a Special Appeal for it, the chair being taken by Mr. Edward
Blount. Mr. McIndoe was the chief speaker and he described
the difficulties the Hospital was having at the time over the
admission and treatment of children, and how necessary it was
to have more accommodation for them. It was at this meeting
that Mrs. Clemetson handed over the first cheque towards the
new Peanut Ward. Despite the hard times the appeal was
quickly successful and over £2,000 was collected by the end of
the year. We shall hear more of this scheme, of how it ran into
difficulties and of its final triumphant success, in subsequent
pages.

Meanwhile the second big project was the building of the
Canadian Wing. In 1942 the Royal Canadian Air Force had
been playing an increasing part in the war in the air and
naturally suffering an increasing number of casualties, and a
Canadian Plastic Surgery & Jaw Injuries Unit under the

command of Squadron/Ldr. Ross Tilley, surgeon, with an anaesthetist and 3 nursing sisters, had been attached to the Hospital for training. At the Board Meeting on January 25th the Chairman disclosed that proposals were under discussion for the addition to the Hospital of a Canadian Wing, and the Board agreed to place some land at the Government's disposal for this purpose. During the next few months much thought was given to the scheme by a special sub-committee, which at first recommended that the new Wing should be built on the ground at the back of Ward III. It was pointed out at the Board Meeting in June, however, that the Canadian Wing was to be a memorial to the Royal Canadian Air Force crews who died in the War, and since it would eventually become the property of the Hospital, and would remain a perpetual memorial, it was thought that it should have a more prominent site. The Canadian Authorities had expressed a wish to erect the building, 270 feet in length and with 50 beds, on Peanut land, where it could have a south aspect, and this was finally agreed, but it necessitated an extra 150 feet of land being purchased, for which, once again, the money was found by the Peanuts; by August the plans were completed and by October the Ward was under construction by the Royal Canadian Air Force. At the Annual General Meeting in June, Mr. McIndoe announced that the Canadian Government had granted £20,000 towards the cost of the building.

Following close upon the heels of this last announcement there came news of the third big expansion scheme. At a Board Meeting on September 27th, the Chairman reported the visit of Mr. Clark Minor, President of the British War Relief Society of America, who, with a deputation from that Society, had been received by Lord Kindersley and himself on behalf of the Hospital. Mr. Clark Minor, he said, had handed them a cheque for £30,000 for the purpose of building a fully-equipped Surgical Unit as a memorial to the work being done by the British War Relief Society in this country; he added that we were greatly beholden to Mr. Kelsey Fry, and to Mr. Le Crohm of the London Dental Society, through whose influence this gift had been made.

One unexpected result of all this money pouring in was a rumour which spread round the Town that the Hospital was now so wealthy that it no longer needed local subscriptions! The Board were naturally anxious to deny this unwelcome suggestion and the Chairman wrote a letter to the local Press pointing out that the money in question had been given for specific objects and that the Hospital, far from being wealthy, still had very great need of the usual subscriptions, which he appealed to the local people to maintain.

Meanwhile, alongside these three important schemes, many other things were happening. The first and one of the most important of these was the appointment in January of Mr. J. H. Peel as Honorary Gynaecologist. This was the first appointment of a Consultant Gynaecologist and it was a most successful choice, for Mr. Peel, now Sir John, is still, 20 years later, serving the Hospital and its community with distinction.

Next, in April we find the House Committee recommending the Board to accept the Rushcliffe Committee's proposals regarding Nurses' salaries, and in May there is news of a Nurses' Recreation Fund being opened. At the same time there was a discussion—perhaps brought to a head by a spell of hot weather—as to whether nurses should wear stockings! Advice was sought from the Sector Matron and also from the Association of Hospital Matrons, both of whom recommended that "all nurses must wear stockings while on duty." In May, still more accommodation being required, it was agreed to rent The Larches as an additional Nurses' Home, with Mrs. Froggatt as Supervisor; and since there were now so many nurses, it was thought necessary for them to have their own Sick Bay, and a room at Warrenside was fitted up for this purpose.

In spite of the rumour concerning the Hospital's wealth, many donations were still being received, amongst others a gift of £400 from South Africa to help maintain the Red Cross and St. John huts. In March the sum of £418 was received from the Working Men's Fund, and in June an Exhibition Golf Match at the Royal Ashdown Golf Course raised the sum of £217. Honeycomb boxes, a part of the Peanut Organisation, during this year brought in no less a sum than £455. Unfortunately, however, later in the year a slight controversy arose owing to the Peanut Organisation having become rather closely mingled with the Appeals Committee. Both were collecting for the Hospital, but since the Peanut Fund was now collecting specifically for a Children's Ward, while the Appeals Committee still had to carry out its original routine function of collecting general funds, the two organisations decided to separate.

In June the Ministry of Health approved the Board's acceptance of Mrs. Norman Laski's kind offer to loan Saint Hill House as a convalescent home for Officers. While on the subject of Officers, it is an astonishing fact that while Officers and other ranks of all services were being treated together in Ward III, the regulations stipulated that they must have different food! The House Committee discussed this matter on June 11th and discovered that it was not possible officially to provide all ranks in this Ward with the same food, but the Chairman was asked to see Mr. McIndoe unofficially about it.

On July 9th came East Grinstead town's own tragedy. In the middle of the afternoon a single German raider dropped a stick of bombs right across the centre of the town causing a large number of casualties, many of them at the Whitehall Cinema, which received a direct hit. In all over 100 people were killed and some 235 injured. Among the casualties were 3 members of the Hospital nursing and domestic staff, one of whom, Kathleen Gladman, was killed. The Hospital naturally received a large number of these casualties and the entire staff worked hard all through the night, treating a total of 57 patients of whom 23 had emergency operations. At their next meeting on the 26th July, the Board recorded "their appreciation and thanks for the magnificent way Matron and her staff, all the surgical and medical staff, and Captain Banham and his staff, handled the difficult situation created by the large number of casualties from the recent air raid; they desire that their congratulations be brought to the notice of all concerned." Subsequently at the Board Meeting of 24th August, the Chairman read a letter from The Director-General of the Emergency Medical Service conveying "the thanks of himself and his colleagues to all concerned for the very good work carried out on that day. Especially he wished to thank Mr. Jayes, Dr. Hunter and the Secretary-Superintendent, as he is very conscious of the burden that fell on them, and of the successful way in which the patients were treated and cared for."

In July Mrs. Dewar resigned from the Welfare Committee and from her many other voluntary duties at the Hospital, and her Mobile Shop was taken over by Miss Spalding. At the same time it was arranged that Squadron /Ldr. Tilley and Flight / Sgt. Blacksell should attend the meetings of the Welfare Committee, which by now had over £5,000 in its Post Office Savings Account, and for whom a special office and store was being erected.

An important step in the growth of the Hospital took place in September. At the Annual General Meeting held on June 28th, Lord Kindersley had mentioned the question of deleting the word 'Cottage' from the title of the Hospital. He said he thought it would be a serious mistake to continue calling the Hospital a 'Cottage Hospital' since the new Canadian Wing with 50 beds would mean that the Hospital bed accommodation would be 230, and it was hardly possible to call this a Cottage Hospital. Dr. Branwell said that not only was the name a misnomer but it did not give the staff the credit due to them; if they changed their Hospital and told future employers they had experience at a cottage hospital, it did not carry the credit for the experience they had actually had, and he did not think it fair to the staff to call the hospital a Cottage Hospital. Lord Kindersley had ended this discussion in June by asking everyone to consider the matter and make up their minds before another year to vote for the alteration in title. Evidently, however, the Subscribers wasted no time in making up their minds on this point, for an Extraordinary General Meeting was called for September 10th. Lord Kindersley was in the Chair and was supported by the Chairman of the Board of Management and 23 other members. He began by reminding the meeting that the reasons for the desirability for dropping the word 'Cottage' from the Hospital title had been clearly set out in the Chairman's letter sent to all members, and he opened the meeting for anyone who wished to speak on the subject, but it is recorded "no one did so." Lord Kindersley then moved the following resolution—

"It is hereby resolved to make application to the Board of Trade that the name of The Queen Victoria Cottage Hospital be changed to The Queen Victoria Hospital, East Grinstead."

The proposal was seconded by Mr. Guthrie Kirkhope and was carried by 23 votes for and 2 against. The President remarked that he would have liked a unanimous vote, but that in any case he held 132 proxy votes from members who had not attended the meeting but who approved of the alteration, thus bearing out the fact that the town, as a whole, was in favour of the change.

Another event of some importance for the Hospital in September, 1943, was the election of Mr. Douglas Stern, M.C. to the Board as the representative for Felbridge in the place of Mrs. McIver, who had resigned. Mr. Stern served on the Board continuously for many years, ultimately becoming its Chairman, and there will be further mention of his valuable services to the Hospital in later chapters. In November Lady Gavin took Miss Margaret Black's place on the Board as representative for West Hoathly.

On December 11th the foundation stone of the new Canadian Wing was laid by Air Marshal Harold Edwards, Air Officer Commanding-in-Chief, Royal Canadian Air Force Overseas. Among those present were Mr. Attlee, the Deputy Prime Minister, Lord Sherwood, the Joint Under-Secretary for Air, Colonel Ralston, the Canadian Defence Minister, and Sir Francis Fraser, Director-General of the Emergency Medical Scheme.

Two sad events overshadowed the Hospital at the end of the year; firstly the death of Mr. Cecil Rowntree which is recorded as follows in a minute dated October 25th—

"The Board of Management deploring the death of Mr. Cecil Rowntree place on record their deeply felt gratitude for the outstanding services which as Honorary Consulting Surgeon, he rendered to this Hospital over a long period of years. To the Board he ever gave benefit of his wide experience and sympathetic co-operation in all matters relating to the Hospital, in which he took a lively and abiding interest. The memory of the great part he played in the life of the Hospital will never be allowed to fade."

Sometime afterwards a plaque was placed inside the main entrance to the Hospital, reading as follows:—

"To the memory of Cecil Rowntree, F.R.C.S. who as

Honorary Consulting Surgeon gave unstinted and devoted service to this Hospital for a period of 27 years."

As has already been stated in an earlier chapter Rowntree was further commemorated by a plaque naming the main theatre 'The Rowntree Memorial Theatre.'

Shortly after this there came in November the sudden death of Mrs. Munn, referred to as follows:—

"By the deeply regretted death of Mrs. Munn the Board have suffered the loss of a valued and highly appreciated colleague. The Hospital mourns the loss of a very devoted friend and experienced Counsellor."

Having been Vice-chairman of the Appeals Committee from 1931 onwards, Mrs. Munn was elected the first Chairman of the new Board of Management when it was formed in 1936, and had remained in that office until 1941. A subscription list was opened to raise the sum of £400 in order to name a cot after her, and, this having been successfully accomplished, a plaque in the Children's Ward now bears permanent testimony to the high esteem in which Mrs. Munn was held by local residents. Mr. McIndoe was elected to take her place on the Board; he also moved into Little Warren, the house until recently occupied by Mr. Rowntree.

It might be interesting at this point to set out for comparison the salaries received by members of some of the ancillary services at the time—a Radiographer received £175 per annum plus board and lodging; a probationer nurse £40 per annum plus board and lodging; a cook £100 per annum plus board and lodging; housemaid £48 per annum plus board and lodging; a masseuse* £235 per annum plus lunches, and the Dispenser £167 10s. per annum plus lunches.

In January 1944, Mr. F. T. Moore joined the staff of the Plastic Surgery Unit. He was at the time a Squadron/Ldr. in the R.A.F. Medical Service, but remained with the Unit on demobilisation and was later appointed Consultant Plastic Surgeon.

* The Chartered Society of Physiotherapy was known as the Chartered Society of Massage and Medical Gymnastics until 1945, and its members, now known as Physiotherapists, were still called Masseuses.

In January also Mr. J. B. Roberts, a member of the Board, gave the Hospital 7½ acres of adjoining land to be used as a Sports Ground, the patients having lost their football pitch when work began on the Canadian Wing. Because of this, together with another piece of ground bordering the Holtye Road which Mr. Wagg presented in February and which was intended for the building of a Nurses' Home, another application had to be made to the Board of Trade for authority for the Hospital to hold, this time, up to 50 acres of land. Lord Kindersley had recently expressed his concern at "the patchiness of the layout of the new buildings and the proposed new Children's Ward" and there had been a meeting at the Ministry of Health between Lord Kindersley, Sir John Maude, Sir Francis Fraser and Mr. Kirkhope to discuss the new Surgical Block; plans were going ahead and estimates being obtained with a view to the building of this block beginning as soon as the Air Ministry granted its approval, and so the Board decided at this stage to lay out the grounds properly, plant trees and try to make attractive surroundings for the new rapidly growing Hospital. Following this meeting, a fine tribute was paid to Mr. Kirkhope in a letter from Sir Francis Fraser on January 10th— "The Emergency Hospital Scheme has I feel contributed some striking successes and among those I include the Queen Victoria Hospital, as it has developed in wartime. This would have been quite impossible without your energy and enthusiasm."

Meanwhile the nurses were again needing more accommodation, but the situation was temporarily saved this time by an unexpected legacy from Miss Lambert, the owner of Gainsborough House in Portland Road, who died and left her house to the Hospital. For some reason the Board decided to sell the house, which fetched £2,000, and then they rented it from the new owner as an additional Home for 13 nurses. There were now, therefore, 3 Nurses' Homes outside the Hospital grounds— Warrenside, The Larches, and Gainsborough House.

Another event that should be mentioned at this point is the taking over of the Convalescent Annexe by Sister Baseley, Sister Stroud having resigned. It would appear that there may have been some disciplinary trouble at the Annexe, for it was now specifically laid down that Sister Baseley was to be in charge solely of the nursing, with Flight/Lt. Wheeler in charge of discipline, while at the same time the Board of Management set up a special Annexe Sub-committee consisting of Lady Kindersley, Mrs. Richards, Mr. Wagg and Mr. Kirkhope, in order to keep a special eye on things there. Sister Baseley was later in the year graded as an Assistant Matron. A further sub-committee had also been formed consisting of Mr. Kirkhope, Mr. Blount and Mr. McIndoe, in order to take charge of the building of the Surgical Block—some £25,000 of the money for this having in the meantime been put on deposit at 1% interest at Barclays Bank.

Charges in the Hospital were under discussion at this time and it was decided that the charge for patients in the General Wards should be raised from 3s. to 6s. per day, to include X-ray and pathology; children to pay 5s. per day instead of 2s., while outpatient attendances and outpatient X-rays were to be charged at the rate of 3s. each, but charges to Contributory Scheme members should not be increased, "in view of the Government White Paper on the Health Services."—the National Health Service was already in this early part of 1944 beginning to cast its shadow ahead. When Dr. Sommerville asked the Board of Management for a statement on the post-war development of the civil side of the Hospital, he got little satisfaction.

On May 29th, a special meeting of the Board's Emergency Committee was held to discuss the replies to be given to a questionnaire sent out by the Sussex Area Committee of the British Hospitals Association, and it was decided to subscribe the requested £4 4s. od. to the Association's campaign. This Association later, in connection with its campaign "to maintain as far as possible the voluntary status and to retain the maximum degree of management by their own Boards of its members," launched an appeal for £600,000, to be divided between Sussex Hospitals on the pre-war bed basis. This very important matter was discussed at a special meeting of the Appeals Committee held on October 5th. It appeared that this appeal was to have an unopposed field and that all other Hospital appeals were to be banned and any monies received were eventually to be distributed on the basis of the pre-war beds; i.e. the Queen Victoria Hospital would count only as 43.

The Appeals Committee discussed this matter at great length and came to the conclusion that the Queen Victoria Hospital would bring in a disproportionate sum of money and they would be very heavy losers by joining the Scheme. Their own appeal funds were at the time coming in so well. They therefore recommended the Board not to join the Scheme, but at the same time pointed out that their not joining the Scheme did not mean they were not backing the continuance of voluntary hospitals.

At the Annual General Meeting on 30th May Lord Kindersley announced that the British War Relief Association of the United States of America had increased their gift for the Surgical Block to £60,000, but that in fact even this large sum was not going to be enough, for estimates had been called for and the lowest estimate, from Messrs. Y. J. Lovell, was for £63,773 for the building alone. On top of this the equipment was expected to cost another £20,000 and the total cost would probably be in the region of £85,000.

At this meeting Lord Kindersley also announced that the Board anticipated being able to embark after the war "on the building of a Children's Ward and a Maternity Wing, which were very badly needed in this district." This statement is of more than passing interest for it appears to be the first official mention at the Hospital of the need for maternity accommodation, though the matter had frequently been discussed by the East Grinstead Urban District Council since its first recorded mention by Mr. George Packer at a Council Meeting as far back as January 6th, 1935.

In June Dr. Barbara Evans was appointed Pathologist under the Emergency Medical Scheme and Mr. Tolley resigned from the Board of Management, his place being taken by Mr. Geoffrey Webb. About this time also comes the first mention of Mrs. Burton-Croyden who, over the next 15 years, worked hard in the service of the Hospital. Mrs. Burton-Croyden, an Officer in the local branch of the British Red Cross Society, arranged for two of the Junior Red Cross workers to come every afternoon to the Hospital and take care of the children in Ward II; in October she was appointed to act as Voluntary Welfare Officer to the civil side of the Hospital, to work in conjunction with the Almoner.

In June a donation of £400 was received from the executors of the Rev. C. L. Norris and shortly after a further £900 was received under the will of the late Miss E. M. Lambert. Meanwhile the Welfare Committee was flourishing and we hear that it now had over £7,000 in its bank account, and proposed to allocate £5,000 towards the equipping of the Surgical Block if it should be required. One of the most successful events arranged by this Committee was the première of the film "Lady in the Dark," which brought in just under £4,000.

June 1944 had seen the invasion of Europe, and a large increase in the number of casualties, evidenced by a note in the House Committee Minutes of June 30th stating that for the time being, all holidays for nurses are to be suspended. Actually this only lasted for a very short time, for in the middle of July we read that nurses' leave may be started again.

Further great news came in July in the shape of a cable from New York, "Tell Lord Kindersley the East Grinstead Hospital now get full £87,000" to which welcome news Lord Kindersley replied by cable, "Many thanks message please convey Clark Minor and associates warmest thanks Victoria Hospital Authorities for wonderfully generous gift." In reporting this to the Board, Lord Kindersley added that it was fully anticipated that this gift from America would cover the entire cost of both the new building and its equipment.

Also reported at the same Board Meeting is the exchange of letters between Lord Kindersley and Sir Philip Chetwode, Chairman of the War Organisation of the British Red Cross Society and order of St. John of Jerusalem. The Executive Committee of this Organisation had unanimously agreed that they were prepared to make a grant of £20,000, preferably for the building and equipment of an X-ray Unit, but otherwise for some other purpose to be designated by Lord Kindersley, which would commemorate the War Organisation's connection with the Queen Victoria Hospital in a permanent and suitable way. The sub-committee which was appointed to consider the best method of spending this money, in due course recommended that it be spent on a Nurses' Home. Lord Kindersley was shortly to interview Sir John Maude at the Ministry of Health to see if he could obtain any information as to the

Ministry's post-war policy regarding the Hospital and whether they would in fact back such a scheme.

Another event recorded at this same meeting was that the Canadian Wing was now partially occupied, 9 patients having been admitted on July 12th. Early in August all 49 beds were occupied, and a bronze plaque was placed in the entrance at the instigation of Mr. McIndoe and Wing/Cdr. Tilley, recording the fact that it was through the initiative and drive of "Air Marshal H. Edwards, C.B., A.O.C. in C., R.C.A.F. Overseas 1942-44, a man of hope and forward looking mind" that the scheme received the approval of the Canadian Government. Another plaque erected about the same time records the equipping by his parents of the dental hut in memory of Flight/ Sgt. C. D. Redgrave of the Royal Canadian Air Force. Shortly after this the Canadian Wing was slightly damaged by an aircraft cannon shell but the damage was very quickly repaired.

The Board decided to buy a number of copies of Squadron/ Ldr. Simpson's book 'The Way of Recovery,' with a view to distributing copies to some of their outstanding subscribers. This book by one of the leading Guinea Pigs described his experiences under treatment at the Hospital. References to the Hospital had also been made by another Guinea Pig, Richard Hillary, in his book 'The Last Enemy.'

Meanwhile, Sister Baseley in the Annexe appears to have been making her mark, for in July the House Committee decided that her salary should be increased and they went to the length of writing her a special letter to express their appreciation of her services. She was later to make her mark in a rather different way.

Early in December a decision was made to prepare plans for the Nurses' Home to be built on the site which had been given by Mr. Wagg especially for that purpose. It was to include a large lounge, a small reception room for visitors, a small kitchen, a duty room, bed and sitting room for Sister-in-charge and roughly 100 bedrooms. Also in December Mr. Jock Millar was appointed to the new post of Maintenance Engineer.

A tribute is paid here to Mrs. Karmel, who resigned her position after two years as voluntary secretary to the Welfare Committee. It is recorded "she has established first-class relations with innumerable organisations in London which enabled the work of the Committee to proceed so smoothly. She has managed the distribution of comforts and the entertainments of the patients in the Hospital with great skill and has proved her willingness at any time of the day or night to work on behalf of the Hospital and its patients." Mrs. Karmel was succeeded by L.A.C. Bernard Arch. It is recorded that the Welfare Committee had by now over £11,000's worth of investments in its name. This money was eventually to be used, as we shall see, to very good effect in the patients' general welfare.

At the Appeals Committee meeting in January 1945 Mrs. Clemetson handed over one cheque for £1,500 to the General Peanut Ward Fund and another £800 cheque to endow two cots. She was able to report that over 13,000 new members had joined the Peanut Club in 1944, that £6,252 had been given to the Hospital, and that the total already collected towards the Peanut Ward was over £8,700. The plans of this ward were now available, but it was pointed out that the Ward for various reasons would cost considerably more than the originally estimated £10,000, and the Committee decided to go ahead and try to raise £20,000 which they thought would more likely be the final cost.

In the early part of the year there was a controversy between the Hospital Authorities and the Working Men's Fund over some £400 which had been raised by the Fund at their Hospital Saturday Appeal. The Working Men's Fund were anxious to give this money for the specific purpose of naming a cot in the new Children's Ward when it was built, but the Hospital Authorities thought otherwise and some considerable argument ensued. Eventually, however, the Hospital agreed that the £400 could be allocated for that purpose.

Other events in January were, first of all the operation performed on Mr. McIndoe in London, when it is recorded that Sister Hall and Sister Mullins were released from their duties in order to go and nurse him. Next, the death of Mrs. W. G. Kirkhope, and only shortly after, the death of Mrs. Banham the Secretary-Superintendent's wife. On both occasions the Board sent a wreath and a letter of sympathy.

In March the late Mr. Harry King left £500 for the endowment of a bed, while Mr. Lambert's estate brought the Hospital £1,650, this money being placed in the Hospital's Capital

Fund, as also was £900 received from the Claud Johnson estate. In April the question of the education of E.M.S. child patients comes up for consideration for the first time. Some of them being long-term cases were missing their education, and it was felt that some efforts should be made to obtain teaching for them while in Hospital. Letters to the County Education Authority received the reply that the project was impracticable. The Board had to accept this, as in any case they were not able to obtain a teacher, nor was there for the present any accommodation.

In May comes the news that the Joint War Organisation of the British Red Cross Society and Organisation of St. John had accepted the Board's suggestion that their gift of £20,000 should go towards the construction of a Nurses' Home. How it was eventually used, though indirectly, for this purpose will be seen later.

In June there comes the gift from the Australian Government of the sum of £5,000 "in special recognition of the treatment afforded by the Queen Victoria Hospital to our Australian Airmen." To this the Hospital replied—"The Members of the Board of Management of the Queen Victoria Hospital, East Grinstead, having been apprised of the munificent gift of £5,000 made to the Hospital by the Commonwealth Government of Australia, place on record their very high appreciation of this so kindly and typical action of the Australian people, and their gratification at having been in a position to receive and treat the gallant Australian patients entrusted to their care." It happened that about this time the Board had the opportunity to acquire a house called 'St. Fillans' in the London Road, which would accommodate a further 22 nurses. Since the cost of the house and re-equipping would come to about £5,000 in all, it was decided to devote the Australian Government's gift to this purpose, and the house was purchased, redecorated, and opened as another Nurses' Home, its name being changed to 'Australia House.'

The Annual Report for 1944 presented at the Annual General Meeting on June 8th, 1945, gives the number of available beds, increased by the 49 beds in the Canadian Wing, as 225. The average cost of each Inpatient per week had been £6 4s. 11d. while the total expenditure for the year was only just short of

£58,000. Towards this the Emergency Medical Scheme had contributed over £48,000.

In June, came a letter from the Ministry of Health, copies of which were sent to all governing bodies of voluntary hospitals which had taken part in the Emergency Medical Scheme, expressing the Minister's deepest thanks to the administrators and staffs of the various hospitals for the part they had played.

The war was over. Three years were to pass before the Hospital was taken over officially by The Ministry; difficult years inevitably, but the machinery at the Queen Victoria Hospital was in top gear, enthusiasm was high and progress continued.

# 7

# Interim

THE period from the end of the war to Nationalisation could easily have been a stagnant one, but so great was the momentum of affairs that, although each of these events produced its own problems, they appear to have been overcome with relative ease.

In June, Air Marshal Johnson, C.B.E., M.C. Air Officer Commanding-in-Chief of the Royal Canadian Air Forces Overseas, had written to say that the Royal Canadian Air Force unit would be withdrawn on September 7th. The handing-over ceremony actually took place on Wednesday, September 5th, when speeches were made by Air Marshal Johnson, Group Captain A. Ross Tilley, and Mr. Frederick Hudd, acting High Commissioner for Canada, the Canadian flag being symbolically lowered by Group Captain Tilley. The Union Jack was then raised by Mr. McIndoe, and the building officially accepted from Mr. Hudd by Mr. Blount, the Chairman of the Board. At a dinner given the previous weekend to the staff of the Canadian Unit, Group Captain Tilley had been officially presented with the Air Raid Warning Siren which had been sited over the Whitehall building where he had lived most of his time in East Grinstead. A number of speakers referred to the outstanding co-operation and friendship which had existed between the Canadian patients and staff and the people of East Grinstead all through their time here. Later, at a meeting in February, the Board placed on record "their sincere gratitude and deep appreciation of the gift of the entire equipment of the Royal Canadian Air Force Wing, which has so generously been made to the Hospital." Authority for this gift had been given by Air Force Headquarters in Ottawa who had decided to include the equipment together with the presentation of the building. It had originally been thought that the Hospital would have to purchase the equipment, and the Chairman stated that "the magnificent gift of all the Canadian Ward and equipment is very largely due to the extremely able manner in which Mr. Kirkhope has handled the negotiations."

The handing over of the Canadian Wing posed a number of problems and a sub-committee was set up to consider how best this great new gift could be used. This Committee decided that the 44 beds should be allocated to the Emergency Medical Service for Plastic Surgery and the private beds in the corridor to Mr. McIndoe for the same purpose. What had been the Patients' Recreation Room became the Board Room and rooms were also set aside in the new building for offices for Mr. Kirkhope, Captain Banham, Mr. Tolley the Treasurer and his clerk, for a General Office and also one for a Royal Air Force Officer. Sister E. R. Hall was appointed Sister-in-Charge of the Canadian Wing. Captain Banham's old office in the main Hospital was handed over to the Matron and still remains her office today.

A big difficulty at this time was that of obtaining domestic staff; amongst others who were leaving was Miss G. Waring who was voted a gift of £25 in recognition of her 18 years devoted service to the Hospital. The Nurses' Recreation Room was being used as a dormitory for Domestic Staff, a very unsatisfactory arrangement, and the Board decided to purchase a house in the London Road just opposite Australia House, called 'Engalee,' which was being offered for sale for £4,000, and this was set aside as a Home for Domestic Workers; it is recorded that the Ministry of Health were very helpful in every way in this matter. Another facet of this particular problem was that for the first time it was decided to employ male cooks, their salary to be 4 guineas per week, non-resident.

There was also the usual shortage of nurses. A number of volunteers who had worked as nurses through the war were now retiring; and all of these were duly noted in the Minutes and thanked for their services. To overcome the shortage the House Committee discussed the question of employing male Nursing Orderlies, but decided before embarking upon this revolutionary step to find out what wages they were paid elsewhere.

In August Miss Holland gave up the voluntary driving duties which together with Mrs. Crichton she had faithfully carried out for 4 years. Mrs. Crichton continued, with the help of Miss Pears and Miss Rutter, on a voluntary basis until 1948 when she joined the paid staff of the Nationalised Hospital and continued then to drive for many years. Also Miss Collett, the Almoner, resigned, her place being taken by Miss Womersley; and Miss Carter replaced Miss Beard in the Occupational Therapy Department, while at the same time the Industrial Therapy Department was closed.

The proposed Maternity Unit also came up for discussion at this point. The East Sussex County Council wrote to ask—"If the Hospital builds a Maternity Ward, can they reserve two beds in it for County Council cases?" The Secretary-Superintendent was instructed to write and tell them, "It is not possible for the Hospital to build at the moment, but when it is, your request will be considered." Towards the end of the year another letter was received, this time from the East Grinstead Rotary Club, asking whether there was any possibility of a Maternity Unit being built. The reply on this occasion was—"While the Board has every sympathy with the object in view the Hospital cannot in the present circumstances commit itself".

In September the whole Hospital was distressed to hear of the very sudden death of Mrs. F. H. Fraser. An indefatigable worker for the Hospital throughout the war years, Mrs. Fraser was in fact preparing to attend one of the Hospital's social functions when she was taken very suddenly ill and died within a few minutes. The Board, at their next meeting on September 24th, recorded in the Minutes their "appreciation of the very valuable service she rendered to the Hospital". Her place on the House Committee was taken by Dr. A. C. Sommerville and she was succeeded on the Board by Mrs. Neville Blond, previously Mrs. Norman Laski and already well-known for her many benefactions to the Hospital and long service on the Welfare Committee.

Another big problem came to a head in September. The business of raising funds locally for the Hospital had not been at all easy since the end of hostilities, and it appears that the functions of the Appeals Committee, which had worked hard and most successfully over the 14 years since 1931, had been gradually taken over by the Welfare Committee and the Peanut Organisation. The Appeals Committee had not met for some months and when they did it was only to decide that they should resign. They wrote a letter to the Board pointing out that Mrs. Devitt had been Chairman of the Committee for 8 years, Mrs. Dempster and Miss Wallis joint secretaries since 1931, and stressing that "the fact that the Hospital was built and equipped at all was due in no small measure to the untiring efforts which have been made by these two ladies". The letter continues—"It is suggested that the present may be a suitable occasion for the Board to consider the future composition and working of the Appeals Committee, and in this connection it is neither practicable nor reasonable to expect this Committee, which possesses neither stenographer nor whole-time staff, to deal with the financial requirements of the Hospital when not only the Canadian Wing, but also the Surgical Block and proposed Children's Ward have been built, equipped, and staffed. It should be noted that the fête held on August 18th this year produced the net sum of £1,000 8s. 10d. This Committee continues to work in the closest co-operation with Aunt Agatha and her Peanut Scheme inasmuch as it carries out the work of organisation of many of the local activities, dances, fêtes, concerts, whist drives, etc." On receiving this, the Board, after giving high praise to the Committee for their great services to the Hospital, suggested that their resignation should be accepted with regret and the whole question of appeals be passed to the Finance & Building Committee for their consideration. A special vote of thanks was given to Mrs. Devitt the retiring Chairman, and to Mrs. Dempster and Miss Wallis.

As an immediate result of this the Welfare Committee decided to extend its activities in future to embrace the whole Hospital, and a Sub-committee was set up to consider the constitution of a new Welfare Committee. One proposal was that Flight/Sgt. Arch should be appointed Welfare and Appeals Secretary to the whole Hospital on a salary and commission basis, but this proposal in the end came to nothing as he was unable to find housing accommodation in the district and left shortly afterwards. The Sub-committee also discussed the best means of using the large amount of capital which the Welfare Committee had amassed and they decided that rather than invest it and use the income for patients' needs, they would instead lend the capital as short-term interest-free loans to assist the immediate needs of patients in their rehabilitation and resettlement; the loans were to be repaid as soon as possible and thus the money could be used again for other patients. This decision seems to have been a very beneficial one and many ex-patients of the Queen Victoria Hospital had reason to be grateful for it.

The marriage of Mr. W. G. Kirkhope to Sister Baseley, who had run The Convalescent Annexe with such success for the last two years, took place on September 6th. Shortly after this Dr. Douglas Robertson and the 7 members of the General Practitioner Staff who had been in the Services returned and again took up their work at the Hospital—Doctors Thornton, Stanley, Sibley, Wilson, Morton Palmer, Dennison and Collin, Dr. Frobisher having returned in 1941. Dr. Lucy Elliott who had been working in Dr. Collin's place had retired during the year, Dr. Newman who had been locum for Dr. Dennison having retired the previous year. Dr. Menczer in place of Dr. Morton Palmer, and Dr. May Bullen acting locum for Drs. Thornton and Sibley, had also left. Mr. Webb resigned from the Board and his place was taken by Mr. F. C. Maplesden; Mr. Nils Eckhoff, the Surgeon, though continuing his work with the Plastic Unit, resigned from the General staff as also did Dr. Paterson and Dr. Franklin, the Paediatrician and Dermatologist.

Mr. McLeod and Mr. Shepherd resigned from the Dental Department, having worked in it from 1940 onwards, together with Mr. Parfitt, who had taken the places of Mr. (now Sir) Wilfred Fish and Mr. Walker some years previously. The thus temporarily somewhat attenuated Dental Department was taken over by Mr. Terence G. Ward, M.B.E. on his demobilisation from the Royal Air Force, in which he had been a Squadron Leader in charge of a Maxillo-Facial Unit. This Department's development in the succeeding years under Mr. Ward, assisted from 1947 onwards by Mr. G. E. Ryba, was to be dramatically successful and we shall hear more of it in the following pages.

Mr. Frank Summers was appointed the Hospital's first full-time fully qualified Pharmacist on October 1st, taking over from Miss Carter who had been appointed Dispenser in 1942. Miss M. I. Dennis was appointed Night Sister, and the Convalescent Annexe was closed.

A minute of the Medical Committee Meeting in October records that it had been decided to invite Mr. McIndoe, Mr. Kelsey Fry and Dr. John Hunter to join the Committee. "It was felt", says the minute, "that by the inclusion of these members of the Maxillo-Facial Unit, the Medical Committee would represent in a fit and proper manner the whole Hospital, and the sub-division into Civilian and E.M.S. spheres would gradually pass into oblivion". This matter had been under discussion on many previous occasions but nothing had been done about it owing to wartime conditions. In any case it had needed an alteration of Rule XII of the Hospital to include Honorary Consultants with Honorary Medical Officers on the Medical Committee, and this alteration had only been made at the last Annual General Meeting of Subscribers.

In November it was discovered that the new Surgical Block was going to exceed the original estimate of its cost, but fortunately a further £10,000 was voted by the British War Relief Society of America to cover what it was hoped would be the total cost. About this time a legacy of £1,200 was received from the will of Mrs. George Simpson, which was distributed —£800 to endow a bed in Dewar Ward and £400 to endow a cot in the new Children's Ward. A letter of appreciation was received from the British Dental Association thanking the Hospital Board and all members of the staff concerned for the Hospital's war work in the services of dentistry.

In December the House Committee voted £25 as a farewell gift to Miss Maddocks for her 6 years voluntary work in the Photographic Department, and they wrote her a letter of appreciation of her work. Following her resignation Mr. Gordon Clemetson, husband of Aunt Agatha of the Peanut Club and until demobilisation a photographic officer in the Royal Navy, was appointed to take charge of this department, and one can only say that it was a very happy appointment, for Mr. Clemetson holds the same position today to which he was appointed in January 1946, and the Department has grown and flourished considerably under his guidance. In December also Warrant Officer Blacksell retired and in the following New Year Honours List was awarded the M.B.E. His retirement was described by Mr. McIndoe as a "major disaster", and he hoped that the Board would give some thought to the problem of how to persuade Mr. Blacksell to return in some position or other. On Christmas Day came the broadcast from Ward III, part of the British Broadcasting Corporation's 'Round the World' programme leading up to the King's speech. This was a great honour for the Hospital and was voted a great success by everybody who heard it.

The year 1945 finishes on a happy note, with the House Committee recommending the Finance & Building Committee to give presents on the occasions of the marriage of Mr. Percy Jayes with Sister Harrington, and of Captain Banham with Miss Holland, both of which events took place about this time. These are only two of the many marriages between patients and staff, and between staff and staff, too numerous to mention individually, which had taken place during the last few years.

Early in 1946 Dr. Sommerville was complaining on behalf of the Medical Committee that there was not sufficient accommodation for local residents either in the General Wards or in the Private Corridor. The House Committee pointed out to him that the imminent re-opening of the Children's Ward, now no longer required as an operating theatre since the opening of the new Surgical Unit, would free the two beds on the balconies of Kindersley and Dewar Wards, so making four extra beds for local patients. However, the House Committee put the matter up to the Board and it was agreed that a further two beds should be made available for local private patients on the Canadian Wing Corridor. At the same time the Board decided to increase the private fees to 9 guineas per week for patients living in the Hospital area and 12 guineas per week for those outside the area.

Another difficulty at this time was the lack of accommodation for male staff, and the Board authorised a Sub-committee consisting of Mr. Kirkhope, Mr. Mitchell, and Mr. Stern, to investigate the possibilities of building on the large piece of land which had been acquired with the house 'Engalee'. This Sub-committee shortly reported back that it would be possible to do this, and in the spring building of two semi-detached cottages was begun.

Thoughts were turning also towards the comfort and convenience of patients' visitors and the Board discussed whether it was possible to arrange some form of transport for them, but came to the conclusion that they were not able themselves to do this. However, later in the year they approached the London Passenger Transport Board, asking them whether they could run special buses from the Town to the Hospital on Visiting Days. This apparently was not possible but the Transport Authority did agree to list the Hospital as an official stopping place in the next issue of their time-tables. For the further comfort of visitors it was decided to open a Canteen which it was hoped would also be available for Hospital workers and patients.

A further welcome gift came in the shape of a cheque for £3,000 from the Government of New Zealand "in recognition of the treatment by plastic surgery of the New Zealand airmen who had suffered burns and become patients in your Hospital". The Board wrote a letter of gratitude to the New Zealand Government for this gift, and invited the Prime Minister of New Zealand to visit the Hospital. £1,500 also was received from the Australian Red Cross Society towards the cost of equipping the Library in the new Surgical Unit.

Towards the end of March all members of the Board were supplied with copies of the National Health Service Act and the relevant White Paper, with the result that in April the various Committees were all showing signs of anxiety as to the possible effects on them of nationalisation. The Welfare Committee set up a Sub-committee to investigate the whole position of Welfare money with a view to safeguarding it, so that in the event of nationalisation "all welfare money can be retained for the purpose for which it has been subscribed". The Finance & Building Committee set up a similar Sub-committee consisting of Mr. Kirkhope, Mr. Blount and Mr. Wagg, with power to consult the Hospital's Honorary Solicitor with a view to taking Counsel's opinion as to how the various Hospital Funds might be affected under nationalisation. Arising out of this there came a letter towards the end of May from the British Hospitals Association, as follows:—

"Your anxiety is shared by many other Hospitals. There is little doubt that Funds already raised for future extensions, but not yet used, would go over to the Minister, together with Endowment Funds. We are obtaining expert legal opinion on this and other points, and we are actively pressing for amendments during the Committee stage to modify the provisions of the Bill in this and other vital respects. Therefore no definite ruling is possible on these matters until the Committee stage has been passed."

and there this very vital matter had to be left for the time being.

In May Miss Helen Davies gave up the appointment of Radiographer which she had held since 1936, having run the Department very efficiently and virtually single-handed for all this time; she was succeeded by Miss Phillips. Miss Grey took over the post of Dietician from Miss Norton. Also in May the Board lost another valuable member in the person of Mr. Alan Huggett and they placed on record their great appreciation of his services over a period of many years. Mr. Harold Brown had also resigned after many years service, and Mr. Tom Peters and Mr. George Packer were appointed in their place.

At the Annual General Meeting on 27th June, Lord Kindersley spoke very largely of financial matters. He mentioned firstly that the Hospital had received £53,000 from the Ministry of Health during the preceding year as against £48,000 the previous year, and went on to mention the wonderful gift of £97,000 from the United States of America for the American Surgical Wing—"In a long life associated with numberless appeals" he said, "I have never experienced such extraordinary ready generosity as we have met with from our American friends." He went on to mention the Australian Government's gift of £5,000 and the New Zealand Government's gift of £3,000—"in further recognition of the world-wide reputation this Hospital has gained". "The gifts referred to" he said, "were specially allocated for specific purposes and I appeal to the public for the continuation of their generous support for the next few years until the Government takes over the responsibility".

In July the Medical Committee recommended the appointment of Mr. E. G. Muir, F.R.C.S. of King's College Hospital, London, as Honorary Consultant Surgeon to the Hospital, and the confirmation of Mr. J. H. Peel, also of King's College Hospital, as Honorary Consulting Gynaecologist, his previous appointment having been a temporary E.M.S. one only; also the appointment of Dr. Phillip Evans of Guy's Hospital, as Paediatrician, and of Dr. Moyle of Eastbourne as Dermatologist. In August the appointments of Mr. R. J. Furlong and Mr. W. H. Gervis as Orthopaedic Surgeons were also recommended, Mr. Gervis's previous appointment having been to the Emergency Medical Service. A further appointment to the Honorary General Practitioner Staff at this time was that of Dr. J. V. MacGregor of Lingfield. The equipment which had been loaned by the Gordon Hospital in 1940 was returned duly repaired and reconditioned.

July 25th 1946, was a great day in the Hospital's life, when Her Majesty the Queen came to open the American Wing. She arrived shortly after lunch and was received by Lord Leconfield, Lord Lieutenant of the County, and Lord Kindersley, President of the Hospital. Among others present were the United States Ambassador, Mr. Averil Harriman, Mr. Clark Minor, President of the British War Relief Society of America, who had arrived in England by air only that morning; Mr. De Cruger, Mr. Gilbert Carr and Mr. Rex Benson, Chairman, Deputy and Vice-Chairman respectively of this Society in London; Mr. W. J. Jordan, High Commissioner for New Zealand in London; the Earl and Countess of Limerick; the Earl of Strathmore; Lady Louis Mountbatten; Lord and Lady Woolton; Admiral Lord and Lady Mountevans; Field Marshal Lord Chetwode; Marshal of the Royal Air Force, Lord and Lady Tedder; Lord Horder; Air Vice-Marshal R. F. McBurney of the Royal Canadian Air Force; Col. Ralph Clarke, Member of Parliament for East Grinstead; Mr. A. J. Golding, Chairman of the East Grinstead Urban District Council; Sir Harold Gillies; Professor and Mrs. Pomfret Kilner, together with Lord Glendyne and Mr. John Dewar, Vice-Presidents of the Hospital, members of the Board of Management and senior members of the staff of the Hospital.

The R.A.F. Regiment provided a Guard of Honour which was inspected by the Queen after the Central Band of the Royal Air Force had played the National Anthem and the Queen's Standard had been broken at the masthead. Her Majesty was presented with a bouquet by 4-year old Betty Streeter.

Mr. Clark Minor recalled that the British War Relief Society of America had been organised within 3 weeks of the outbreak of war, and was supported by a million loyal friends of Great Britain. They were indebted in East Grinstead, he said, to Lord and Lady Kindersley for the inspiration which had enabled them in the United States to co-operate in the establishment of this great American Centre. He continued—"It is our hope that this building shall remain throughout the years as a symbol of Anglo-American goodwill, and shall be regarded as one of the greatest international co-operative efforts ever known in the world to relieve human suffering. Those things which have inspired your friends in the United States to help in this war are things of permanent value in our friendly relationship. May this continue throughout the years."

He then presented the key of the American Surgical Block to Lord Kindersley who, speaking briefly before handing it to Her Majesty, said—"This great generosity of the American people touches the hearts of all men and women, and cements especially international goodwill and friendship."

Her Majesty then spoke and, expressing her pleasure at being present she referred to "This fresh example of the co-operation which during the last 6 years has brought our two peoples closer than ever before." She then mentioned the great and efficient work that had been quietly going on in the Hospital for many years prior to the war. "It has been a Hospital", she said, "made possible by the generosity of the people who lived in the neighbourhood. When war came, it became a centre for burns and face injuries and was recognised for its skilled work all over the world". Referring first to the Canadian Wing, Her Majesty continued, "I feel this is a suitable opportunity to express our deep gratitude to the Canadian Government"— and then to the American Block—"in this wonderful building we see something more than just a new wing to your Hospital. It is a symbol of the love of freedom, and of the desire to relieve suffering in the world, which unites our two peoples. We have shown how our two nations can work together, and as we so continue, our faith in the future is more than justified".

Her Majesty having unlocked the door, entered the new building where she unveiled the plaque commemorating her visit. The United States Ambassador then unveiled a companion plaque commemorating the gift of the building.

Following the Queen's visit Lord Kindersley received a letter from her Private Secretary in which the following sentence occurred—"Please convey to the Surgeons, the Nursing Staff and the Domestic Staff of the Hospital Her Majesty's great pleasure at the success of their arrangements. Throughout the visit Her Majesty was impressed by the evidence on all sides of cheerfulness, efficiency and co-operation. To the patients also Her Majesty sends her greetings and good wishes. The occasion of this visit will long remain with the Queen as a happy and inspiring memory."

The Board were also informed that it was Her Majesty's intention to send a large signed photograph of herself to be hung in the Board Room or other appropriate place. At the next meeting Miss Beale proposed a vote of thanks to the Sub-committee who had made all the arrangements for the visit, and the Chairman remarked that the main weight had fallen on Mr. Kirkhope's shoulders. In this connection the following sentence from a letter written by Mr. Wagg to Mr. Kirkhope is relevant—"I am writing at 5.15 p.m. whilst the impression of this afternoon is still strong, to congratulate you on today's triumph of organisation, which I know almost better than anyone, was principally due to you".

In October the Finance & Building Committee had the unpleasant duty of reporting an overdraft on the various Hospital accounts at the Bank, amounting in all to approximately £8,000. There was, it appears, a variety of reasons for this large overdraft, interest on which incidentally was most generously waived by Barclays Bank. The principal reason was that the Ministry of Health's payments to the Hospital were still being based on 1945 costs of upkeep, whereas in fact today's costs were considerably higher. The average cost per Inpatient at this time, it was estimated, was £8 5s. 8d. per week, although the full charge made in the General Wards amounted only to £7 5s. od. The following month the Finance & Building Committee was able to report that the Ministry of Health had made an immediate payment of £13,000, which not only cleared the overdraft but represented payment in advance for the next few months' costs. They had agreed also to accept new figures for the cost of wages and fuel, etc. and the Committee expressed the opinion that this new agreement should cover the running costs.

In November Mr. C. R. McLaughlin was appointed a member of the Plastic Surgery Unit, as was also in an Honorary capacity Mr. H. Osmond-Clarke, Consultant Orthopaedic Surgeon to the Royal Air Force. In November also a further effort was made to persuade the London Passenger Transport Board to run a bus service on Sundays; this time the Transport Board agreed, and from now on 2 buses were run from the Hospital grounds every Sunday afternoon—a very great help to patients and their visitors.

One of the difficult problems arising from the war and peculiar to this Hospital was the rehabilitation of the long-term plastic cases, long-term because in order to complete their treatment many of them needed multiple operations which would extend over—in some cases—many years. The Welfare Committee made itself responsible for these cases and was strengthened now by the addition of Dr. Russell M. Davies, Mr. Blacksell and Mr. Arch; meetings were arranged between representatives of the Welfare Committee, the R.A.F. Benevolent Fund, the British Red Cross Society, the Air Ministry Rehabilitation Department and the Guinea Pig Club, in order to try and co-ordinate the granting of re-settlement allowances and various other matters. It was agreed amongst all these bodies that the Guinea Pig Club would be largely responsible for co-ordinating the various Services in this respect and it was reported in February 1947 that no less than 85 of these long-term cases were being helped in various ways for periods up to as much as 2½ years. It is at this point also that we hear of Mr. McIndoe's success in persuading the authorities to defer discharge from the Services of these long-term patients; the Minister announced in the House of Commons that they would not be discharged until their treatment was complete.

Another problem was the X-ray Department. The spacious accommodation provided in the new American Wing was adequate to cope with the tremendous increase in work that had taken place in the war years, but quite obviously one Radiographer and a part-time Radiologist were not, and it is recorded that there were certain complaints both from patients and doctors that the Department "was not co-operating as it did in

129

Miss Davies's day", and as a result of this it was decided to put all calls for weekend radiography direct to the Matron! In February 1947, however, Dr. William Campbell was appointed full-time Radiologist and with the assistance of Miss Naomi Mills, newly appointed Radiographer, quickly got the Department into efficient running order, since when under his expert guidance it has contributed enormously to the general efficiency of the Hospital. Miss Mills left after some 2 years and was succeeded by Miss Beryl Phillips. The number of X-ray photographs taken has increased from under 2,000 in 1947 to an annual rate of well over 7,000 at the present time, and the Department now has 4 Radiographers; nor since Dr. Campbell's arrival have there been any further complaints of lack of co-operation. The old X-ray Department was converted for use as a small emergency ward, the Dark Room being separated off to become the sluice-room of the Private Corridor. It was decided to call this small ward The Edward Blount Ward, "in order to honour the many years service given by the Chairman to both the old and the new Hospitals".

The X-ray Department was not the only one to benefit from the extra accommodation in the new American Wing. The Dispensary, which had hitherto been housed in the main building in the small room now used as Kindersley Ward's Linen Cupboard, moved over to the room which is now the Anaesthetic Department's office. In fact, the building up of the old Dispensary into a fully grown and meticulously efficient Pharmacy under Mr. Summers, keeping pace step by step with the steady growth of the Hospital is a success story in itself. Miss Carter, who had left on Mr. Summers' appointment, returned as his Assistant, in which post she remained until the end of 1960. In 1950 the Pharmacy took on the extra job of dispensing for the nearby Edenbridge & District War Memorial Hospital of 32 beds. In 1956 an Assistant Pharmacist was appointed and the Department spread, first into the room now used by Dr. Robertson, then into part of the X-ray Department, until its final home was reached in the Canadian Wing as will be heard later.

But the greatest benefit of all came to the Outpatient Department, at last released from its tiny and totally inadequate accommodation in the main building. Spacious new consulting rooms, examination rooms, changing rooms and a Sister's Office had all been included in the new building, and at last the Department was able to cope with the steadily expanding work that was coming to it.

The 4 theatres themselves were the last word in modern design; the Recovery Ward with its 10 beds was a totally new feature; the Lecture Theatre, the Library, the Secretariat and spacious accommodation for the Pathological and Photographic Departments all played their part in the tremendous expansion of the Hospital's work which the building of this new wing made possible.

In February there comes news also of another matter of considerable importance to the growing Hospital. The Chairman of the Board announced the setting up of the Marks Fellowships, the money for these having been most generously provided by Sir Simon Marks* and his 2 sisters, Mrs. Neville Blond and Miss Mathilda Marks.† The Board in its gratitude addressed the following resolution to each of the donors:—

> "The Board having been informed of the 3 Fellowships in Plastic Surgery of £740 per annum each, founded by Sir Simon Marks, Miss Mathilda Marks and Mrs. Neville Blond, under a 7 year covenant and tenable at this Hospital, desire to place on record their very high appreciation of this most outstanding and valuable action, and to express their deep gratitude to the generous and far-seeing donors."

At the Annual General Meeting later in the year Lord Kindersley, referring to the scholarships, said they were "a great contribution to surgery". At the same time the Ministry of Health established 3 more Fellowships in Plastic Surgery of the same value. Mr. John Watson was the first to be appointed to a Marks Fellowship, with Mr. P. H. Beales and Mr. A. L. Schofield second and third.

In March came the resignation of the Almoner, Miss Bye, only a year after her appointment, and the Board decided that for the time being the appointment should be left vacant, but Miss Kemp to be appointed as Enquiry Officer; later in the year Miss Kemp's status was changed to 'Social Worker'.

* Now Lord Marks.
† Now Mrs. Terence Kennedy.

131

Another resignation at the same time was that of Sister Walker, who received a farewell gift and a letter of thanks for her "exemplary service over 7 years". H.M.S. Argus sent a cheque for £311 and in recognition of this the Board gave approval to fix a plaque to a cot in the Children's Ward.

At this point there came a fundamental change in the representation of the Medical Staff. The old Medical Committee was abolished and instead all members of the Medical Staff were to be members of a new Queen Victoria Hospital Medical Society. The Society elected annually an Executive Medical Committee which had in fact the same powers as the previous Medical Committee, and it was specifically laid down that this Executive Committee would consist of 5 General Practitioners, 5 Maxillo-facial representatives and 3 Consultants. The Executive Committee appointed its own Secretary who was also the Secretary of the Society. Apart from representing the Medical Staff in the administration of the Hospital, the main function of the Society was the arrangement of monthly lectures and an Annual Dinner, and there can be no doubt that, though the clinical meetings and lectures—at first highly successful—gradually petered out for lack of support, nevertheless the Annual Dinner and the social side of this Society succeeded very well in one of its main objects, which was to weld together the various sections of the Medical Staff whose functions within the Hospital and clinical outlook seemed sometimes to be at variance. Two additional members over and above Mr. McIndoe and the Secretary of the Society Dr. Sommerville, were elected to the Board of Management, Mr. Percy Jayes and Dr. Eric Sibley. Dr. Douglas Robertson who had helped very largely in putting this Medical Society on its feet was elected its first President, Mr. F. T. Moore filling the position of Assistant Secretary, to be in charge of the initial programme of lectures.

In May members of the Board and all Sub-committees were re-elected en bloc "in view of the fact that this will probably be the last year of the Board as at present constituted".

In June there came the announcement of a knighthood for Mr. McIndoe, and at the end of the month Mr. Blount opened the Board Meeting by offering Sir Archibald the Board's congratulations, while the minutes record their pleasure at the recognition thus bestowed upon him. This honour was, of course, very well deserved, rewarding as it did 7 years outstanding and continuous work, not only for the Hospital but for surgery in general and plastic surgery in particular, and for the country and its war effort as well. Sir Archibald had by this time fully established himself at the head of the Hospital, and his was the chief inspiration which had led to its enormous growth during these years and the world-wide reputation which it now enjoyed.

Dr. P. H. Cardew was appointed to the Medical Staff in July in the place of Dr. Wilson of Dormansland, who had resigned some months previously.

Later in the year, the Hospital was once more overdrawn, to the extent of £10,000 and there was a sum of £5,600 still owing on the American Surgical Centre. Lord Kindersley most generously loaned the money to pay off this account from his own pocket, but the financial situation was desperate and the help of the Ministry had again to be asked. £15,000 was sent immediately to clear the overdraft and the loan, while the method of finance was radically revised. In future the Ministry were to make Block Grants from time to time, sufficient to cover all the E.M.S. expenses in advance and thus avoid as far as possible any overdraft. In spite of this, by September the account was again £9,000 overdrawn, so that another grant was required from the Ministry, and this appears to have been forthcoming. It is hardly surprising that at the Annual General Meeting Mr. Blount was moved to refer to "our excellent relations with the Ministry of Health", and to add, "the Hospital has never lost by its association with the Emergency Medical Service".

The Ministry of Health had for some time been talking of building accommodation for Nurses in the Hospital grounds. There had also been a proposal to acquire a nearby mansion 'Oakleigh' as a Nurses' Home, and in November as well a Special Meeting of the Board was held to consider the purchase of Warrenside, the lease of which was due to expire on the 25th March the following year. But at the same time the Hospital urgently needed convalescent beds since the old Annexe had been closed, and the opinion was expressed that the Plastic Unit could almost double the present number of operations if only beds were available. It was finally decided therefore that the Ministry would rent Oakleigh as a Convalescent Home and that the Board would buy Warrenside with the British Red Cross & St. John's Joint War Organisation gift of £20,000, which had been given for the purpose of providing a Nurses' Home. "There is not the remotest prospect of our building a Nurses' Home for many years to come", says the Minute, "and in all probability the Joint War Organisation donation will pass to the Ministry of Health when the Hospital is taken over in July 1948".

Another matter of some importance arose in August when a letter was received from Mr. W. R. Murray, Managing Director of the Kent & Sussex Courier, asking for the return of all monies raised by the Peanut Club and at present held in trust by the Hospital. As will be seen later this request was a most long-sighted one and subsequently was to prove of tremendous value, but at the time the Board were a little worried about their legal position regarding this money. Mr Kirkhope had written to Mrs. Clemetson in May saying—"We here have come to the conclusion that money raised for a specific purpose will not be touched", and had had a reply back by return, saying "Mr. Murray and I cannot agree with your conclusions. We ourselves feel no such optimism". In fact, after taking Counsel's advice in the matter, the Hospital decided to return the money and the transfer of these funds was completed in September, the new Trustees being Mr. Murray, Mrs. Clemetson and Mr. F. S. Harries of Tunbridge Wells.

As a commentary here on the old voluntary system, we hear for the first and only time of legal proceedings being taken against 3 ex-patients for the recovery of charges, although there are many records of impecunious patients being unable to pay and having their charges reduced or even in extreme cases cancelled. There are also cases reported from time to time where certain members of the Board "undertook to investigate the case of '——' ", and one suspects that quite often these members of the Board put their hands in their own pockets on behalf of the patients. Certainly in these pre-nationalisation days the matter of unpaid accounts does not seem to have loomed very large, and the fact that legal proceedings were taken would almost certainly have been reported through one or other of the various committees. It is probable therefore that these proceedings—the only ones mentioned in all the Minute Books—were in fact the only ones taken.

In September there came the formal announcement of Nationalisation in a letter from the Minister of Health, notifying the Board of Management that he had advised the Regional Hospital Board that this Hospital was transferable to him on the appointed day. "If the Board of Management feel the Hospital should be disclaimed, the Minister asks to have an early opportunity of considering any reasons in support of that view". The Board agreed that no action be taken with reference to the last sentence. Indeed the Board must have known that they had no option in the matter, for the Hospital by this time was so large that it would have been quite impossible to support it by local voluntary donations.

Towards the end of the year Dr. Russell Davies was able to give the Welfare Committee a very satisfactory and encouraging account of the working of the recent R.A.F. Welfare Co-ordinating Committee, and reported that the Emergency Health Service of the Red Cross & St. John Organisation was proving both generous and expeditious in rendering financial assistance for this purpose. Flight/Lt. Wheeler at this time was being pressed to return to his former employment with the Birmingham Education Committee, while at the same time the R.A.F. had told him he was unlikely to be retained at the Queen Victoria Hospital any longer than the end of the year as there was no longer an R.A.F. Establishment here to justify his post. He told a Welfare Committee Meeting of his keen disappointment that he would be unable to finish the work of rehabilitation and resettlement which he had started and had hoped to see through. Mr. Blount expressed the Committee's keenest regret and paid high tribute to the value of his work.

A number of minor changes took place early in 1948. The Patients' Sitting Room in the Canadian Wing was fitted out as an Ophthalmic Department. At the same time the Surgeons' Mess was moved into what had been the Officers' Recreation Room, while the old Surgeons' Mess became a Patients' Rest Room; it is now used as the Hospital Linen Store. The Red Cross Shop, run by Miss Spalding, had served such a useful purpose that although the source that had originally subsidised it had dried up, a sum of money was voted by the Board to save it, while they determined to make efforts to make it self-supporting. The total expenditure for the year 1947 is given in the Annual Report as £101,466, of which over £80,000 had come from the Government's Emergency Hospital Scheme.

Shortly after this the Ministry of Health sent an Accountant down to examine the details of The Endowment Fund in order to ascertain how much of this was 'free money'. It appeared that the whole of The Endowment Fund would pass to the Ministry of Health for redistribution on the appointed day and since this Hospital was considerably more favourably situated than some, the amount allocated from the total pool was likely to be a great deal less than the sum put into it. The Finance & Building Committee therefore decided to realise as much as possible of this money—£2,877—with a view to spending it before the appointed day.

East Grinstead and District Farmers had by now collected £349 out of the £500 required to endow a bed; the Chairman remarked that their efforts had been interrupted by wartime conditions, and on this account the Board decided to name 'The Farmers Bed', it being understood that they hoped to collect the balance of the money.

At a meeting at the end of March, 1948, the Chairman of the Board opened by making sympathetic reference to the passing of Mr. F. E. Richards, a lifelong member of the Board—

"In the deeply regretted death of Mr. F. E. Richards, the Board have suffered the loss of a greatly valued and highly appreciated colleague. Mr. Richards has been associated with the Hospital for many years, was a life member of the Board of Management, Vice-chairman of the Finance & Building Committee and had taken the keenest interest in all the affairs of the Hospital. The Board mourns the loss of a very devoted friend and experienced counsellor and extends to Mrs. Richards its very sincere sympathy in her great loss."

The Chairman then went on to read a letter informing the Board that this Hospital would in future be one of a group of 18 hospitals comprised in Group XII of the South-East Metropolitan Region, and he also read a letter from the Regional Board asking for nominations to the new Group Management Committee. Dr. Haldin-Davis was elected to represent the

Board on this Committee, with Dr. Russell Davies to represent the Medical Committee. The Finance & Building Committee had pointed out the very considerable amount of work which would be needed to bring our buildings into first-class condition before being handed over on July 5th, and Mr. Kirkhope and Mr. Mitchell were asked to go into the matter, with power to act. This sentence—"Mr. Kirkhope and Mr. Mitchell to investigate, with power to act" recurs again and again in the Minutes during these post-war years, particularly in connection with any matters concerning finance or property, and it is obvious that their experience in such matters was of incalculable value to the Board.

In April comes the resignation of Captain Banham after 12 years devoted work in the Hospital. His resignation was accepted, and in June is recorded the appointment of Mr. Anthony Esdaile Whitworth to succeed him, the appointment to be in the first place for 3 years, and to include the loan of a free house; this house, Tudor Cottage, where Captain Banham had lived for the last few years, had previously been the property of Lord Kindersley, but was now purchased by the Hospital as a permanent house for its Secretary.

From this point onwards preparations are being made for the nationalisation of the Hospital. It is reported that a House Committee is to be appointed as from July 5th, its constitution and duties as yet undecided. The Medical Committee recommended the appointment of a House Surgeon to the general side of the Hospital, to work under the direction of the Honorary Medical Officers. They also recommended the appointment of Mr. John B. Musgrove to be additional Consulting Surgeon to the Ear, Nose and Throat Department. Mr. Musgrove had acted as locum during Mr. Scott-Brown's recent illness, and was well-known to the Medical Staff. At the same time they recommended the appointment of Dr. Frank Dudley Hart, Physician of the Westminster Hospital, as additional Honorary Physician. They also recommended that it would be desirable for the various Consultants to be asked to appoint their own deputies during holidays or illness. "We hope by these measures", said Dr. Sommerville, "to consolidate the position of the Hospital regarding the attendances of Consultants, and this, together with the appointment of a Resident Medical

Officer, means that no stones can be thrown at this Hospital in the future by any representative of the Ministry, as the work of all Departments will thereby be adequately covered".

In June come the final meetings of the various Committees. The old House Committee, meeting for the last time on June 18th, passed a vote of thanks to their Chairman and Vice-chairman for all their valuable work. The final meeting of the Finance & Building Committee on June 21st was concerned about Mr. Kirkhope's position as Bursar, for apparently the National Health Service had no provision for such an appointment; they decided to leave the matter in abeyance.

At the final Board Meeting on June 28th, it was decided that the Minutes of the final meetings of the various committees should be approved and signed by the respective Chairmen on the spot in order to finalise the Minute Books. Dr. Haldin-Davis expressed the regret felt by all that this was the last Board Meeting to be held under the Chairmanship of Mr. Blount. He paid tribute to Mr. Blount's ability, tact and assiduous devotion to the welfare of the Hospital over a long period of years, and expressed his pleasure that his connection with the Hospital would still be maintained. In reply Mr. Blount said that his labours had been greatly helped by the kind co-operation he had always received from the Board, and he thanked everyone most sincerely. On June 30th he wrote to Mr. Alfred Wagg, who had been his Vice-Chairman for the last few years—"I am possibly the only one who knows how great has been your influence among the staff, the patients, and the sometimes touchy and temperamental medicos and surgeons. Your unobtrusive diplomacy has often quieted a rising storm and restored a placid atmosphere to the advantage of all concerned". This personal appreciation from the Chairman to his Vice-Chairman gives us evidence of the co-operation that existed on the Board and we have one of the very few hints of any differences that may have occurred over the years between the Board and their medical colleagues. He wrote also to Mr. Kirkhope thanking him for his help—"No one knows better than I do the immense value of the services which you have rendered to the Hospital in every direction. Much of the success of the Hospital has been due to your untiring efforts".

The final Annual General Meeting took place on June 22nd

with Lord Kindersley in the Chair, supported by Mr. Blount, Chairman of the Board, and 46 members. The Kent & Sussex Courier, reporting this meeting, said "there was an atmosphere of mourning for the passing of the old regime and of foreboding for the future. General regret was expressed at the change after some 85 years during which East Grinstead had successfully provided for its sick and had even led in the field of medical and surgical service. One note of optimism, however, for the future was struck by Dr. Haldin-Davis who pleaded for the new system to be given a chance to prove itself,—'with those in control freed from the financial terror which had hung over the heads of the Voluntary Boards.' Lord Kindersley said, 'I think we may claim that the Town has kept up its record as leaders in hospital work until today. We in East Grinstead have nothing to be ashamed of in that respect. The Hospital is going to be taken over by the State on July 5th, but had it been left undisturbed there were 3 additions which would have materialised in the course of very few years. The first was a Nurses' Home, the second would have been a Children's Ward and the third a much needed Maternity Unit.' He paid a personal tribute to the Matron, Miss Caroline Hall—'I have never seen her without a smile on her face and I think it is that happy nature which has carried her through so many difficulties'. 'We also' he said, 'owe a great debt of gratitude to Mr. Edward Blount, Chairman of the Board of Management, who has been looking after the Hospital for 48 years, and to the Bursar, Mr. W. Guthrie Kirkhope'. 'I shall disappear from the scene so far as the Hospital is concerned', continued Lord Kindersley, 'but I shall still watch its progress with interest, and if it can maintain that happy atmosphere to which I have already referred, then, as far as I am concerned, I shall not be entirely satisfied at the change, but I shall be reassured.' "

# 8

# Nationalisation

ON the appointed day, July 5th 1948, the Queen Victoria Hospital, along with nearly every other hospital in the country, passed into the hands of the Government as part of the National Health Service. There seems to have been remarkably little to mark this change; indeed so far as the Hospital records go the take-over would appear to have been followed by a period of stunned silence, for there is no record of any meetings of any kind until August 6th.

It was Dr. Haldin-Davis who alone, at the final Annual General Meeting in June, had defended the Act—"I do not take the pessimistic view of the future which has been taken by those who have preceded me" he said, "I have been associated with the new Group Management Committee, and the Regional Board, for the last month or so and I find that it is composed of very much the same people as ourselves. They are all people who have been, and are, interested in hospital management. They recognise the work that has been done in the past and think it can be carried on in the future. We may have to put in an extra supply of red tape but the spirit of the administration, as far as I can see, is entirely the same spirit which characterises our own hospital—the spirit of benevolence, charity and general friendliness, and they are anxious that this should continue. I think that this is going to come out a great deal better than we are inclined to believe. I think the future of the Hospital is as bright as the past has been."

The Medical Staff were now under contract to the Regional Board, a remote and unknown quantity, and many of them did not like it. A new category of Junior Consultant was introduced, the Senior Hospital Medical Officer, Consultants themselves were subdivided into full or part-time according to the proportion of their time spent on National Health work or private practice; even the General Practitioners, with their 85 years tradition of service to the Hospital, felt that their future was fraught with uncertainty. Wisely, the Ministry and the Board gave time for them all to sort themselves out, and, as it happened, the general side of the Hospital, instead of being closed to the Family Doctors as some had feared, was opened even wider (there are now 22 on the General Practitioner Staff as against only 15 in 1948) and in the Plastic Unit 4 full Consultant Surgical appointments were made, Mr. F. Braithwaite, Mr. P. H. Jayes, Mr. C. R. McLaughlin and Mr. F. T. Moore, in addition to Sir Archibald McIndoe and Mr. N. Eckhoff. On the clinical side the Hospital appeared to be little affected by the new Act.

On August 6th the new House Committee met for the first time, and the following were present:—

| | |
|---|---|
| Miss H. M. Beale | Lady Kindersley |
| Mr. Edward Blount | Mr. J. H. Mitchell |
| Mr. R. C. Burgess | Mrs. E. D. Richards |
| Alderman R. H. Burslem | Mr. John Simons |
| Dr. Russell M. Davies | Miss M. Spalding |
| Dr. H. Haldin-Davis | Mr. Douglas Stern |
| Sir Herbert Eason | Mr. A. R. Wagg |
| Miss F. H. Hanbury | |

Mr. Burslem and Mr. Simons being Chairmen respectively of the Group Management and Group Medical Committees. An apology was received from Miss I. P. Wallis. Mr. W. G. Kirkhope, under the new name of House Governor, and Mr. A. E. Whitworth as Secretary attended the meeting. The first business was the election of Mr. Edward Blount as Chairman with Mr. J. H. Mitchell as Vice-chairman. Though it was understood that no sub-committees would have any statutory powers, nevertheless it was decided to set up (1) a Nursing Staff Subcommittee, consisting of Lady Kindersley, Mrs. Richards, Miss Beale, Miss Spalding, Miss Hanbury, Dr. Russell Davies and Mr. Burgess, and (2) a Finance Sub-committee, consisting of Mrs. Richards, Dr. Haldin-Davis, Mr. Wagg and Mr. Stern, with Mr. Blount and Mr. Mitchell ex-officio members of both committees. Sir Archibald McIndoe, Mr. T. G. Ward and Dr. E. J. Dennison, who had succeeded Dr. Sommerville as

Secretary, represented the Medical Society on this new House Committee.

The only other items of any interest at this first meeting were the announcements that Oakleigh had been leased for 12 years and that plans were being prepared for building a new Dental Department.

At the following meeting 3 weeks later with the Matron and Miss Kemp, now Almoner, in attendance, Sir Archibald McIndoe asked for 150 extra beds, 50 for women, 50 for children and 50 for dental cases. The present total of 205 beds including 10 Recovery being, he said, inadequate to provide the necessary facilities for specialist training in Plastic Surgery which the Ministry of Health had agreed should be one of the functions of this Hospital.

One of the first tasks of the Nursing Sub-committee which met on 20th August and elected Lady Kindersley as its Chairman with Mrs. Richards as Vice-chairman, was to consider a Memorandum on the nursing services of the Hospital which had been prepared by Dr. Russell Davies. Among the recommendations made in this Memorandum was the formation of a Nurses' Representative Council, and this Council was later elected, with Dr. Russell Davies as its first Chairman. Another proposal was the presentation of a Badge which Lady Kindersley agreed to give annually, plus 5 guineas, to the best nurse in the Hospital.

The Finance Sub-committee met on August 24th and elected Mr. Kirkhope as its Chairman. At the next meeting of the House Committee, however, Mr. Burslem pointed out that this appointment meant that an Administrative Officer of the Hospital was Chairman of one of its Committees, a situation which seemed rather improper; so at the next meeting of the Finance Sub-committee Mr. Kirkhope stood down and Mr. Mitchell, who had been elected deputy, became Chairman instead.

In the middle of October, Mr. C. E. Tolley died. He had been first a member of the Board of Management of the old Hospital and then its Treasurer since 1941, and the Finance Committee recorded "its sense of loss of an old and valued friend", while the House Committee recorded:—"as Treasurer he had devoted all his time and ability to the service of the

Hospital whose accounts in consequence had been kept in a way so exemplary as to receive praise from many quarters. The whole Hospital had regarded him with affection and his loss was one deeply felt by all who knew him." Following Mr. Tolley's death the Finance Sub-committee appointed Mr. A. W. FitzAucher to take his place, with Mr. Eric Clark as his assistant, and 2 clerks, for they regarded 4 as the essential minimum to staff the Treasurer's Department. This arrangement, however, was not accepted by the Group Management Committee who ruled that:—

1. The appointment of Treasurer would not be filled, though Mr. FitzAucher might remain in his post for such minor matters as administering petty cash, receiving various monies collected at the Hospital, and so on.
2. The checking and payment of all accounts were to be transferred forthwith to the Finance Department at Tunbridge Wells, this to include the Samaritan and Amenity Funds.
3. Preparation sheets for salaries and wages were also to be forwarded forthwith to the Finance Department.

Mr. FitzAucher promptly resigned and Mr. Clark accepted the somewhat reduced post of Financial Administrator. One of the consequences of this change in the financial administration was a letter the following month from the Group Finance Officer, Mr. B. G. Spencer, requesting the closure of the Hospital's existing account at Barclays Bank, and the opening of an account instead at the Westminster Bank. The Minute recording this goes on to say—"in view of the association between the Hospital and Barclays Bank over a period of 50 years, the proposal was accepted with the greatest regret." This break with the past was followed later by a similar break with Messrs. Whitley, Hughes & Luscombe who had been Honorary Solicitors to the Hospital for many years, and also with Messrs. Charles Kingham & Company of Dorking, who had supplied the Hospital with provisions and groceries since 1940. In each of these cases the House Committee sent letters of appreciation for past services.

Amongst the most important developments which came early after nationalisation was that of the Dental Department. Mr.

Ward reported to the House Committee on August 30th that the Dental Consultative Committee of the Regional Board had recommended that the Dental Department at this Hospital should be developed in order to provide facilities for specialist work for the whole South-eastern Region, plus training facilities. Two trainees were to be appointed and a Resident House Surgeon, with 3 more Mechanics.

Another development was the installing of a Registration Office and Mr. R. P. Barrowman, who previously had worked in the R.A.F. Office, was asked to organise it. With increasing outpatient work as a consequence of the National Health Service, and more inpatients resulting from the opening of Oakleigh, this was an essential and obvious step. The new Registration Office opened in the American Wing on April 4th, 1949, in what is now the Almoner's Department.

In November Dr. Charles Palmer of Copthorne was appointed to the General Practitioner Staff, followed shortly after by Dr. E. M. O. Bullen of Dormansland.

The House Committee meeting on January 31st, 1949, did some important business. Firstly we read that—

"Her Majesty the Queen having graciously consented to become Patron of the Hospital, it was proposed by the Chairman and unanimously resolved to tender to Her Majesty the thanks of the Committee in the following terms—
    'The House Committee of the Queen Victoria Hospital, East Grinstead, with their humble duty to Her Majesty the Queen, beg her to accept their grateful thanks for her gracious consent to become the Patron of their Hospital.'
This signal mark of the Queen's interest and sympathy will give the utmost satisfaction and encouragement to all who have been, are now and will be connected with the Hospital."

At the same meeting it was proposed by the Chairman that Lord Kindersley should be invited to become the Honorary President of the Hospital. This proposal was carried with acclamation and at the next meeting we hear that Lord Kindersley has accepted the appointment. Also at this same meeting comes another Minute:—

"The meeting having been informed that the project for the new Children's Ward had been rejected by the Regional

The retiring Management Committee July, 1948.

Sir Archibald McIndoe introduces his mother and his new wife
to Lady Kindersley and Mrs. Blond.

Hospital Board, largely on grounds of finance, it was reported that the Trustees of the Peanut Club were holding the sum of approximately £27,000 originally collected for this object. In view of the fact that the Hospital was now the Regional Centre for children suffering from burns and congenital deformities, many of which entailed a stay of upwards of 6 months, it was agreed to recommend (1) that the Trustees of the Peanut Club Fund should be approached with a view to obtaining their consent to the use of this sum in providing a complete new Children's Ward, and (2) that subject to such consent being given a fresh approach to the Regional Hospital Board should be made."

This fresh approach was in fact made, and in March we hear that the Trustees have decided to make £24,000 available for the purpose on the conditions (1) that it is paid in interim payments as the work proceeds, (2) that they are allowed to see the plans and (3) that they are allowed to affix any plaques to the building that might be appropriate. Mr. Burslem, Chairman of the Management Committee, wrote officially to thank the Trustees, and on April 29th, 1949 the Kent & Sussex Courier reported:—

"The Regional Board has accepted with gratitude the offer of the Charitable Trust of £24,000, to provide a Children's Wing at the Queen Victoria Hospital".

The offer having been made and accepted, it appears from available records that the matter must have been pigeon-holed at this point, for it was another 12 months before anything at all was heard about it. After that progress was very slow indeed and in fact in October 1950 there came a personal letter from Aunt Agatha to Mr. Kirkhope, complaining "another summer has come and gone since the Trustees agreed to pass the money under certain conditions. There is so much delay and there have been many enquiries from subscribers to the fund; one has already asked for the return of his £400 donation." A further year after this, when a move was finally made, it was a somewhat surprising one, as will be seen later.

On the 1st March the Hospital heard with regret of the death of Dr. Haldin-Davis. Having been a member of the Board of Management of the old Hospital for many years, he was one of the original representatives of this Hospital on the Group

145

Management Committee, and had done much to smooth the change-over to the new regime. Later Sir Archibald McIndoe was elected to join the Group Management Committee in his place, and Dr. Russell Davies succeeded him on the Finance Sub-committee.

Oakleigh opened on March 28th, with Mr. and Mrs. T. H. Hearnshaw in charge, and with these 52 extra beds the Hospital now had a total of 252. The first outpatient clinic for early Mental Diseases was held on April 5th by Dr. Fitzpatrick from Hellingly Hospital.

Another matter under discussion at this point was—what was to become of the Kindersley Bowls and Darts Cups and the Richards Football Cup? Were they to pass into the possession of the State? The Ministry of Health advised that the Cups should not pass to the State but should be handed over to the care of some independent body. This fitted in very well with the plans of the recently formed League of Friends of the Queen Victoria Hospital, and in fact at the end of April the Cups were handed over to the League in order that competitions could be continued under its auspices and the proceeds added to its funds. The League, following a pattern which was developing at the time in connection with many nationalised hospitals in other parts of the country, came into being as a result of a meeting called by the then Chairman of the East Grinstead Urban District Council, Mr. L. W. E. Dungey, who became its Founder Chairman, remaining in this position for some years until he was succeeded by Mr. W. G. Kirkhope. Mr. A. S. Robinson became its first Secretary. Its intention was both to provide extra comforts and amenities for the Hospital patients which might not necessarily be provided by the Health Service, and in addition to provide a central organisation to correlate the many voluntary activities which hitherto had almost entirely maintained the Hospital but for which there was otherwise no outlet under the new regulations. Nobody knew at first in what sort of ways the League might help the Hospital, but everybody felt that some such organisation was necessary, and in fact in the succeeding years it has proved to be so, the Hospital having benefited in many ways, as will be seen in the following pages.

In April it was reported that the Ophthalmic Committee of

the Regional Hospital Board had officially recognised the institution of a Corneo-Plastic Department at this Hospital in charge of Mr. Benjamin W. Rycroft, with 10 beds, though the Unit had in fact been functioning for some time already. On receipt of this news Mr. Rycroft asked for the appointment of a full-time Ophthalmic Sister, and this appointment was filled by Sister King, who joined the Staff on December 2nd and still remains in charge of the Department today.

On April 29th the Hospital was inspected by the Vice-President of the Royal College of Surgeons with a view to the possibility of recognising the House Surgeon post for the purposes of the Primary Fellowship examination; the post was later approved for this purpose and subsequent to his visit he wrote:—

"The Plastic Unit under the able direction of Sir Archibald McIndoe has a recognised place in the national training of Plastic Surgeons and an international reputation in this field. The Unit is magnificently appointed and equipped. A written description would fail to do justice to the Unit. It has to be visited in order to understand its exceptional merits and activities."

In June came the news that the Matron, Miss Caroline Hall had received the O.B.E. The Chairman of the House Committee congratulating her, remarked, "No honour could be more richly deserved and it was one which would give the greatest pleasure to many in all parts of the world."

Several changes in the staff took place during the summer; Miss Carter, the Occupational Therapist, resigned and was succeeded by Miss H. M. Prentice; Miss A. M. Parker, Superintendent Physiotherapist resigned and was succeeded by Miss Rosemary Wootton; later in the year Miss Kemp resigned her post as Almoner and Miss G. M. Wise, a member of the Institute of Almoners, was appointed in her place. Miss Wise expressed a wish to be resident in the Hospital for her first 3 months in order to get to know the life of the Hospital. It was the policy of the Ministry of Health at the time that 1 Almoner should have the care of approximately 80 cases, and since the total beds in the Hospital were 250, the House Committee recommended that 2 additional Almoners should be appointed.

For some reason only 1 appointment was made at the time, Miss Sheila Motton, and it was some 3 years later before Miss Edge-Partington became the third member of this Department. On March 6th, 1950 Mr. B. G. Spencer, the Group Finance Officer, attended the House Committee meeting to answer questions about the new financial arrangements, seen in tabular form on page 149.

He talked also about the expense of maintaining the Hospital for the previous 9 months, which added up to the enormous sum of £129,729. The only income to set against this was £13,625 derived from private patients' fees, staff board and lodging fees, the Road Traffic Act, canteens, occupational therapy, inquest fees, rents of the cottages, etc.

By this time it was becoming apparent that the Nursing Sub-committee was not fulfilling any useful function; in fact Lady Kindersley herself described it as 'a waste of time'. It was therefore amalgamated with the Finance Sub-committee with Mr. Mitchell remaining as Chairman and Lady Kindersley as Vice-chairman.

Accommodation for Resident Medical Officers had been becoming rather short and in March the Assistant Nurses' sitting room was converted to an additional flat for this purpose. There were now 3 Resident Medical Officers, 2 surgical and 1 for anaesthetics; nor were they all of the same sex, and for the first time it was necessary to provide separate accommodation for women residents. Dr. Ronald McKeith of Guy's Hospital was appointed Paediatrician in the place of Dr. Phillip Evans who had resigned some months previously.

In April the House Committee received a reproof from the Management Committee, the subject being the new Dental Department. The House Committee had asked Mr. Troup to design this building, and the letter from the Group Management Committee reads:—

"The Regional Hospital Board has agreed to the payment of Mr. Troup's professional fees. The Buildings Committee of the Regional Board however deprecated the manner in which instructions had been given to the Consultant, and requested the Group Management Committee to inform the House Committee that instructions should not be given to Con-

ENDOWMENT AND AMENITIES ACCOUNTS

| | | | Ministry of Health Hospital Endowments Fund | |
| --- | --- | --- | --- | --- |
| | | | Ministry of Health | Regional Hospital Board |
| *Sources of Income* | Legacies and Bequests and Interest | Gifts of small amounts and allocations from General Endowments and Interest | | |
| *Accounts Credited* | Individual Hospital Endowment Funds | Individual Hospital Amenities Funds | Group General Endowments Fund | |
| *Authority for Expenditure* | Finance Sub-Committee | House Committee | Finance Sub-committee | |
| *Purposes for which Used* | Items of Capital nature, Research, Conference Fees, etc. | Wireless, Television, Furniture, Christmas festivities, Entertainments, etc. for Patients and Staff | Allocations to Individual Hospital Amenities Funds | Specific items for Research, Nurses Prize Awards, Conference Fees, Group Ball, etc. |

sultants for Capital Work without their prior approval in future."

This 'was duly noted'.

However, to offset this some praise came their way in the shape of a letter from Sir Hartley Shawcross, a member of whose family had recently been treated in the Hospital, as follows:—

"It is often so difficult to combine high efficiency with a happy and friendly atmosphere, that I think special congratulations are due to your Hospital for having attained it in so marked a measure. My own observations impressed me with the great efficiency with which the Hospital was run."

On April 6th a preliminary discussion took place between Mr. Cecil Burns the Architect, Mr. Burslem and Mr. Wagstaff the Chairman and Secretary of the Group Management Committee, and Mr. Kirkhope, as to the proposed form of the new Children's Ward, the construction of which had been agreed to by the Regional Board a year previously on the condition that its cost did not exceed the sum provided by the Peanut Club.

The following month a representative of the General Nursing Council visited the Hospital and agreed that Warrenside was a suitable site for the proposed new Training School for Nurses. This was subsequently agreed by the Regional Board and it was suggested that 12 pupils should be admitted every term with the expectation that they would in due course be absorbed into the wards of the various hospitals in the Group.

The Red Cross Organisation informed the House Committee that they could no longer run the patients' Library free of charge, and they proposed to do it on a basis of a 5s. fee per year per occupied bed. This offer was accepted and it was agreed that the Library, under the able control of Miss Ethel Truby, should be continued on this basis, the money being found by the Amenities Fund.

In July the Hospital received a £100 legacy from a Trust dating back to 1923, the income of which had been left to the deceased's wife and on her death the capital was to go to the Queen Victoria Hospital 'if still in existence'. The wife had died in February and the Queen Victoria Hospital, still very much in existence, was glad to add this sum to its Endowments

Fund. Later in the year the Fund also benefited by another legacy, of over £1,800, from the Willis-Homes-Hunt estate, plus a further £600 from the Claud Johnson Estate.

In July Dr. G. E. Hale Enderby was appointed Consulting Anaesthetist and Mr. John Watson, formerly the first holder of a Marks Fellowship, was appointed Consultant in Plastic Surgery in the place of Mr. Fenton Braithwaite who had resigned on taking up another appointment in Newcastle. In July also we hear that the total expenditure of the Hospital for the year ending March 31st, 1950 was £183,087. It was reported that a proposed central boiler house was to cost £5,000 and that this money might be spent from the Hospital's own Endowment Fund.

In September Mr. W. G. Kirkhope resigned his position as Senior Administrative Officer. The Chairman and several other members of the House Committee spoke with much feeling of the incomparable service which Mr. Kirkhope had rendered to the Hospital for more than 20 years, and it was with the greatest regret that his resignation was received. A recommendation was made to the Group Management Committee that he be elected a member of the House Committee. On this occasion Mr. Kirkhope received many letters paying him tribute, among them one from Mr. J. E. Blacksell—"as a representative of the Guinea Pig Club may I say what a splendid job of work you have done for the Hospital in particular and for patients everywhere. Your wisdom, kindness and energy have always been available for anyone in need." At a special ceremony at the Hospital he was presented with an inscribed silver salver, and at the following meeting on October 2nd Mr. Whitworth was appointed Senior Administrative Officer in his place.

In October members of the Committee of the League of Friends visited the Hospital to try and find out in what particular ways the League could help, and they decided that curtaining of the Wards and care of the garden should have first priority. In December another visitor was Mr. Blenkinsop, Parliamentary Secretary to the Ministry of Health, who was shown round the Hospital together with Mr. K. I. Julian the Chairman of the Regional Hospital Board.

At the House Committee meeting on December 4th Mr.

Blount resigned, saying that he felt himself unable for personal reasons to continue as Chairman, and at the following meeting on January 8th, 1951 the Committee elected Mr. W. Guthrie Kirkhope in his place. Mr. Kirkhope's first action on election was to refer to the services which Mr. Blount had rendered to the Hospital for the last 50 years, having been elected to the Board of Management in the year 1900. He had placed the Hospital, he said, before all his many interests in East Grinstead, and that he had now felt it necessary to resign his chairmanship was a very great loss, only mitigated by the fact that he was able to continue as a member of the Committee. Sir Archibald McIndoe moved a vote of thanks and congratulations to Mr. Blount on his completing half a century of association with the management of the Hospital. Mr. Mitchell was elected Vice-chairman.

At this meeting in January 1951 it was reported that a further meeting had taken place between Mr. Burns, Sir Archibald McIndoe, Mr. T. G. Ward, Mr. Guthrie Kirkhope, the Matron, Mr. Wagstaff and Mr. Whitworth, in order to discuss the plans for the new Children's Ward. Following this meeting came a letter from the Group Management Committee asking for an estimate of the cost of furniture and equipment, and for a statement setting out in detail the reasons for the need for this accommodation, to forward to the Ministry for approval. To this letter Sir Archibald had replied that the cost of the equipment and furnishings could only be the balance of what was left of the Peanut Club Fund after paying for the building. As regards approval by the Ministry of Health for the scheme, he had informed the Chairman and Secretary of the Group Management Committee that this must be forthcoming immediately if the Trustees of the Peanut Fund were not to be informed that it was useless for the Architect to continue the drawing up of plans, with the consequent accumulation of his fees. On hearing this the House Committee gave its full approval, endorsing Sir Archibald's action in writing this letter. Rough plans were in fact submitted to the Ministry the following March.

At the same meeting with the Architect Mr. Burns on December 9th, extensions to the Dental Workshop had been discussed. The Department by this time had 2 Consultants,

3 Registrars and a House Officer, and was in dire need of more accommodation. The plans included more surgeries, offices and a waiting room, to be added to the existing building, with an extensive laboratory and work rooms above. The total cost of this fine new building which was completed and opened during 1951, was some £15,000.

The January House Committee meeting also decided to write a letter of congratulation to Mr. William Kelsey Fry on the knighthood which had been conferred upon him in the New Year Honours List. Dr. F. Dudley Hart, one of the Consultant Physicians, had recently been appointed Sub-Dean of the Westminster Hospital Medical School and in consequence had to resign his appointment. He was succeeded temporarily by Dr. Richard Tonkin, also of the Westminster Hospital, until the following November when Dr. Douglas Robertson was appointed Consultant Physician in his place. Dr. Gardiner-Hill continued to visit the Hospital as its Senior Physician on an Honorary basis.

It is possibly worth noting here that there was an epidemic of smallpox in Brighton at this time and owing to the astonishingly large number of contacts between local people and Brighton in some way or another, large numbers of people in the town of East Grinstead and surrounding districts were vaccinated, including 200 members of the Hospital Staff.

On January 29th the House Committee decided that children could be visited during normal visiting hours unless the Paediatrician advised otherwise. This may seem a curious decision to look back on, but up to this time the visiting of children in Hospital had nowhere been encouraged and in most Hospitals throughout the country, including the Queen Victoria, it was totally banned, on the grounds that visitors might bring infection to the child patients and that the psychological upset of them leaving at the end of their visit might delay the child's recovery. This almost universal ban included even the children's own parents! A swing of opinion in favour of visiting was sweeping the country at the time, and the Committee's decision recorded here was therefore bringing the Hospital into line with modern thought on this matter. It was some 2 years later that the *daily* visiting of children in this Hospital was actively encouraged, and as recently as 1960 the decision was made to allow completely unrestricted visiting in the Children's Ward.

In April came the resignation of the Matron, Miss Hall. She wrote "It is with regret that I ask you to accept my resignation. I find it necessary to do this owing to unforeseen circumstances at home. Please accept my resignation as from April 1st to terminate my appointment on July 1st. If the Committee can release me sooner I would appreciate it. I have given this matter a great deal of consideration and it seems that it is the only thing to do. I shall leave with many regrets. The years I have been Matron here have been very happy ones." Her resignation was accepted with the deepest regret, and actually it was not until September that her successor Miss Cook was appointed and she was finally allowed to leave.

As a result of a Group Management Committee recommendation, a Joint Consultative Committee was set up to bring together all sides of the Hospital to discuss matters of common interest. The administration was represented by Mr. Wagstaff and Dr. Russell Davies, the Matron and Mr. Whitworth; while all grades of the Staff were to send their representatives. This committee met for the first time on May 22nd and continued in existence until December 1956, when it ceased to exist owing to lack of interest; the Nurses never agreed to join it as they had their own committee. A further effort was made to restart this committee in 1962, and so far it appears to be successful.

In June Mr. Douglas Stern presented a Dual-programme Radio Service installation to every bed in the Hospital. Miss N. J. C. Starling was appointed Occupational Therapist. Dr. J. F. Pelmore was appointed Consultant Anaesthetist and an additional appointment of Senior Anaesthetic Registrar was made. The Pathological Laboratory was becoming busier and now had a full-time Pathologist and 4 full-time Technicians. In July the East Grinstead Sanitary Laundry closed and the House Committee wrote a letter to the Directors expressing their appreciation of the 50 years service which they had given to the Hospital. In July also the doctors were evidently finding themselves a little oppressed for we find the following note:—

"The Medical Committee wish to impress upon the House Committee their opinion that the principle of treating the

154

sick should be given priority over the maintenance of the administrative machinery."

One symptom of this was the controversy that arose over the prescribing of beer in the Hospital. On July 2nd the Chairman and Secretary had decided that with very few exceptions indeed, there was no need for beer to be prescribed for any patient and they therefore suggested that in future no beer be ordered by the Hospital. Mr. Ward wrote to say that beer was an essential part of the diet of some of his jaw cases, so the House Committee recommended that no beer be prescribed except for jaw cases. In September this controversy was taken a step further by Dr. Morton Palmer who wrote to the House Committee saying that it might be necessary to prescribe beer for a patient and what would the procedure be then? To this the Commmittee replied, "It is not the wish of the Committee to withhold beer prescribed by any General Practitioner who feels that no other medicine could possibly replace it from the pharmaceutical point of view. The Senior Administrative Officer will be empowered to make such arrangements as he thinks fit in exceptional cases."—and there the matter was left.

In September Mr. S. G. Tuffill, Ll.B., F.R.C.S. was appointed Consultant Urologist to succeed Mr. Yates-Bell, who had held this post since 1948.

On September 17th Miss Hilda Cook, the new Matron, arrived. She had previously been Matron of the Plastic & Jaw Unit at Rooksdown House, Basingstoke. On September 22nd a Garden Party was held at the Hospital attended by large numbers of the Staff, patients and ex-patients, who came to say goodbye to Miss Hall. Mr. Kirkhope in a farewell speech said that he thought there could be few people in East Grinstead who did not owe something to Miss Hall. "It is claimed" he said, "that East Grinstead is a happy Hospital with a happy staff and patients. This is largely due to the Matron's happy nature." He then presented her with a cheque for £235 which he said "had been subscribed to by endless people in small and large amounts", and a handsome leather toilet case with a card reading "Presented to Matron Caroline H. Hall, O.B.E. from her friends in the Queen Victoria Hospital and the town of East Grinstead and its neighbourhood as a token of their affection and high regard for her many years of devoted service to the patients entrusted to her care". The resignation of Caroline Hall was followed at the end of the month by the resignation of her sister, Cherry.

The new Matron lost no time in asking for the appointment of an Administrative Sister in addition to the Assistant Matron. This appointment was in due course recommended by the House Committee and Sister Dennis was appointed as Administrative and Homes Sister. It was also decided that the Matron needed secretarial assistance. There had been disappointingly few applicants for the new Training School for Nurses opened in March with Sister Tutor Miss Barry in charge, in spite of advertising locally and in the Nursing papers, and a decision was made to advertise further afield in the local press in Yorkshire, Scotland and Wales. In passing we might notice that the number of Nurses employed at the Hospital had increased from 80 in September 1948 to 113 in June 1951, the increase being largely due to the 48 hour week which had been introduced on July 5th, 1948, and to the acquisition of Oakleigh and the new Preliminary Training School.

September 1951 brought a rude shock in the shape of a blunt letter from the Ministry of Health to the Trustees of the Peanut Fund, saying that under the National Health Service Regulations the money subscribed for the Children's Ward belonged to the Ministry, and requesting them to hand it over immediately. The letter went on to say "the cost of the Children's Ward, if and when built, will be borne by the Exchequer".

Not unnaturally, this totally unexpected demand caused considerable public reaction and local feeling ran high. On September 5th Mr. Fred Dart, Chairman of the Local Trades Council, said "If this money goes into a pool, East Grinstead will lose sight of it. Those who collected it want to see the money used for the purpose for which it was intended". The Courier on September 14th said, "if this outrageous piece of official robbery goes unchallenged in East Grinstead, it will succeed elsewhere in Britain. The Peanut Trustees will fight and the people of East Grinstead must stand solidly behind them, for watching the outcome will be every freedom-loving individual in the country."

A Public Meeting was held at the Whitehall on September

17th, with Lord Kindersley in the Chair, supported on the platform by Sir Archibald McIndoe, and Mrs. Clemetson. The latter in a vehement speech declared "I intend to fight to the last ditch. Having spent 10 years asking people to raise this money I feel most strongly I have a duty to those who supported me. I will not sign the money away under any circumstances." And a resolution in the following terms was passed:—

"This public meeting of the people of East Grinstead has heard with the greatest indignation of the demand made by the Ministry of Health that the money collected by the Peanut Club, all of which was subscribed for the definite purpose of building a Children's Wing at the East Grinstead Hospital, should be handed over to the Ministry of Health for the National Hospital Service, without any promise as to the use to which it will be put. They give their full support to the Trustees of the Peanut Club in resisting such a demand in every legal way unless the Ministry give a clear and definite assurance that the money collected is within an agreed specified time devoted to the object for which it was raised, namely the building of the Children's Wing at the East Grinstead Hospital."

Even this violent reaction failed to move the Ministry, for 18 months later, in another personal communication from Aunt Agatha in February 1953 there appear the words—"I think the delay perfectly disgraceful. It may even be necessary to give a bit more publicity before long". Finally it was another 2 years after that before the Children's Ward came into being, 6 years almost exactly from the Regional Board's acceptance of the Peanut Club's Offer. Of the final triumphant conclusion of this episode more will be found in a later chapter.

At the end of 1951 comes the resignation of Mr. W. G. Scott-Brown, the Ear, Nose and Throat Surgeon, on account of ill health. Another resignation at the same time was that of Dr. Roger Stanley who left the neighbourhood after having been on the Staff for 20 years. Mr. Barrowman also resigned, having been appointed Medical Records Officer to the Birmingham Children's Hospital and the Committee congratulated him jointly with Mr. Whitworth on their successful development o the Medical Records Department; he was succeeded by Mr.

J. G. Myson. Miss I. G. E. Martin, the Assistant Matron, resigned with effect from the end of February after 5 years at the Hospital to become Matron of the Royal Isle of Wight County Hospital at Ryde; she was succeeded first by Miss M. Roberts and after a few months by Miss H. M. Davies. The Hospital's first peacetime male nurse, with urological experience, was engaged for Kindersley Ward. It is recorded here also that a patient who died on December 7th had been in the Hospital for 915 days; this was at the time easily the record length of stay for any one patient, though of course it has now been exceeded since the opening of the Geriatric Wards.

In January 1952 there was a meeting between the Regional Board's Consultant Architect and their Catering Adviser, with Mr. Kirkhope, the Hospital Catering Officer and Mr. Whitworth, to discuss alterations to the E.M.S. Kitchen with a view to providing a central kitchen to serve the whole Hospital. Obviously this would effect a great saving of time and efficiency over the present arrangement with the additional kitchens in the Main Hospital and the Canadian Wing.

In the meantime the importance of the work being done by Mr. Rycroft and the Corneal Grafting Unit was steadily gaining recognition and it is recorded in the House Committee Minutes that as the result of Press publicity "large numbers of people have offered their eyes for use after death". A letter of explanation had to be sent to these people in the following terms:—

"Thank you for your letter. We would accept your offer with gratitude though in the present state of English Law it is difficult to advise you how to ensure that your wishes are carried out. A person cannot bequeath their body by will, but separate evidence of your wishes can be given to your next-of-kin and it is a matter for them to decide. The use of your eyes after death lies with them. They should send an urgent telephone call to the Corneo-Plastic Unit at the Queen Victoria Hospital notifying us *immediately* of your death in order that suitable arrangements may be made from there. Your help is greatly appreciated in furthering work which is of increasing importance to those suffering from diseases of the eyes."

On December 11th a meeting took place at the Hospital under

the Chairmanship of Mr. Kirkhope of representatives of local organisations, at the instigation of Mrs. Clemetson. The meeting was attended by Mr. Gerald Williams, Conservative Member of Parliament for Tunbridge Wells, and Dr. Horace King, Labour Member for the Test Division of Southampton, and was convened mainly to hear Sir Archibald McIndoe and Mr. Rycroft explain how great was the need for donor eyes in the Unit. "We have all the facilities we require here at this Hospital" said Mr. Rycroft, "but there remains the problem of donor eyes; our waiting list grows week by week." An immediate result of this meeting was the 'Sight for the Blind' Campaign and the distribution of forms by the Women's Voluntary Service for use by those who wished their eyes to be used after death for corneal grafting, and the decision to issue a certificate signed by Sir Archibald to all who completed the forms.

The publicity arising from this meeting, which was fully reported in the local papers, spread rapidly, and was soon taken up both by the National Press and other provincial publications. Mr. Rycroft himself appeared in a television programme entitled 'Second-hand Sight' in the following March, and the programme received high praise from the critics. The ground was in fact well prepared by the time Mr. Gerald Williams, supported by Dr. Horace King, introduced his Private Member's Bill. This Bill is itself of historical interest for, having had its first and unopposed reading in the House of Commons on May 14th, 1952 it had its second and third readings and its Committee stage all passed on May 21st. It was only the second Bill to be passed under the 10 minute rule, and the first since the war to pass through 3 stages in 1 night. By the middle of June the Bill had passed through the House of Lords. It was said of it at the time that "few attempts to introduce alterations to British Law have met with such remarkable success in an atmosphere of mutual goodwill from both sides of the House, and it is probably one of the quickest bills to have got through both Houses."

Under the new Law it was now possible for people to bequeath their eyes for use in corneal grafting after death, and the eyes could be so used without permission having to be sought from the next-of-kin. This was a big step forward in the work of corneal grafting and the supply of eyes increased considerably from then on, though even today it is never sufficient, and the need to donate eyes remains as pressing as ever.

At the end of the year it was decided as a measure of economy that the meetings of the Finance & Nursing and the Planning Sub-committees should be discontinued, thus leaving the House Committee as the only local administrative body, with the exception of the Medical Committee, which had advisory powers only. There is, however, evidence that the Welfare Committee, the only pre-nationalisation committee to survive, was still going strong, though its functions of course were not administrative under the Health Act, and it also was soon to come to an end. At the final meeting of the Finance & Nursing Sub-committee it was reported that the state of the funds was:—

| | |
|---|---|
| Samaritan Fund | £2,990 |
| Amenity Fund | £430 |
| Endowments Fund | £763 |

with a note that the Endowments Fund also contained the sum of £5,049 which was to be devoted to the building of the new boilerhouse.

The main event in the summer of 1952 was the resignation of Mr. Whitworth from his post as Secretary. The Minutes record:—

"The Committee regrets losing his services and congratulates him on receiving a better appointment. He has devoted himself wholeheartedly to the work entrusted to him and we are greatly in his debt for many improvements which have been carried out in the administration of the Hospital."

He was succeeded by Mr. G. A. Johns, previously Secretary of the Kent & Sussex Hospital, who has held the appointment and continues to do so, with great success, to the present day. Mr. Dennis Glass was appointed Orthodontic Specialist in the Dental Department to deal particularly with congenital dental abnormalities, and Dr. F. B. Briggs was appointed to the General Practitioner staff.

Also in June we hear that the wife of a patient who died in the Hospital in November 1950, is to bring an action against the Management Committee which will be heard in July at the Lewes Assizes. This is the only record in the Hospital's

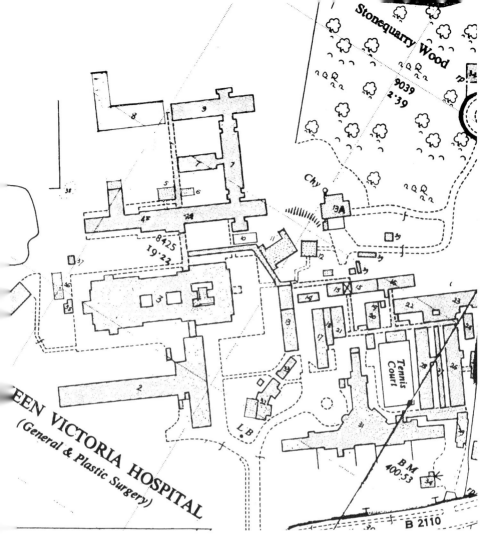

Ground Plan of the Hospital Buildings in 1962.

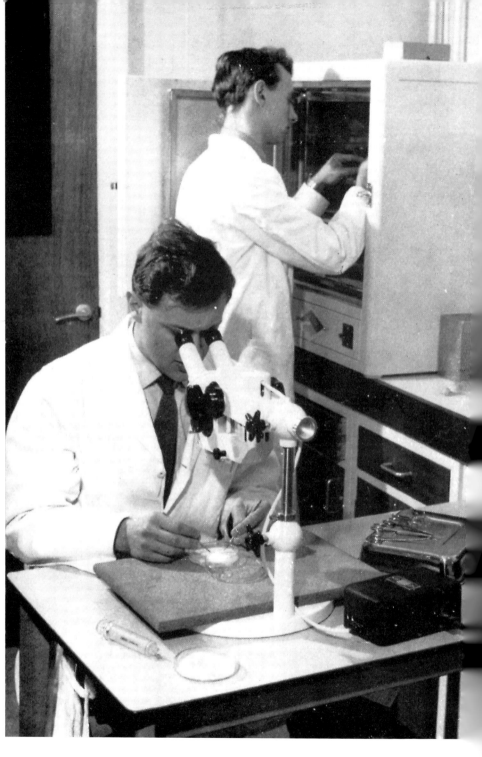

At work in the Blond Research Laboratories.

history of any such action, and after going to the High Court, it resulted in combined damages of over £10,000 being given against the Committee and a member of the junior resident staff.

There was considerable talk at this time about Civil Defence, and this Hospital was selected for the provision of extra beds to be devoted entirely to this purpose; they were to consist of 2 Units of 27 beds each with living accommodation for Nursing Staff, and were to be sited to the north of the American Surgical Wing.

Early in August the House Committee received a letter from the Medical Committee, drawing attention to the fact that although the local population had increased by approximately 10 per cent since 1939, the beds available for their treatment had suffered reduction owing to the necessity of accommodating chronic cases. The House Committee pointed out that when the Civil Defence Wards and the new Children's Ward were completed they would provide additional accommodation, and they resolved to reconsider the matter when more information was available as to the precise intended use of the Civil Defence Wards. However, in November Dr. J. O. Collin, who had now succeeded Dr. Dennison as Secretary of the Medical Committee, wrote a letter to the Chairman of the Regional Hospital Board with a copy to the House Committee, requesting additional beds for general cases, and the result of this was a meeting of representatives of the Medical Staff and the House Committee to investigate the matter. This Sub-Committee, consisting of Mr. Kirkhope, Sir Archibald McIndoe, Mr. Mitchell, Dr. Collin, Dr. Sommerville, Mr. F. T. Moore and Mr. Johns, met on December 1st and recommended as a short-term measure that 10 beds in Ward I be loaned for the use of General Practitioner cases and that more would be considered later depending on the use of the Civil Defence Wards. The House Committee at the same time endorsed a recommendation from the Medical Committee that—

"In view of the shortage of general beds application be made for early additional ward space so that a further 30 beds be allocated to the General side of the Hospital".

Dr. Joan Godfrey of Felbridge joined the General Practitioner Staff on December 1st, while Dr. Orr-Ewing left at the end of February. Dr. W. T. Rougier Chapman, partner of Dr. J. V. MacGregor of Lingfield, joined the Staff in March. Mention should be made here of the Postgraduate Training work being done by the Plastic Unit; every month the House Committee published a list of surgeons under training; this list, varying from 7 or 8 up to as many as 20 at a time, with the countries of origin spread all over the world, is a most impressive monthly tribute to the fame of the Plastic Unit.

Towards the end of 1952 the matter of the Nurses' accommodation came to a head. A Sub-committee appointed in September, consisting of Mr. Kirkhope, Lady Kindersley, Mrs. S. M. Looker, O.B.E., who had only recently joined the House Committee, Mrs. Richards and Mr. Mitchell had recommended that Stoneleigh in College Lane should be purchased to accommodate 23 nurses, but the Regional Board had turned this idea down. The Matron had made a strong plea for another Nurses' Home—"I do not exaggerate the position" she said, "when I say that unless something is done we will very soon be engaging a lower standard of nurse because of the accommodation offered". Mr. Kirkhope wrote a letter to the Group Management Committee telling them that we had 22 nurses non-resident, 39 at present sharing rooms out of a total of 116, and that any applicants for positions here went away when they heard that they had to share a room. The Larches and Gainsborough House leases were both due to expire on June 24th, 1953, but it was thought that accommodation for Nurses in the Civil Defence Wards could be available before then. As a result of all this came a letter from the Group Management Committee saying that they were of the unanimous opinion that the only solution was the building of a Nurses' Home within the curtilage of the Hospital, to be commenced immediately, and that they had arranged a meeting with the Regional Board early in the New Year to discuss this. The meeting took place on January 23rd and it appears that the Board representatives were not optimistic about this building owing to lack of money. The Civil Defence Wards were no answer, they said, as it was intended to use these for patients soon anyway, and it was possible that compulsory extension of the leases of The Larches and Gainsborough House by the Minister of Health might be resorted to. At this point Mr. Douglas Stern suggested that the required accommodation could be built as a second floor to the Canadian Wing, the Surveyor agreeing that such a project was possible. Mr. Stern offered to contribute £5,000 towards the cost on condition that the work began before July 1st. He also suggested that the £5,000 in the Endowments Fund which had been earmarked for spending on the new boilerhouse was not now going to be required for that purpose, and might therefore be added to his own contribution. These suggestions were recommended to the Board with a copy to the Management Committee, and later we hear that Mr. Kirkhope and Mr. Stern were to meet the Board and Management Committee representatives on March 3rd to discuss it; meanwhile it was anticipated that some nurses could be accommodated in the Civil Defence Wards when they were handed over by the builders at the end of the month, but that failing this the shortage of nurses might soon mean closing some beds. At the end of March Mr. Burslem reported that the Regional Board had decided to provide Nurses' accommodation in the Hospital grounds and to contribute £5,000 in addition to the offers of similar amounts from Mr. Stern and the Hospital Endowments Fund; plans, he said, were being prepared for a separate building which would accommodate approximately 25 nurses and which could be extended. Later a further meeting between representatives of the Board, the Management Committee, and the House Committee agreed that a number of similar villas might be erected.

At the House Committee meeting on March 2nd Mr. Kirkhope paid tribute to the late Mr. Edward Blount and expressed the Committee's sincere regret at his death. Mr. Blount had retired from the House Committee at the end of the year and thus finally terminated his long association with the Hospital, the longest service given by anybody to the Hospital in its whole history. Mr. A. S. Robinson, Secretary of the League of Friends, took his place on the House Committee.

In May Dr. Michael Worlock was appointed to the General Practitioner Staff. At the same time the House Committee asked the Medical Committee to appoint one General Practitioner as a Staff Medical Officer. This proposal was not accepted by the Medical Committee, who held the view that every member of the Staff should be free to choose her own doctor as was the general public.

In June there was a complaint from the Management Committee that the East Grinstead Hospital was more expensive to run than the other Hospitals in the Group. The total expenditure during the 12 months ending March 31st, 1953 was £254,934, giving a cost per patient per week of £24 18s. 2d. The House Committee considered this and, agreeing that it was so, maintained that there were special reasons for it; firstly because it was largely a specialist unit, secondly it had a high preponderance of surgical cases which meant theatres, dressings, anaesthetics, etc., and thirdly because the special treatments carried out here frequently involved expensive X-ray and pathological investigations, all of which were unique to this Hospital and therefore not in any way comparable to the other Hospitals in the Group. This explanation seems to have satisfied the Management Committee temporarily though they returned to this question again some 12 months later. In June a television set was lent to the Hospital for the use of Ward I for Coronation Day, this being the first official mention of television in the Hospital.

In August 1953 there occurred the death of Dr. John T. Hunter. One of the most universally popular members of the Staff, he had arrived with Archie McIndoe at the outset of the war as Anaesthetist to the new Maxillo-Facial Unit. He had been a tower of strength in the early days and had unobtrusively played a big part in building up the Plastic Unit, particularly the anaesthetic side. Well described by Richard Hillary in his book 'The Last Enemy' as "vast and genial", John Hunter was indeed a big man physically and in many other ways. It is difficult to say whether he will be remembered more for his quietly confident professional skill or for his hearty presence on all social occasions, for both were outstanding. He had been ill for some months and had been nursed partly in the Hospital and partly by his wife at their home in Ashurst Wood. He lived just long enough to know that his efforts, together with Dr. Russell Davies, to obtain recognition for this Hospital for teaching purposes for the new Fellowship examination of the Faculty of Anaesthetists had been successful. At the House Committee meeting of August 31st, Mr. Kirkhope paid tribute to his work throughout the war years. Early the following year

Dr. Anthony Edridge was appointed Consultant Anaesthetist in his place.

A decision by the Management Committee to start a Chest Clinic at the Hospital brought criticism from Mr. Kirkhope. Reporting that Dr. C. R. H. Weekes the Chest Physician "would require 5 rooms for his Clinic, and it is therefore exceedingly difficult to comply with the Management Committee's ruling that accommodation be found so soon as September 1st", he added that he felt the Management Committee should not have reached their decision without first consulting this Hospital; the matter, he said was still being investigated. The Clinic was in fact opened on October 1st.

On October 5th Matron reported that the Pupil Assistant Nurses' Training School at Warrenside had had 42 pupils since it opened in 1951 and that it served a most useful purpose; it had helped to improve the standard of nursing at the Hospital, and if it were closed it would be even more difficult to obtain nurses and this was a good reason for continuing it. The House Committee accepted Matron's opinion on this and recommended that the School be continued. Dr. J. V. MacGregor of Lingfield resigned from the General Practitioner Staff and was succeeded by Dr. J. F. Paxton, the successor in his practice in Lingfield. Miss B. Williams succeeded Miss Grey as Catering Officer on October 1st.

At the October House Committee Meeting Mr. John Simons made known how serious the position was in the Group regarding Geriatric cases. The Management Committee had previously recommended the use of Oakleigh for these cases, and they now wrote to say that Dr. P. T. Cooper of Tonbridge would be responsible for the admissions and that cases would only be admitted through him. The House Committee asked the Management Committee to reconsider this, and to allocate 7 beds only to Dr. Cooper, the 7 remaining beds to be under the control of our own Staff; the Management Committee, however, would not accept this and went only as far as to say that preference would be given to East Grinstead cases.

Amongst other things being considered at this time was the inadequacy of the present Casualty Department and the possibility of having a new Casualty Department in the old Canadian Wing Kitchen when that was closed, but the Medical

Council, while agreeing on the need for a new department somewhere, thought this site would not be sufficiently central. Another question was that of overcrowding in the Physiotherapy Department—no less than 1,539 treatments had recently been given here in one month. Dr. Ronald Maggs was appointed Consultant Psychiatrist in the place of Dr. G. Fitzpatrick. Miss Taylor became Catering Officer and Mr. H. C. (Peter) Wintle became Steward in the Surgeons' Mess. At the end of March Mr. John Simons retired from the Hospital Management Committee and ceased to be a member of the House Committee. Sister Sayers resigned from the Outpatient Department and was succeeded by Sister Wood, the present holder of this office. Early in May Mr. J. Myson who had succeeded Mr. Barrowman as Medical Records Officer only a few months previously, resigned and was succeeded on July 16th by Mr. J. D. Crane who still holds this position. A second Night Sister was appointed with effect from May 10th.

It is rather remarkable to discover at this point that all admissions to the General side of the Hospital have up to now been the responsibility of the Matron. No wonder she needed a second Administrative Sister and extra secretarial help! In June 1954 the responsibility for routine admissions was transferred from her care to that of the Registration Office, and for emergency general admissions to the General House Surgeon.

Another event which took place about this time and was of some considerable significance to the Hospital was the re-marriage of Sir Archibald McIndoe. If the first Lady McIndoe concerned herself at all in the affairs of the Hospital, there is no record of it in any official document, but from now on the situation was very different. Mrs. Constance Belchem, who became the new Lady McIndoe in July, soon began to appear with her husband at the Hospital social functions and we have a delightful photograph of her doing so, taken in a group which also included his mother, Mrs. McIndoe. Later she took her place on various committees, and now plays a very active part in the life of the Hospital.

On August 30th Mr. Kirkhope referred at the House Committee Meeting to the loss the Hospital had sustained recently by the death of its President, Lord Kindersley. He expressed the Committee's sympathy with Lady Kindersley and her family, and recalled Lord Kindersley's magnificent work on behalf of the Hospital and his unfailing interest in all its activities. At the same meeting he referred also to the recent death of Mr. John Dewar, who in addition to being a great benefactor to the Hospital had also been a regular visitor, especially to the ward which bore his name. Subsequently Gladys Lady Kindersley was invited to succeed her late husband as President of the Hospital, an honour which she accepted 'with appreciation'.

Again the question of the high cost of running the Queen Victoria Hospital was raised. The Management Committee had fixed 26s. per week as the proper cost of food per patient, and a letter came complaining "in spite of economies the figure is still 31s. 6d." The House Committee's answer to this was that comparison with other Hospitals in the Group was not possible owing to the high proportion of jaw cases that could not take solid food for the greater part of their stay in Hospital; also the special high nutritional diet which was essential in the treatment of serious burns cases; furthermore that there were many patients undergoing plastic surgery who were not confined to bed and therefore were able to eat normal meals. In spite of these, one would think, very reasonable arguments, it was decided that the Regional Catering Officer should visit the Hospital in October to meet a Sub-committee and discuss the Catering. The outcome of this meeting was the formation of a permanent Catering Sub-committee consisting of representatives of the Medical and Nursing Staff and the House Committee, with the Hospital's Catering Officer; Miss Taylor, the holder of this office at the time, resigned shortly afterwards and in the following August was succeeded by Mr. E. J. Wragg. In October Dr. H. N. Hardy and Dr. G. F. M. Carnegie were appointed to the General Practitioner Staff.

On November 1st we hear that the Regional Board was unable to make any additional finance available for opening the Civil Defence Wards. Mr. Summers, who was by this time bursting out of his small dispensary next to the Recovery Ward, was therefore granted permission to use a room in one of the wards as an Aseptic Laboratory until the new Pharmacy could be built. The House Committee decided at this meeting also that the recently completed new Nurses Villa should be known as "Douglas Stern House". The Reverend Dr. G. Golding-Bird, Vicar of St. Swithun's Parish Church, resigned his post as Church of England Chaplain to the Hospital on leaving the district, and was succeeded by the new Vicar, the Reverend H. C. F. Copsey. At the end of November the League of Friends agreed to provide curtains in Dewar Ward at an approximate cost of £350, and the House Committee decided that they would themselves curtain Kindersley Ward, the cost to be divided between the Amenities and the Endowments Funds.

The Library again comes in for discussion at this point. The joint Committee of the Red Cross and St John Organisations had decided to increase the charge per occupied bed per annum from 7s. to 10s. 6d. This the House Committee thought was too much and they decided to ask the East Sussex County Council, the Welfare Committee and the League of Friends, whether they had any alternative suggestions to make. As a result of this the County Council offered to provide a library service for the Hospital at a charge of 5s. This was more satisfactory, but still the Committee decided it was not sufficiently advantageous, and they came to the conclusion that the best thing would be to terminate the Red Cross and St. John agreement at the end of March and for the Hospital to organise its own library, starting with a donation of £50 from the Amenities Fund.

At the end of the year Sir Archibald McIndoe resigned from the Group Management Committee, his place being taken by Mr. Douglas Stern. This appointment, though it was not obvious at the time, was ultimately to prove of considerable significance.

A special sub-committee appointed early in the new year met on February 9th and fully discussed the shortage of nurses at the Hospital. It had been necessary for the last 3 weeks of January to restrict admissions for the first time in the history of the Hospital owing to lack of nursing staff due to sickness, holidays and a number of unfilled vacancies. This Committee decided it was essential to retain Australia House for accommodating nursing staff. Meanwhile the Pre-student Nurses Course from Pembury Hospital, with 9 members, was transferred to this Hospital, but there were only 2 applicants for the new Pupil Assistant Nurses Course.

At long last, The Peanut Club having won their struggle to retain the money they had collected for it, the new Children's Ward was nearing completion, and this same sub-committee decided that in view of its anticipated early opening, the old children's ward should be used as an annexe to Dewar Ward to accommodate 6 extra patients, but to bear in mind the possibility of converting it into a new Casualty Department some time in the future. They resolved also to investigate the possibility of adapting the old Canadian Wing Kitchen, which was not thought suitable for a Casualty Department, as a Dispensary.

At the House Committee meeting on April 4th, Mr. Kirkhope paid tribute to the memory of the late Dr. W. E. Wallis, who he said "had served the Hospital and East Grinstead for many years". In fact Dr. Wallis for some time held the record equally with Dr. W. H. Marshall for any medical staff appointment, having been a member of the General Practitioner Staff for 35 years.* He was its senior member for at least 20 of these years. It was later decided to commemorate him by naming the old Children's Ward after him and this ward is now known as 'Evershed Wallis Ward', a very suitable tribute to an outstanding record of service.

Another important matter was also mentioned at this meeting in April; there was a letter stating that "the General Practitioners have considered the provision of a Maternity Home and are of opinion (a) that there is a great need for maternity beds, (b) that 10 beds will provide adequate cover, (c) that Oakleigh would be suitable for such accommodation". "There are approximately 30,000 patients registered with the Queen Victoria Hospital General Practitioners" the report continues, "of whom it is expected some 400 per annum will have babies, of which about half will require Hospital deliveries. Since the Ministry of Health gives an official figure of 1 bed to 19.2 patients per year, it is therefore evident that 10 beds will suffice." At this the House Committee resolved to recommend to the Management Committee that a 10-bed Maternity Unit

* This record has now been exceeded by Dr. H. B. Shaw and Dr. G. K. Thornton.

169

be provided at Oakleigh as soon as possible. With such a strong recommendation from the local medical profession, it seems very remarkable, and indeed a poor commentary on the present system of central planning, that at the time of publication 8 years later, we still have no maternity beds in East Grinstead. One cannot but feel that the old pre-National Health Service Management Committee, if only it were still in existence, would have done better than this for its local population.

One effect of the appointment of the Reverend H. C. F. Copsey as Church of England Chaplain to the Hospital on April 1st, was that he made a strong representation to the House Committee to free the Chapel, which up to now had been used largely as a Mortuary, for his use for Church Services. This seems to have brought to a head a matter which had obviously to be considered soon anyway; the building of a new Mortuary. The House Committee decided to investigate the possibility of doing this, while at the same time they notified the local police that the Hospital could no longer offer them mortuary facilities; it was decided that the Chairman should discuss this matter of mortuary accommodation with Dr. A. C. Sommerville, Her Majesty's Coroner for East Sussex.

Early in May Mr. Peter Williams, partner in the firm of Whitley Hughes & Luscombe, who had been Honorary Solicitors to the old Hospital for many years, was appointed to fill a vacancy on the House Committee and Dr. J. D. W. Hunter was appointed to the General Practitioner Staff. Mrs. M. D. Crichton, driver of one of the Hospital vehicles, resigned and received a letter of appreciation from the Committee for her services over the last 15 years. This left Mr. W. Payne and Mr. F. Maynard, the present Hospital drivers, working full-time with only one vehicle, in use 15 hours every day, between them. The Nursing Staff requested that the ground surrounding Douglas Stern House should be made into an attractive garden and themselves contributed the sum of £40 towards this, the Committee deciding to grant a further £60 from the Amenities Fund. The House Committee recommended the appointment of a second Administrative Sister, to which post Miss M. E. Doyle was later appointed.

Looking back at this point over the first 7 years of nationalisation, one finds an unexpected amount of progress. It might have been thought, after the great gifts of the Canadian Wing and American Surgical Block, that time would be needed to absorb these new expansions; in spite of them however, and of the big change-over in administration resulting from national-isation, progress, though on a reduced scale, had continued. To start with the Dental Department had enormously increased in size and importance during these years; the Corneal Grafting Unit had come into being; the Registration Department, the Nurses' Training School, the Nurses' Residential Home, were all new, with Oakleigh and the Civil Defence Wards providing added accommodation; the League of Friends had taken over the voluntary work previously done by the Welfare and Appeals Committees; and now the Children's Ward was under construction and there were plans for a central kitchen, a new Pharmacy, and a new Casualty Department, altogether quite an impressive total.

# 9
# Ends and Beginnings

WEDNESDAY, July 6th 1955, was, in the words of the East Grinstead Observer, "a date that will be recorded by future historians as one of great importance to the Town", for it was on that day that the new Children's Ward was officially opened by Her Majesty Queen Elizabeth the Queen Mother. The approach to the Hospital was lined with Officers and Cadets of the Air Training Corps, the Men's Detachment of the British Red Cross Society, the St. John Ambulance Brigade, the Boy Scouts and Girl Guides. Amongst the first to greet Her Majesty were 2 children, Ann Clifton and Robbie Hodgson, both of whom were Gold Peanuts, a high honour awarded to those who have enrolled 500 new Members to the Peanut Club. Mr. Guthrie Kirkhope the Chairman of the House Committee presented to Her Majesty Miss Hornsby-Smith, Parliamentary Secretary to the Ministry of Health, Mr. K. I. Julian, Chairman of the South-East Metropolitan Regional Hospital Board, Alderman R. H. Burslem, Chairman of the Group Management Committee, Sir Archibald McIndoe, Mr. John Simons, Chairman of the Group Medical Committee, Mrs. Neville Blond, Mrs. Douglas Stern, Councillor E. J. Dakin Chairman of the East Grinstead Urban District Council, Mr. W. R. Murray, the Managing Director of the Kent & Sussex Courier, and a Trustee of the Peanut Fund, Dr. W. H. Marshall, Senior General Practitioner Member of the Hospital Staff, the Right Reverend Geoffrey Warde, Bishop of Lewes, the Reverend H. C. F. Copsey, Vicar of East Grinstead, Mr. Cecil Burns the Architect, Mr. P. F. Wilson, the Director of the Colour Council who was responsible for the colour scheme in the new Children's Wing, Mr. W. H. Price, the builder, Mr. E. A. Wagstaff, Secretary of the Group Management Committee, Mr. G. A. Johns, the Hospital Secretary, and Miss G. M. Wise, the Almoner. The Central Band of the Royal Air Force was in attendance and with Her Majesty on the platform were the Duke of Norfolk, Lady Kindersley, Mrs. Clemetson and the Matron. There were 500 invited guests and no less than 400 members of the Peanut Club, including many children. Lady Kindersley in welcoming Her Majesty, reminded us that it was 9 years previously, in 1946, that she had opened the American Wing of the Hospital,—"So you can see that she has more than fulfilled her obligations and duties as Patroness of this Hospital." Lady Kindersley then spoke of the Peanut Club which had really been responsible for the building of this beautiful wing for children. "We thank them" she said, "and we thank especially Mrs. Clemetson, known better to us as Aunt Agatha, from the bottom of our hearts. Membership today" she said, "is over half a million people." Her Majesty in her speech said, "It gives me very real pleasure to be with you today as Patroness of this Hospital. A great Hospital must always be a living, growing thing if it is to fulfil its duty to the needs of those whom it serves. I am delighted therefore in the completion of this new Children's Wing. It is pleasing to think the children themselves should, by their own enthusiasm, have given such an impressive sum of money towards their own Ward. I pray that every blessing may rest on all those whose skill is devoted to the great work of healing." Prayers of dedication were said by the Reverend H. C. F. Copsey, followed by dedication by the Bishop of Lewes. Her Majesty then made her way to the Ward, her route being lined by members of the Staff; on the way she spoke amongst others to Mr. Fred Maynard who had been a Theatre Orderly at the Hospital for nearly 10 years and to Mrs. J. Burton-Croyden, Commandant of the local Red Cross Detachment. The Wing had been built at a total cost of about £36,000, towards which the Peanut Club had subscribed £30,000, and it was one of the most modern examples of Hospital building in the country. One of the children in the Ward presented Her Majesty with a children's book written by Aunt Agatha, a present for Princess Anne.

In August came the news that the Civil Defence Wards would open on October 1st, and that they were to be used for plastic surgery cases, and to be known as Wards V and VI. Ward I was to be used for 24 Female Geriatric patients and Oakleigh for Male Geriatric cases. Edward Blount Ward was to be used as a Recovery Ward for children. On September 25th Ward IV was opened with 20 Corneo-plastic beds. Miss E. Macdougall, head of the Secretariat for some years, retired on October 8th, while Mr. Derek Agate began work in the Registration Department on November 14th.

A further meeting took place in October, this time between Mr. Kirkhope, Mr. Peel, Mr. Grasby and Dr. Collin to discuss Maternity accommodation; they came to the conclusion that it was desirable to have this at the Hospital where all facilities would be available in emergencies, rather than at Oakleigh, which had been suggested, and a recommendation was put forward that Ward I should be turned into a Maternity Unit of 15 beds. This recommendation was in due course considered by the Management Committee and put forward to the Regional Board, a point of some interest, for it was about this time that there was considerable public outcry in the Town about the lack of maternity accommodation and it was generally believed that nothing was being done at the Hospital to try to alleviate the situation. This report—and others in previous and subsequent pages—shows how wrong this belief was. Some months later the Regional Board stated "A general review of the Maternity Services of the Region is being conducted and consideration will be given to the needs of East Grinstead in the course of this examination".

At the beginning of November the Management Committee wrote to the House Committee conveying a request from the Ministry of Health for co-operation in assisting the Government during the present difficult economic situation by making sure that expenditure was kept within the sums allocated; but when following this the House Committee decided to close Ward VI and transfer its staff to other wards, there came another memorandum from the Management Committee calling for details of the closure of beds. It stated "no beds should be closed at the Hospital without the Management Committee's approval, as before beds can be closed in the Group it is necessary for the Management Committee to obtain the authority of the Regional Board".

The early part of 1956 brought a number of minor but nevertheless important changes. There had recently been complaints from the Resident Medical Staff as to the inadequacy of their quarters, and a sub-committee consisting of Mr. Kirkhope, Mrs. Looker, Dr. Russell Davies and Mr. Mitchell, recommended the taking over of Tudor Cottage for their use since they did not consider it essential for the Secretary to live so near the Hospital. This recommendation was duly carried into effect, Mr. Johns being given time to find himself alternative accommodation.

At the meeting on January 30th, 1956, Miss Hilda Cook resigned her position as Matron after 4½ years at the Hospital. She finally left at the end of April in order to be married. Mr. F. Eland succeeded Mr. Wragg as Catering Officer with effect from January 9th. After several years as part-time Teacher to the Hospital School, Mrs Monk was appointed full-time teacher by the County Education Committee. Mr. A. S. Robinson resigned from the House Committee on leaving the district and Mr. Simon Montfort Bebb, a member of the Welfare Committee and son-in-law to Sir Archibald McIndoe, was appointed to take his place, while Miss L. Cowling became the new Secretary of the League of Friends. Miss M. H. Davis, the Assistant Matron, also resigned at the end of April, at the same time as the Matron. Major-General Albert Sachs, C.B., C.B.E., M.D., M.Sc., M.R.C.P., lately Consulting Pathologist to the Royal Army Medical Corps, was appointed Consultant Pathologist to the Hospital with effect from April 9th.

A donation to the Amenity Fund of 10 guineas from the Neville and Elaine Blond Charitable Trust should be noted here. The significance of this gift may well have been missed at the time; probably nobody realised that it marked the beginning of a period of immense generosity to the Hospital by Mr. and Mrs. Blond, about which more will be heard later.

It was in April 1956 that the Hospital was rocked to its foundations. At a meeting on the 3rd of the month Mr. Kirkhope read to the House Committee a copy of a letter he had written to the Management Committee in which he tendered his resignation as Chairman. It appeared that since he was not a member of the Management Committee he was no longer eligible to hold this post. Mr. Kirkhope having read this letter invited Mr. J. H. Mitchell, Vice-chairman, to take the chair and left the meeting. Members expressed their strong disapproval of the instructions from the Regional Hospital Board which had apparently led the Management Committee to request Mr. Kirkhope's resignation. Mr. Wagg, feeling strongly about it stated that he would resign from the House Committee at the end of the meeting, which he in fact did, and the following resolutions were passed:—(a) "the House Committee registers with deep regret the resignation of our Chairman, Mr. W. Guthrie Kirkhope, but at the same time we have pleasure in recording our sincere thanks and appreciation of his unfailing devotion and service to the Hospital during the last 30 years"; (b) that Mr. J. H. Mitchell as Chairman of the Meeting should personally convey to Mr. Kirkhope the Members' regrets and thanks; (c) that Lady Kindersley as Honorary President of the Hospital, be authorised to write a letter on behalf of the Committee to the local press and to the Chairman of the Regional Board, expressing the House Committee's strong disapproval of the manner in which Mr. Kirkhope's appointment as Chairman of the Hospital had been terminated; (d) that a Sub-committee with Lady Kindersley as Chairman should consider the matter of a presentation to Mr. Kirkhope.

This apparently had all begun in a specially appointed Sub-committee of the Regional Hospital Board which recommended to the Group Management Committee that they should revise their terms of reference to the House Committee in order to avoid fragmentation of the Hospital Service. "The Management Committee and not the House Committee should take responsibility for the day-to-day running of the Hospital" they said; "We think that special emphasis should be laid on the House Committee's responsibility for staff welfare as their primary function. The Chairman of the House Committee should be appointed by the Management Committee and they should, in the case of this Hospital and in the interests of direct administration, appoint one of their own members. In brief, the daily administration of this Hospital should be carried on by the Management Committee and its Officers in the ordinary approved manner. The Board hope that the Management Committee will give earnest consideration to these recommendations and will in particular take the earliest opportunity that offers of implementing the last recommendation above." The unpleasant news was conveyed to Mr. Kirkhope personally by Alderman Burslem, the Management Committee's Chairman, who pointed out to him that as he was not a member of this Committee, they had no alternative but to request his resignation and appoint another Chairman. There was apparently no suggestion that Mr. Kirkhope might be appointed to the Management Committee, and thus possibly retain the chairmanship.

The next edition of the East Grinstead Courier referred to "the infamous story of the enforced retirement of Mr. Kirkhope which would shock the people of East Grinstead profoundly". The Editorial continued, "faith in the Tunbridge Wells Group Management Committee and the Regional Board has been wearing very thin for a long time now. This scandalous example of ruthless disregard for a life-time of service to the community will do nothing to restore it. Mr. Guthrie Kirkhope's services to the Hospital are known to everyone in the Town. No-one has done more to create and maintain that fair atmosphere of wellbeing and freedom for which it was famous until the soulless tentacles of nationalisation began their work of reducing everything to a common denominator, and stifling initiative. The method of the move to bring about Mr. Kirkhope's retirement savours very strongly of trickery and the conduct of the Tunbridge Wells Management Committee is not above reproach in the matter. By the simple expedient of appointing him a member of that Committee he could have retained his position as Chairman at the Hospital. The conclusion can only be drawn that Mr. Kirkhope's removal from the Chair was for some reason considered necessary. If that were so the honourable thing would have been to tell him so and give him the reason. The Town will not easily forget this shameful page in the history of its Hospital. Public confidence in the administration has suffered a severe blow from which it will take years to recover." Another article in the same paper stated, "For nearly 30 years the names of W. Guthrie Kirkhope and the Queen Victoria Hospital have been synonymous. He is numbered high among the handful of pioneers whose passionate zeal and enthusiasm have made the Queen Victoria Hospital outstanding among its contemporaries. No man has done more than he to raise funds both for the building of the Hospital and for the extra comforts and amenities that it enjoys. Much of his drive is behind the formation of the local League of Friends.

To East Grinstead, dubbed during the War as 'the little Town with the big heart', Mr. Kirkhope has been a vivid and colourful personality. His enforced resignation is a bitter disappointment to him and the Town."

In discussing the future of the Hospital, Mr. Kirkhope, in an interview, said he was confident that remote control would never achieve what the close association of local men and women on the House Committee could do by their personal interest in Hospital welfare. "For so many years" he said, "I have striven to keep alive local interest in our world-famous Hospital and the people of East Grinstead have never failed me. Everything I have asked for has been given. Remote control will inevitably sap, and eventually kill, the voluntary spirit which has done so much to make our beloved Hospital unique". Lady Kindersley, writing in the same paper, as President of the Hospital, said—"I think it is quite disgraceful that he should be treated by the Regional Board as he has been treated, and I wish to register a strong protest. I think it should be made clear to everyone what a loss he will be to all those who work for and have the interests of the Queen Victoria Hospital at heart". Sir Archibald McIndoe wrote "the indecent haste with which the Group Management Committee have carried out the directive of the Regional Hospital Board will do nothing to reduce the stature of our Chairman, Mr. Guthrie Kirkhope. He will be sustained by the affection and respect in which he is held both by the Hospital Committee and by the people of East Grinstead. He was one of the triumvirate of outstanding citizens who created the Queen Victoria Hospital. Lord Kindersley and Edward Blount, if they were alive, would stand aghast at this inconsiderate termination of the life work of their successor. Guthrie Kirkhope has amply justified their confidence. For 25 years he has given his services wholeheartedly to this and other projects in East Grinstead. He has always been a man of independent opinion and forthright action, qualities which would appear to have little meaning today."

The storm reached even the National Press. The Courier again the following week described it as "this shameful piece of bureaucratic scheming. Why was it necessary to rush this resignation through to the extent of appointing a new Chairman before Mr. Kirkhope's resignation had been placed before the

Committee and even before he was acquainted with the Committee's decision?" It appeared in fact that Mr. Douglas Stern had been appointed to take over the Chairmanship when Mr. Kirkhope resigned. Mr. Stern, interviewed by the paper, said that in accepting the new office he was very conscious of the fact that the House Committee was henceforth to be deprived of many of its administrative functions. Hitherto the House Committee and its Chairman had been permitted a measure of discretion in the day-to-day administration and running of the affairs of the Hospital which had not been enjoyed by other Hospitals in the Group or in general throughout the country. Now, however, the Regional Board had directed that the Queen Victoria Hospital must fall into line, and the Chairman of the House Committee must be appointed by the Group Management Committee from one of their own members. "As Mr. Guthrie Kirkhope does not have that qualification" said Mr. Stern, "he has resigned and I have been appointed Chairman in his place for a period of one year. The day-to-day administration of the Hospital will, in future, be almost entirely in the hands of the Group Management Committee at Tunbridge Wells, with their representatives at the Queen Victoria Hospital, the principal of whom are the Hospital Secretary and the Matron."

The House Committee when they next met on April 30th sent a letter to Mr. Kirkhope in which they expressed their hope that he would continue to serve on the Committee. His immediate personal reaction to his dismissal was to lie quiet for a few months, but in July after careful consideration he wrote to the Committee offering his resignation, saying that he would always take a keen interest in the work and welfare of the Hospital and would watch its progress with interest. On receipt of this letter the Committee wrote again to him that it was their unanimous wish that he would reconsider this decision, and in fact he finally decided to remain a member of the Committee and attended the meeting on July 30th, when he was warmly welcomed by the Chairman and members. Mr. Wagg, however, went ahead with his decision to resign, and received a letter expressing the Committee's deep regret and sincere thanks for his long and devoted service to the Hospital. As he had been appointed to the end of March 1957 this left a vacancy, and out of a number of nominations Mrs. Neville Blond, previously a member of the pre-nationalisation Board of Management, was elected to take his place. Mrs. I. Graham Bryce, M.A., of Colemans Hatch, a member of the Hospital Management Committee, had also been appointed to serve on the House Committee and attended her first meeting on April 30th.

Following the departure of Miss Cook, Miss T. Fagelman, Matron of Pembury Hospital, was seconded temporarily to the Queen Victoria Hospital, pending the appointment of a new Matron. On May 22nd there is reported the arrival of Miss J. E. Flunder as Assistant Matron, and in due course at the end of July Miss A. T. Monteath was appointed Matron. Miss F. Wilde was appointed secretary in the Pathological Department. Miss E. Vine resigned her post as House Warden at Engalec and received a letter of appreciation from the Committee.

Dr. Sachs lost little time in voicing his dissatisfaction at the inadequacy of the accommodation in the Pathological Department, and wrote to the House Committee suggesting possible methods of providing additional accommodation. This letter was referred to the Medical Committee, who reported back that they agreed that the Laboratory accommodation was inadequate for maximum efficiency and that it should be enlarged; the extensions they thought should include a new mortuary and post-mortem room.

An interesting innovation here was the formation and the first meeting on June 19th of a special Sub-committee with Mr. Mitchell as its Chairman, to consider the proposed reorganisation of the Hospital kitchens and dining accommodation. This Sub-committee decided that the E.M.S. Kitchen could cater for the whole Hospital—the Regional Board had already provisionally agreed the plan to convert the disused Canadian Wing Kitchen into a Dispensary—and it therefore recommended also closing the General Hospital Kitchen, which it thought might be seriously considered for conversion to a Casualty Department. This special Sub-committee is interesting because it appears to have been the forerunner of the 'Working Party' of which we shall hear more, which was formed in February the following year.

Another point of interest here is a letter from Dr. J. O. Collin who signs it as Secretary of the Medical Council, the last letter from him having been as Secretary of the Medical Committee. It will be remembered that the Medical Society had been formed in 1947 in order to bring all members of the Medical Staff together and it had elected from among its members a small Executive Committee known as the Medical Committee. This change from Committee to Council meant that every single member of the Staff had an equal voice in the discussion of the Medical affairs of the Hospital thus widening the medical representation. One of the first acts of the new Medical Council was to consider steps to reduce the possibility of infection in the new Children's Ward: during the previous summer this Ward had had to be closed twice, first because of a case of chicken pox and on the second occasion a case of poliomyelitis having been inadvertently admitted. The obvious answer was that all children should be medically examined before being admitted to the Ward, and this decision later led to the construction by the Peanut Club of the admission block. During the discussions that preceded this building, Mr. Kirkhope disclosed that the original plans for the Children's Ward had included an Isolation Block, and that this had been deleted by the Ministry.

Early in 1957 there is a note that following a serious road accident in the district there were no less than 7 patients in the Casualty Department at the same time, and the House Committee resolved once again to draw the Management Committee's attention to the total inadequacy of the facilities for the reception of casualties at this Hospital. Mr. R. L. Beare, F.R.C.S. was appointed Senior Registrar in Plastic Surgery on January 4th.

On February 11th there took place the first official meeting of the newly formed 'Working Party'. Mr. Mitchell was in the chair and the members were Mr. S. Montfort Bebb, Mr. Kirkhope, Mrs. Graham Bryce, Mrs. Looker, Dr. Collin and Mr. Stern, Dr. Russell Davies and Mr. Peter Williams: Mr. Wagstaff and Mr. Johns being in attendance. In opening the meeting Mr. Mitchell said he had given some thought to the reference terms of this Working Party, and finally it was decided that they should be as follows:—

"To consider the immediate and future needs of the Hospital and to make recommendations to the House Committee."

The setting up of this Working Party followed the special Sub-committee previously referred to and, while its coming so soon after the quarrel with the Management Committee over the chairmanship of the House Committee may have been incidental, one cannot help having the feeling that this was an attempt by the Queen Victoria Hospital authorities to assert some form, if only an attenuated one, of their own independence. In any case, the Working Party appears not to have been completely acceptable to the Management Committee, whose Chairman is reported twelve months later to have said that while he recognised the valuable work done by the Working Party, nevertheless he felt that its term of office should end with the summer recess; "it has taken on the appearance of a standing sub-committee and it is therefore contrary to the constitution of House Committees". Later, in July 1958, he again expressed his views on this point as follows:—"If the House Committee desires that it should continue, it is open to them to recommend to the Management Committee that Standing Orders should be changed so as to permit all House Committees in the Group to appoint Planning Sub-committees". This the House Committee decided to do; they recommended that the present Working Party should continue until the end of March 1959 and then should be re-appointed. Later in the year the Management Committee agreed "that the Working Party set up at East Grinstead shall, as constituted at present, continue in office until March 31st, 1959". It goes on to say:—"House Committees shall not appoint standing Sub-committees without the consent of the Management Committee, but shall, if so directed by the Management Committee, appoint Catering or other Sub-committees, with such terms of reference and for such periods as the Management Committee may direct. The Working Party, or Planning Sub-committee as the Management Committee proposed to call it, was in fact reappointed on April 1st, 1959, and it is interesting to note that it is still functioning in 1963.

However, to return to its first meeting in February 1957, the Working Party approved the previous recommendation that the Canadian Wing Kitchen should be converted for use as a Pharmacy, and confirmed the recommendations that the Main Hospital Kitchen would be suitable for a Casualty Department; they stressed that any such new Casualty Department must be properly staffed and run. These matters were finally settled at the end of February when the Senior Administrative Medical Officer of the Regional Board, Brigadier Glyn Hughes, visited the Hospital with Mr. Druitt the Deputy Secretary of the Regional Board and Mr. King the Deputy Architect. Whatever was said about this Working Party, it certainly seems to have got things done. Later they noted the need for a Nurses' Recreation Room, towards which the Welfare Committee had promised up to £3,000. The Matron having stated that "there is nowhere in the Hospital where large functions such as prizegivings, dances, etc. can be held", the Chairman remarked that a suitable hall would cost between £12,000 and £15,000.

In March Dr. K. B. Chambers was appointed consultant anaesthetist in the place of Dr. J. F. Pelmore, who had resigned.

In March also Miss N. J. C. Starling the Occupational Therapist, resigned; she was subsequently succeeded by Miss C. G. Letcher. Miss Margaret Williams who had worked voluntarily in the Department for over 4 years, also left to be married. In April came the resignation of Miss B. F. Phillips from her post of Senior Radiographer and her replacement by Miss E. F. Storey; also the marriage of Mr. R. H. Millar, the Senior Porter, to Miss V. M. Oswin the Assistant Catering Officer. A concert at the Whitehall Theatre, on April 12th, organised by Mr. Cyril Fletcher, was an immense success, as was also the new Guinea Pig Public House on the nearby Stone Quarry Estate, named after the Guinea Pig Club, and opened by Sir Archibald McIndoe.

At the House Committee meeting on April 1st, Mr. Johns read a letter from the Group Secretary, referring to the revised regulations regarding the constitution, powers and duties of House Committees which had been adopted by the Management Committee at its meeting on February 25th. In accordance with Paragraph 8 of these Regulations the Management Committee had exercised its right to appoint the Chairman of the East Grinstead House Committee, and Mr. Douglas Stern would continue to serve as Chairman until such time as the Management Committee resolved to the contrary. At this meeting we hear also that Dr. J. O. Collin has been appointed to serve on the Group Management Committee.

On April 11th there is reported the meeting of a Sub-committee which was appointed to consider the school-teaching arrangements at the Hospital. Mrs. Looker was Chairman of this Sub-committee and Mr. Burgess and Miss Wallis were members, with Mr. Johns and Miss Monteath, the Matron, in attendance. Sister Baker, in charge of the Children's Ward, gave her opinion that it was not always practicable to send children to the school, which was situated some distance from the Ward, owing to the shortage of staff and also to the visits of doctors who needed to examine the children in the Ward; in her opinion, the teaching of bed cases was perfectly satisfactory. Mrs. Monk, the teacher in charge, also referred to the difficulties arising from the distance between the schoolroom and the Ward, and the Sub-committee decided that it was impossible for one teacher to undertake the task; they therefore recommended that 2 full-time trained teachers be employed plus a part-time unqualified helper.

One matter very much in mind just now was the necessity to develop a community spirit and social life in the Hospital. The Welfare Committee had come to the conclusion that there was no possibility of a hall being built for several years, and Lady McIndoe, who was now President of the Nurses' Social Club, put forward a plan for enlarging the existing building, towards which the Welfare Committee had agreed to pay some £1,100. In September however, it became known that the Regional Board had approved in principle the building of a new Nurses' Recreation Hall, and both the Welfare Committee and the League of Friends agreed to subscribe to it. Meanwhile the Group Management Committee accepted the Welfare Committee's offer to improve the present building. On July 13th the Group Nurses' Prizegiving Ceremony was held at this Hospital with Lady Limerick presenting the prizes.

In July Mr. W. J. Moore succeeded Mr. Eric Clark as Assistant Hospital Secretary. Miss Grace Garcia resigned after 11½ years on the secretarial staff and received a letter of thanks from the Committee. Dr. W. H. Marshall retired after 35 years on the Staff, having thus equalled Dr. W. E. Wallis's long record; he was given a farewell dinner at nearby Gravetye

Manor Hotel by his medical colleagues. Miss Motton the Assistant Almoner, retired at the end of August. At the beginning of September Assistant Nurse I. J. Batchelor resigned after 17 years at the Hospital, on account of her forthcoming marriage. Shortly after this the death of Miss Faith Hanbury occurred, and the Chairman referred to her 21 years devoted service to the Hospital.

Dr. C. R. H. Weekes, in charge of the Chest Clinic, retired at the end of 1957 and was succeeded by Dr. S. J. Sutton. The Medical Council considered using the Library Room in the old hospital as a Recovery Ward for the Main Operating Theatre, in order to release Edward Blount Ward for general cases, for it was reported that owing to the shortage of general beds in the Hospital at least one case a day was being turned away and sent to the Kent & Sussex or Pembury Hospitals. Decision on this matter was however deferred until the nursing situation had improved, and it is worth recording that this identical matter was again under discussion at a meeting of the Medical Council nearly 5 years later in July 1962!

Early in the New Year the old Staff Nurses' Dining Room in the main building was converted into a Nurses' Sick Bay, and the League of Friends generously gave £350 towards equipping it, together with a Sitting Room and Isolation Room; they also provided curtains for all the beds in Ward I. In March the Resident Medical Staff moved into Tudor Cottage. There was a suggestion, but it was not followed up, that Warrenside Cottage should be converted into quarters for married Residents.

On March 3rd, 1958, the Chairman of the House Committee welcomed Lt. General Sir Euan A. M. Miller, who had recently been elected Chairman of the Group Management Committee in place of Mr. Burslem, and was attending his first House Committee meeting here. The Queen Victoria Hospital by this time was becoming very well known and increasing numbers of individuals and organisations were visiting it. The British Council frequently sent parties and at the end of April the Royal Society of Health sent the delegates to its Annual Congress, while in May the Royal Society of Medicine sent a party of visitors. As a result of these and very many other visits it was decided to establish a Chairman's Hospitality Fund starting with the sum of £50 from the Endowments Fund, in order to pay for the entertainment of these visitors.

May brought news first of Mr. Kirkhope's serious illness, and then death, and on June 2nd members attending the House Committee meeting stood in silence as a tribute to him. Only a short time before this illness he had been presented by his friends with his portrait in oils. At the next meeting Lady Kindersley proposed, and the meeting agreed, that Ward I should be named after him in recognition of the tremendous debt the Hospital owed him. Later a commemorative plaque was put up in the Ward. In July Lady McIndoe and Mr. Simon Voss were appointed to the House Committee in place of Mr. Kirkhope and Mr. Montfort Bebb, who had recently retired. Another resignation about this time was that of Mr. Nils Eckhoff, who had been on the Surgical Staff of the Hospital since 1940. The Committee wrote thanking him for his long and valuable service to the Hospital.

The 10th Anniversary of the National Health Service on July 5th, 1958, was marked by a letter from the Chairman of the Management Committee to the Chairman of the House Committee, also by a donation of £500 to the Amenities Fund by Mr. Douglas Stern. Unfortunately it was also marked by an acute shortage of nursing staff and no less than 58 of the Hospital's total of 301 beds were closed for this reason. In September Miss V. R. Hardy was appointed Assistant Catering Officer in place of Mrs. Millar.

In November we hear that the Peanut Club has offered to provide a schoolroom near the Children's Ward, this in addition to the Admission Block, Laundry and Saline Bath Unit, which they had already promised to provide for the Ward. There is further news of the Hospital Chapel; a meeting attended by the Venerable H. J. L. Morrell, Archdeacon of Lewes, agreed that the required alterations to the Chapel should include the construction of a Vestry. Lady Kindersley agreed to give an Altar Cloth and new curtains, the League of Friends to contribute £100 towards the furnishings, and arrangements were agreed upon for the Chapel to be dedicated the following April, when members of the Roman Catholic and Free Churches might be invited to take part in the services. At the end of the year Miss Truby resigned from the position of Hospital Librarian, which she had held for over 20 years and she was succeeded in this post by Mrs. Colin Hunter, a member of the Committee of the League of Friends.

1959 opens with a number of changes. First there is the resignation of Miss Marjorie Spalding after 23 years on the Management Board or House Committee, together with that of Mr. Simon Voss, their places being taken by Mr. Geoffrey Place and Lt. General Sir Frederick Harris. Mrs. Graham Bryce also resigned from the Committee on leaving the district. Shortly after this Mr. Peter Williams was appointed to the Management Committee, becoming thereby its representative on the House Committee, and leaving a vacancy on this Committee to which Mr. John Oliver was elected. Dr. Peter A. J. Smith, M.R.C.P. was appointed Consulting Dermatologist to succeed Dr. R. D. Moyle. Mrs. Belton was appointed to the new post of Orthoptist at the Hospital, thus saving local patients many journeys to Tunbridge Wells, previously the nearest place where this treatment could be obtained. Lady Dorothy Macmillan was asked to present the prizes at the Nurses Annual Prizegiving. Mr. Peter Griffits became Chairman of the League of Friends in place of Mr. Kirkhope, Mr. Hugh (Pip) Parratt having recently succeeded Miss Cowling as its Secretary.

We should pause in April 1959 to look back at what has happened during the 12 months just ended; (1) the former Canadian Wing Kitchen and Boilerhouse have been converted into a Pharmacy: (2) the Red Cross & St. John Recreation Building has become a Central Diningroom adjoining the Main Kitchen, which has been enlarged: (3) the new Mortuary and Postmortem Room have been built: (4) the Chapel has been redecorated and furnished and the former Postmortem Room converted into a Chapel Annexe: (5) the Main Hospital entrance has been re-designed and a coloured paving strip with flower beds and lawns made in front of the general wards; this was done by the Peanut Club as part of their undertaking to beautify the Hospital grounds: (6) Percy Lodge has been converted into a Sewing Room, with a bedroom and bathroom retained for relatives of seriously ill patients: (7) the Sisters' diningroom in the Canadian Wing has become a second Waiting Room while a loudspeaker system has been installed in the Outpatients Department: (8) an additional room off the main corridor between the Recovery Ward and the Laboratory has been built for the Registration Department: (9) a Nurses' Cloakroom has been provided: (10) Sister's Office in Kindersley Ward has been reconstructed: (11) the former Staff Nurses' Diningroom has been converted to a Nurses' Sick Bay. In addition to all this, work is about to begin on:—(1) the Admission and Isolation Block with a Saline Bath and Laundry for the Peanut Ward: (2) the School building adjacent to the Peanut Ward: and (3) extensions to the Physiotherapy Department. All these added together make an impressive total for the 12 months. None of them large, together they increased the efficiency of the Hospital very considerably.

A Sub-committee set up some 15 months previously with Mrs. Graham Bryce as Chairman, reported in April 1959, and made the following recommendations:—(1) a 44-hour week and 3-shift system for Nurses should be adopted as soon as possible: (2) Clerks would be useful in some Wards: (3) Experimental Ward Teams consisting of a Staff Nurse, Pupil Assistant Nurse and Auxiliaries: (4) a central linen exchange and a central syringe service: (5) an efficient call system: (6) the appointment of a Domestic Staff Superviser. The Committee also thought that nursing in the future would probably derive its main pool of work from young married women on a part-time basis. Most of these recommendations have since been put into effect.

The month of June saw a remarkable personal demonstration of affection for the Hospital, in connection with the Peanut Club's offer to provide a new schoolroom adjacent to the Peanut Ward. Materials having been provided, the erection of this building was entirely carried out by Mr. Fred Dart, J.P., an ex-chairman of the East Grinstead Urban District Council, with the help of his son and their friends working voluntarily in their spare time. They received a well-deserved letter of thanks from the House Committee. The dedication of the Chapel went according to plan and the first service in it took place on June 7th; the new altar furniture was presented in memory of Dr. W. H. Marshall who had recently died at Canterbury. The original residential accommodation of the Civil Defence Unit, now occupied largely by Nurses from the West Indies and other parts of the Commonwealth, was officially named 'Commonwealth House'.

In September came the resignation of Miss Wise; she had been Chief Almoner since September 1949, and during her tenure of this post had not only greatly increased the size of the Almoner's Department, but also vastly enhanced its value to the Hospital. This was recognised by the House Committee, who wrote a letter expressing their appreciation of her long service, regretting her resignation, and asking her to reconsider and withdraw it. She refused however to do this and left at the end of the year. She was succeeded by Miss V. F. Gardiner.

In the autumn comes the first mention in the House Committee records of the possible establishment of a Research Unit at the Hospital. It had been known for some time that Sir Archibald McIndoe was keen to establish a special laboratory for research on Tissue Grafting, and that the means to establish such a unit might be forthcoming through the generosity of a voluntary donor. Though there were as yet no definite plans the Regional Board wrote to ask the House Committee for their views regarding a suitable site for it. The vacant ground opposite 'Commonwealth House' was chosen, and work went ahead on the building and establishment of this unit during the following 12 months.

The Hospital was by now becoming so large and busy that for some time past difficulties had occurred in patients finding their way about it. This problem was resolved by a decision to install receptionists at the entrance to the American Wing. Mrs. Colin Hunter undertook to organise a rota of voluntary helpers, and, though it was not for some months that they actually began their duties, when they did they soon established themselves as a most necessary and valuable part of the Hospital administration. About the same time various re-arrangements in the Outpatient Department were suggested; the Almoner's Office to become Sister's Office, the Outpatient Reception Room to become an Almoner's Office, the Inpatient Reception Room to become a Waiting Room and the present Waiting Room to be extended and made into a Reception and Records Department, with a new corridor to do away with the necessity for so many people walking through the Outpatient Department on their way to other Departments. These alterations were to be paid for by the Welfare Committee, but owing to the financial constitution of the Hospital Service this could only be done if they first gave the money to the Amenities Fund, and the Fund would then pay for them! They were in fact carried out later, and the cost of £1,200 was borne, as above, by the Welfare Committee. At the end of September Dr. J. M. Frobisher of Forest Row, retired from the General Practitioner Staff, while Dr. H. C. I. Bywater of Lingfield was appointed to it.

Plans were now being prepared for a new Canteen which the League of Friends had offered to provide at a cost of £850, and it was decided that the Welfare Shop which had been run so successfully for so many years by the Welfare Committee should be amalgamated with the Canteen. The old Canteen would thus be freed and one suggestion was that it might be used as a Central Linen Pool.

In December Miss P. M. Carter who had been part-time assistant in the Pharmacy since 1942, resigned. She received a letter of thanks and appreciation from the House Committee for the work she had done so assiduously for the Hospital over such a long period; she was succeeded by Mrs. James. In December also Miss M. E. Doyle, the second Administrative Sister, resigned and was replaced by Sister Page. On December 15th the record number of 35 operations was performed at the Hospital in one day, and in the 6 days December 15th-20th no less than 119.

Early in 1960 the nursing situation improved slightly and a suggestion was made to accommodate some of them at Oakleigh, but the Medical Council advised against this "in view of the forthcoming Group Review". This is the first mention of the new 'Hospital Plan for the Nation' which caused so much speculation in the next few years and the full effects of which on our Hospital are still to be seen. The decision was made to call Ward V 'McIndoe Ward' and Ward VI 'Kelsey Fry Ward' in recognition of the early work and influence of these two great men on the Hospital. In April Sir Charles Key was elected to the House Committee.

April 12th, 1960 was one of the saddest days in the Hospital's long history, for it brought the news of the death of Sir Archibald McIndoe. Having been to a dinner the night before and come home late to his flat, he went to bed and died in his sleep. The news reached the Hospital during the morning and was officially broadcast to the nation in the B.B.C.'s 1 o'clock news bulletin. The work of the Hospital went on uninterrupted, though, as one of the Sisters said shortly afterwards—"We all felt like closing the doors until we'd had time to recover". The only outward and visible sign that day was the empty place beside the main entrance to the American Wing where his maroon-coloured Rolls-Royce had customarily stood whenever he was in the Hospital.

Tributes to Sir Archibald were paid in many different places—amongst others in the House Committee: when it next met the Chairman referred to the great loss which the Hospital had sustained and the members stood in silence in his memory. A full and well-deserved public tribute was paid also by the British Broadcasting Corporation in a radio programme narrated by Bill Simpson, one of the leading Guinea Pigs and one who had known Archie well. The programme included contributions by Dr. Charles Mayo from the Mayo Clinic; by Air Marshal Sir Harold Whittingham; by Sir William Kelsey Fry; by Dr. Ross Tilley; by Mr. Bernard Arch, Secretary of the Guinea Pig Club, and a number of its members; by Sir John Cordingly, Comptroller of the R.A.F. Benevolent Fund; by Mrs. Clemetson; by Sir Simon (now Lord) Marks, a close and personal friend, and by Sir Harold Gillies.

Archie McIndoe was the first New Zealander and the first Plastic Surgeon to be elected to the Council of the Royal College of Surgeons and he became one of its Vice-Presidents. He was heavily involved in the great task of raising funds for the re-building of the College and was so largely instrumental in the success of the appeal that the Council of the College decided that one of the buildings in their new premises should bear his name as a tribute to his great work for humanity.

Of the many hundreds of people who over the years have contributed to the growth and fame of the Queen Victoria Hospital I think all would agree that the name of Archie McIndoe must come at the top of the list, and it is a fitting tribute that the Research Laboratory, which was now being built and in which he was becoming deeply interested at the time of his death, should be named after him.

There was, as was to be expected, much uninformed speculation as to which of the remaining Consultant Plastic Surgeons would take McIndoe's place as Head of the Plastic Unit. It was soon however silenced by the Surgeons themselves, Mr. Jayes, Mr. McLaughlin, Mr. Moore and Mr. Watson, who organised themselves into a Committee to administer the Unit, and elected Percy Jayes as Chairman of this Committee, to take Sir Archibald's place on the House Committee.

The Hospital never closed its doors, but it was very considerably shaken. He had built it up and moulded its policies over the last 20 years, and was as much a part of the Hospital as it was of him. Some felt at the time that its best days were over, but fortunately his influence remained and his very good friends Neville and Elaine Blond were determined that the work which he had inspired should continue, as we shall see in the following pages.

On Friday, April 29th, the extension to the Physiotherapy Department was opened by Lord Limerick. This Department, with 4 physiotherapists working in it had been grossly overcrowded for some years, and the extension provided by the League of Friends at a cost of some £2,500, doubled the space available for treatment of patients. At the opening Mr. Peter Griffits described how the League of Friends had been formed soon after the nationalisation of the Hospital, in order to provide amenities not normally provided by the State, and pointed out that though they had made many minor benefactions to the Hospital, this was their first "major job in bricks and mortar".

When the House Committee next met on May 2nd, the Chairman Mr. Stern, referred to the lack of a suitable building for events such as the Nurses Prizegiving, especially now that 'McIndoe Ward,' which had been used for this purpose on a few occasions, had been opened for patients. He announced that he and Mrs. Stern were willing to meet the cost of building and equipping a suitable hall, which they thought would be best sited alongside the covered way between the Dental Department and the American Wing. The House Committee unanimously recommended the acceptance of this most generous offer, and it was in due course accepted by the Management Committee and the construction went ahead.

In June the Birthday Honours List contained the announcement of a knighthood for Mr. Benjamin Rycroft in recognition of his outstanding contribution to ophthalmic surgery. July saw the formal ending of the Welfare Committee, the purposes for which it had originally been set up in 1941 no longer existing under the National Health Service; on the realisation of its assets, the money was to be shared between the Guinea Pig Club and the Amenities Fund and, the Chairman added, he anticipated that the latter Fund would receive approximately £700. The Committee recorded their appreciation of the work done by the Welfare Committee for the Hospital over so many years. Mrs. Blond and Mr. Wagg were the only original members who had served continuously throughout nearly 20 years of the Welfare Committee's existence.

The Matron, Miss Monteath, had resigned earlier in the year, and on September 19th Miss M. A. Duncombe was appointed to succeed her. There had been an interval of some months since Miss Monteath had left and the Chairman referred at the next meeting to the efficient way in which the Matron's duties had been carried out during this interval by the Assistant Matron, Miss Flunder. Miss Duncombe had previously been Lady Superintendent of Nurses at the Evelina Children's Hospital.

Monday November 7th was a busy day at the Hospital. First of all Lady McIndoe opened the new extensions to the Peanut Ward—a Reception and Isolation Unit, with a Saline Bath Unit and Laundry—all of which had been made possible by donations from the Peanut Club. Mrs. Clemetson, founder of the Club, was present, with Mr. Douglas Stern, Mr. John Watson, the Matron and Mrs. Baker, Sister in charge of the Ward. Lady McIndoe spoke of the supreme importance of the Hospital to us because of the wonderful work that was done in it, and Mrs. Clemetson added "It is our great sorrow that Sir Archibald McIndoe is not here with us in person to see the completion of the work, but that he is here in spirit I have no doubt whatever". Turning to Lady McIndoe she said "I had set my heart on having you with us on this occasion so that you can set the seal on the work which Sir Archibald helped to plan".

Later that same afternoon, in the presence of 150 invited guests, Lt. General Sir Euan Miller, Chairman of the Group Management Committee, officially accepted the new Assembly

Hall on the Hospital's behalf from Mr. and Mrs. Stern. In his speech he referred first to Mrs. Stern's work as a V.A.D. Nurse during the war and of her help in the Operating Theatre, then mentioned how she had in 1945 endowed and named a cot in the Children's Ward, and in 1955 had been presented to Her Majesty the Queen Mother in recognition of 14 years service to the Hospital. "Mr. Stern's 20 years administration, with 5 of them as Chairman of the House Committee is well known to us" he said, "and apart from already having given a Radio Installation, a Nurses' Home and many other items, these generous people have now presented this Hall. This is a great record of generosity and service, culminating with this gift which will be a great asset and was badly needed". The Hall, the building of which had only begun in July, had cost some £7,000. The first ceremony to be held in it was the Nurses Prizegiving on November 26th, with Lord Kindersley giving away the prizes.

The House Committee met later the same day and discussed the question of closing Oakleigh and transferring the male Geriatric patients to Ward II. Amongst other reasons for doing this was the fact that Sister Young, who had run Oakleigh for so many years, had resigned. The Geriatric cases were in fact transferred to Ward II temporarily, but they soon returned to Oakleigh with Mr. Jennings in charge of them instead of Sister Young. The final decision not to close Oakleigh was due largely to the views of the Plastic Surgeons, who said that without the convalescent beds, there would be a drop of at least 300 in the number of operations performed per annum. This number in 1960 was a record, at 4,851.

History was made on November 19th when for the first time a Helicopter landed in the Hospital grounds, bringing a severely injured patient from East Anglia with, amongst his other injuries, a fractured jaw.

At a Committee Meeting later that month we find Matron mentioning for the first time the lack of central facilities for the sluicing of dirty linen. This job had always had to be done on the Wards and it was considered that this might be one factor that made it difficult to get nurses, as it was an unpleasant job and should be done centrally.

January 1961 brought news of the awarding of the C.B.E. in

the New Year Honours to Mr. T. G. Ward for his work in the Dental Department. Dr. Roger Orcutt from West Hoathly was appointed to the General Practitioner Staff, followed shortly after by Dr. Peter Steel of Groombridge and Dr. Raymond Evans of Hartfield, bringing the total of the General Practitioner Staff to 22.

At the House Committee meeting on March 6th, Mr. Douglas Stern resigned his position as Chairman. At the subsequent meeting Mr. J. H. Mitchell was appointed Chairman in his place, and his first action was to propose a vote of thanks to Mr. Stern both for his services as Chairman for the last 5 years, and for the gifts and time which he had given so generously to the Hospital. Mr. Peter Williams was elected Vice-chairman of the House Committee on his resignation from membership of the Management Committee.

March 22nd was another important day in the Hospital's history when the Minister of Health, the Rt. Hon. J. Enoch Powell, opened the McIndoe Memorial Research Unit in the new Blond Laboratories, which had recently been completed through the generosity of Mr. and Mrs. Neville Blond. After formally opening the Laboratories the Minister addressed a large meeting in the Assembly Hall, including amongst others Sir Arthur Porritt, President of the Royal College of Surgeons, and Professor P. B. Medawar, F.R.S., of the University of London. Mr. Blond, presiding at the meeting, in his opening remarks told how Sir Archibald McIndoe, "that unique and lovable man", had first suggested to him that such a Unit might be built, and that the suggestion had been warmly supported by Mr. John Watson, Dr. Russell M. Davies and Mr. Robin Beare. He paid tribute to the pioneer service of Mr. Watson in organising the Unit, and also to the co-operation given by Mr. Stern, Chairman of the House Committee, and Sir Euan Miller, Chairman of the Group Management Committee. He concluded by saying it was hoped that if anything was achieved in the Research Laboratories it would be something which they would be able to show the whole world.

Mr. Powell, Minister of Health, opened his speech by saying that he thought the afternoon's ceremony was important not only because of the Unit itself, but because also it had proved that it was possible for such a thing to happen and in such a way at this time. He thought the history of the Queen Victoria Hospital brought together and symbolised all the strands and threads that have flowed into the National Health Service as we know it today, starting off with the voluntary efforts and local initiative which produced the original Hospital, followed by the present Hospital on this site which was added to by the Emergency Medical Service during the war—which Service, he said, was one of the creative sources which had helped to bring the National Health Service into existence. He referred then to the Royal Air Force, the Royal Canadian Air Force and the American help which had added in such a distinguished way to the original Hospital, and then to cap it all the advent of the National Health Service. All these things, he said, had gone to produce the organisation which we had today, but still, even since the National Health Service, the voluntary efforts continued. First of all the Peanut Ward, now today this Research Unit which had been financed by the generosity of Mr. and Mrs. Blond. "What a wonderful story this tells", he said, "of how State and voluntary efforts can be blended together. We all recognise that this voluntary effort is still very much alive and flourishing and I consider it my duty to foster and encourage it. It is supremely right to seal this Research Unit with the name of Sir Archibald McIndoe. Britain has for the last 20 years been proud of East Grinstead, and in years to come will I am sure be proud of this Unit. For myself and my Office I am proud and grateful to perform this ceremony."

Sir Ivor Julian spoke briefly, referring to the great privilege it was to have known Sir Archibald McIndoe, how his greatness had inspired so many things apart from his own work, not only the Hall in which we sat but now this Research Unit, and he felt sure that this was not the end and that other things would follow, similarly inspired. He paid tribute to Mr. Powell, who, he said, we were very lucky to have as our Minister, and concluded by thanking him for coming.

The new Unit, designed to provide facilities for research into the problems of transplantation of tissue and wound healing—with particular emphasis on investigation of the problem of homo-grafting, i.e. tissue transplanted from one individual to another, one of the major surgical necessities of the time—was unique in being the only Research Unit in the country devoted entirely to this problem. Its maintenance was provided for by a grant of £4,000 per annum for 7 years by Sir Miles Clifford, Chairman of the Leverhulme Trust, together with a similar grant of £3,000 by Messrs. Johnson & Johnson of Great Britain Ltd.

April brought another complaint from the Medical Council that the number of general beds, which was approximately the same as in 1936, was inadequate to meet the needs of the local community, which had doubled in size in the last 15 years and was continuing to grow. The House Committee, however, suggested that a quicker turn-over of patients and whenever possible their earlier return to their homes was the only possible way to alleviate this situation for the present.

On May 1st Mr. Peter Williams was elected Chairman of the Planning Sub-committee. In June Dr. R. M. Lodge was appointed to the General Practitioner Staff. On July 8th the Dowager Lady Reading presented the prizes at the Nurses Prizegiving. Later in July it is reported that the League of Friends had undertaken to furnish the Waiting Room in the new Casualty Department and to provide cubicle curtains and office curtains. There was at first some concern over the question of staffing this new Department, but in spite of this it was opened on September 22nd and in the first 10 days no less than 130 patients were treated in it. A letter was written by the House Committee to Sister England of Dewar Ward giving her their thanks and appreciation for the way in which she coped with the difficulties of running the old Casualty Department in addition to running her own Ward. August brought the resignation of Sister Bailey after many years in charge of the American Theatres.

The Annual Guinea Pig weekend which had been held continuously since 1941, was marked this year by a very special and delightful ceremony. The Guinea Pig Club had expressed a wish to mark their connection with the Hospital by presenting a portrait of the late Sir Archibald McIndoe, and this portrait, painted from a photograph, by Frank Eastman, was unveiled on September 23rd by Lady McIndoe in the presence of no fewer than 150 members of the 600-strong Guinea Pig Club.

December brings the first appearance of the Hospital Magazine, 'The Q-Vic Times'. This was started, with Mr.

197

G. H. Hunter as editor, mainly with the idea of making available to all members of the staff information of official and social activities within the Hospital, but it includes also various articles of general interest. It is produced monthly and has achieved a circulation of some 500 copies. The end of the year saw the termination of another long spell of service when Mr. K. A. Grieve, the Chief Engineer, resigned after more than 10 years. He was succeeded after a short interval by Mr. J. Carswell. The end of the year saw also another innovation in the opening of a Central Foul Linen Sluice, the first to be provided in the Group. Dirty Linen could now be placed in plastic bags at the patient's bedside and taken direct to the new plant, thus saving an immense amount of time and limiting the spread of infection, while incidentally relieving the wards of what had always been a distasteful task.

January 1962 opens with a proposal to introduce the metric system to the Hospital's Dispensary in place of the apothecaries' system of weights and measures. The Medical Council however suggested that the time was not appropriate to do this and recommended that its introduction should be postponed until the following year when it was expected that the British Pharmacopoeia and the country generally would be making the change; they thought it would be confusing if both systems were in operation at the same time. The change was in fact made a few months later, in order to fall into line with the other Hospitals in the Group, and the Pharmacists got over the difficulty by labelling drugs, where there was any possibility of a misunderstanding, with both quantities simultaneously.

In January also the Chairman of the League of Friends wrote a letter regarding the shortage of accommodation at the Hospital. The House Committee in their reply pointed out that the Ministry of Health's proposals for a new 'Hospital Service for the Nation' were expected shortly, and that the need for additional accommodation for patients within this area had already been brought to the notice of the Regional Hospital Board.

In February Dr. I. A. Williams was appointed Consultant in Physical Medicine to the Tunbridge Wells Group and held his first weekly outpatient session at the Queen Victoria Hospital. It was not long before he was adding his weight to the demands for enlargement of the Occupational Therapy Department, proposals for which had already been considered some time previously and rejected on the grounds of expense. February brought also the appointment of Mr. L. Cotton, F.R.C.S., of Kings College Hospital, as Honorary Consultant in General and Vascular Surgery. Two of the Hospital Sisters visited a Burns Unit in a hospital in Paris and were granted study leave for the purpose; the expenses of this journey being met by the Jill Mullins Fund, a fund consisting of money subscribed in memory of Sister Mullins and administered by the Matron for this and other purposes. In this month also the Hospital Staff Consultative Committee which had been defunct for some time, was reconstituted with Sir Charles Key as its Chairman. Early in March the long awaited Ministry of Health 'Hospital Plan for the Nation' was announced, and copies of the relevant plans for this Hospital and Group were circulated to the House Committee, and a brief discussion took place at the meeting on March 5th.

At the end of March Lady Kindersley resigned from the House Committee. She had been either on this Committee or on the previous Board of Management and on, previous to that, the Hospital Management Committee of the Queens Road Hospital, since the year 1927—a total service of committee work of 35 years; years of hard work, great generosity and dedicated service, almost unequalled in this story. Lady Kindersley consented to remain as President of the Hospital though she retired from the day-to-day administration of the Hospital which she had so largely influenced for so many of these years. Her name will stand forever very high on the list of those who have contributed to the continued success of the Hospital. She was succeeded on the House Committee by the Chairman of the League of Friends, Mr. Peter Griffits.

Friday, March 30th, was another big day in the Hospital's history, when the extensions to the Blond Laboratories were officially opened by Sir Arthur Porritt, K.C.M.G., K.C.V.O., C.B.E., President of the Royal College of Surgeons. This Unit, originally built 12 months previously to house the McIndoe Memorial Research Unit had increased its activities so rapidly that in less than 12 months it had outgrown its original building. In September 1961, Dr. Morten Simonsen, M.D. of the University of Copenhagen, a scientist of international repute for his work on homo-transplantation, had been appointed Director of the Unit, with Dr. A. D. Barnes, a Leverhulme Research Fellow, to assist him. This appointment was made and the increased staff that accompanied it were made possible, by the generous gift of £5,000 per annum for a period of 5 years, by Mr. and Mrs. Terence Kennedy. It had very quickly become evident that the Unit was outgrowing its building and that nearly double the space would be required to meet its requirements. Mr. and Mrs. Neville Blond once again generously gave the sum of £10,000 to make this possible together with an annual grant of £600 for the provision of essential services and maintenance of the building. The Research Unit is organised by the East Grinstead Research Trust with Mr. Neville Blond, C.M.G., O.B.E., as chairman and Mrs. Neville Blond, Sir Miles Clifford, K.B.E., C.M.G., General Sir Euan Miller, K.C.B., D.S.O., M.C., Douglas C. Stern, M.C., Robin L. B. Beare, F.R.C.S., Russell M. Davies, F.S.A., R.C.S., John Watson, M.A., F.R.C.S.E., (Hon. Secretary), as members and with Professor P. B. Medawar, F.R.S., and Professor D. Slome, Ph.D., as Scientific Advisers.

Mr. Neville Blond presided at the opening and spoke of the great privilege and pleasure of having Sir Arthur Porritt with us that day. Sir Arthur in his speech referred to his own friendship with the late Sir Archibald McIndoe, and the great work which he had initiated and was now inspiring in this new Research Unit. Mr. John Watson, thanking Sir Arthur mentioned that the Unit had formed a focal point for all homo-graft research, some of which had previously been carried out in rather scattered places, and he mentioned also how this new Unit formed the basis of the teaching of the Plastic Surgery Post-graduate Teaching Unit. Sir Ivor Julian rounding off the occasion gave his opinion that the Hospital had never had any greater friends than Mr. and Mrs. Blond, and hinted that there was in their minds some even greater benefaction to the Hospital of which we were likely to hear more very shortly, in the shape of a special Burns Research Unit.

In May the Hospital began to think of celebrating its own Centenary and a Committee was formed representative of all Departments of the Hospital, to make the arrangements. The

House Committee decided to give £250 from the Amenities Fund towards the celebrations and in due course the Management Committee agreed to augment this by a further £250. It was at this time also that the question of Nurses' Pay was being discussed and on May 18th Mrs. Evelyn Emmett, Member of Parliament for the East Grinstead Division, came to the Hospital to have a personal discussion with the Nurses about it. The new scheme of training had just been introduced to the Hospital allowing for part-time training of pupil nurses over a period of some 2 years, and it was hoped by this means to augment the still slightly depleted numbers of the nursing staff.

Monday, June 4th, saw the handing over to the Hospital by Mr. and Mrs. Douglas Stern of their latest gift in the shape of a new Games Room for the use of the Hospital Staff, equipped with table tennis, billiards, and other spare time relaxations. At a House Committee meeting later the same afternoon Mr. Mitchell officially thanked the Sterns for their generous gift.

Thursday, June 21st, saw the official opening of the new Swimming Pool for the use of the nurses, at the rear of the Hospital, by Lady Constance McIndoe. The pool was provided by the joint efforts of the Peanut Club and the Nurses' own Barclay Club which raised more than £1,000 towards its cost, and it included a sun chalet with changing-rooms which was provided largely through the kindness of Lady McIndoe who, at the opening ceremony, expressed the wish that it should be dedicated to the memory of the late Sister Jill Mullins who had been a member of the original plastic team with Sir Archibald throughout the war, and to whom a plaque was erected at the Pool in her memory. The Peanut Club undertook responsibility for laying out the surrounding grounds.

In July the League of Friends provided a 'Staff Location System' at a cost of £700, and in August the Peanut Ward was redecorated by the Peanut Club. Visiting hours, which had remained unchanged since 1888 were in September considerably relaxed, visiting being officially allowed in all main wards from 2 p.m.—8 p.m., with only a short interval for nursing purposes.

The weekend of October 13th-14th was the 21st anniversary of the founding of the Guinea Pig Club and the occasion was suitably celebrated by some 200 members of the Club who journeyed to East Grinstead for the Club's annual weekend. With H.R.H. the Duke of Edinburgh now its President in place of the late Sir Archibald McIndoe, this Club continues unabated the rehabilitation work for which, along with its social activities, it originally came into being in 1941, and it is the proud boast of its Committee, of whom Squadron Leader Tom Gleave, Dr. Russell M. Davies and Welfare Secretary, Mr. J. E. Blacksell, are leading members, that every member of the Club is now a fully-functioning economic unit; most are making their own way and the few who are unable completely to do so are aided by rehabilitation grants and help from the Club's own resources. The East Grinstead Hospital still remains the base to which Guinea Pigs the world over return, as one of them expressed it on this occasion, "to recharge their batteries".

# 10

# The Hospital To-day

THE Queen Victoria Hospital, in June 1963, and in the presence of its Patron, Her Majesty Queen Elizabeth the Queen Mother, is about to celebrate the Centenary of its foundation. It has come a very long way from Dr. Rogers' original 7-bedded Cottage Hospital with its 'profusion of flowers', and though there are still plenty of flowers, they are now spread over a total of nearly 33 acres of grounds. The main Hospital site at Holtye Road comprises some 25 acres, the remainder of the total area being made up by the Oakleigh Annexe with 2 acres, Australia House, Engalee, Warrenside and Tudor Cottage.

The Hospital is situated within the area of the South-east Metropolitan Regional Hospital Board and is one of the 13 Hospitals administered by the Tunbridge Wells Group Hospital Management Committee, the present Chairman of which is Lt. General Sir Euan Miller, and Secretary Mr. E. A. Wagstaff: Gladys Lady Kindersley is its President, and the present House Committee excluding the Matron and Administrative Officers who attend all its meetings, is as follows, the figure after each name being the number of years that each has been associated with the Hospital in some capacity or another:—

J. H. Mitchell, Esq. (*Chairman*) (27)
P. A. Williams, Esq., D.S.C., (*Vice-chairman*) (8)

Miss H. M. Beale, O.B.E. (27)
Mrs. Neville Blond (22)
R. C. Burgess, Esq. (29)
Dr. J. O. Collin (25)
Dr. Russell M. Davies (23)
P. Griffits, Esq. (4)
G. S. Hall, Esq. (3)

Mrs S. M. Looker, O.B.E. (11)
Lady McIndoe (9)
Lt. Gen. Sir Euan Miller, K.C.B., K.B.E., D.S.O., M.C. (5)
J. Oliver, Esq. (4)

| Lt. Gen. Sir Frederick Harris, | G. Place, Esq. (4) |
|---|---|
| K.B.E., C.B., M.C., Ll.D., | Mrs. E. D. Richards (27) |
| M.B. (4) | D. C. Stern, Esq. (20) |
| P. H. Jayes, Esq., F.R.C.S. (24) | Miss I. P. Wallis (32) |
| Sir Charles Key, K.B.E. (3) | T. G. Ward, Esq. |
| | C.B.E. (17) |

In addition to the House Committee there is a Planning Sub-committee made up of the following members:—

Mr. P. A. Williams (*Chairman*)

| Mr. R. C. Burgess | Miss I. P. Wallis |
|---|---|
| Mrs. Looker | Dr. J. O. Collin |
| Mr. J. H. Mitchell | Dr. R. M. Davies |
| Mr. D. Stern | Sir Frederick Harris |

and the House Committee is advised also on medical problems by the Medical Council of which the present Chairman is Dr. A. Sachs, with Dr. J. D. W. Hunter as Secretary. The Joint Staff Consultative Committee, representing all branches of the Hospital employees and administration, also from time to time makes proposals for discussion by the House Committee, and a Catering Sub-committee under the chairmanship of Mr. John Oliver, makes recommendations regarding the catering.

The Chief Administrative Officer is Mr. G. A. Johns, with Mr. W. J. Moore as his Chief Assistant, and the Hospital employs in all 26, mostly full-time but some part-time, Secretaries and Clerks in its various departments.

The Matron, Miss M. A. Duncombe, with Miss J. E. Flunder as Assistant Matron, Miss M. I. Dennis and Miss L. A. Page as Administrative Sisters, has in all some 30 Sisters, 50 Staff Nurses, and 80 other nurses, some State Enrolled, some Pupil Nurses and Nursing Auxiliaries, with 25 Ward Orderlies under her charge. The Pupil Nurses Training School can take 44 students, though there are at present a number of vacancies, and it offers a 2-year training course resulting in registration as State Enrolled Nurse. The course, which is essentially practical rather than theoretical, can be taken on a part-time basis and may then extend over 3 years or longer, the only qualification for entry being that applicants must be aged 18 or over. There are also a number of Pre-student Nurses, aged 16-18, who perform a variety of useful tasks in all departments of the Hospital. The Hospital employs in addition some 70-80 domestic workers.

There is a total of 316 beds, 50 of which are at the Oakleigh Annexe, 14 of these being Male Geriatric and 36 convalescent beds. There are 13 Recovery Beds and, while there may be minor variations from time to time, the official allocation of the other beds is as follows:—

| Plastic Surgery | 136 | Female Geriatric | 21 |
| General | 53 | Corneo Plastic | 20 |
| Dental | 23 | | |

One of the most remarkable things about the Queen Victoria Hospital is that although administratively it is, as briefly outlined above, one single institution, it is in fact divided medically into 2 very distinct sub-divisions. With the large and renowned Plastic Surgery and Jaw Injuries Centre making up one of these sub-divisions, it has nevertheless maintained its original function of providing general hospital care for the local population through the other sub-division—a busy and fully staffed General Practitioner Unit. This particular combination is unusual in the Hospital service and at the present time when the entire service is being replanned, the fact that it works so supremely well deserves further study by those responsible for the planning.

The General side of the Hospital consists of 45 beds in the main building, 22 for women, 14 for men, 3 staff beds, and 6 private rooms, with 8 children's beds and cots in the Peanut Ward, making 53 'acute' beds available for the local population. There are always a few local patients in the Women's Geriatric Ward I, and a number in the Men's Geriatric beds at Oakleigh, so that it is not possible to say how many beds in the Hospital are specifically available for the local population at any one moment, as the number varies slightly from day to day. A count, however, conducted one day in the summer of 1962, showed 70 inpatients registered as being under the care of the local General Practitioner Staff.

There are 22 General Practitioners on the Staff of this Unit with overall responsibility for the cases sent in by them, though they are assisted by a Resident House Surgeon and have the following full complement of Consultant Staff to advise them:—

| | |
|---|---|
| Mr. J. E. H. Cogan | Ophthalmic |
| Mr. L. Cotton | Surgical (Hon.) |
| Mr. R. Furlong | Orthopaedic |
| Dr. H. Gardiner-Hill | Medical |
| Mr. W. H. Gervis | Orthopaedic |
| Mr. E. D. Y. Grasby | Gynaecology |
| Dr. R. MacKeith* | Paediatrician |
| Dr. R. Maggs | Early Nervous Disorders |
| Mr. E. G. Muir | Surgical |
| Mr. J. B. Musgrove | Ear, Nose and Throat |
| Sir John H. Peel | Gynaecology |
| Dr. D. Robertson | Heart and General Medicine |
| Dr. P. A. J. Smith | Dermatology |
| Dr. S. J. Sutton | Chest Diseases |
| Mr. S. G. Tuffill | Urology |
| Dr. I. Williams | Physical Medicine |

The General Practitioners, in order of appointment, are:—

| | |
|---|---|
| Dr. H. B. Shaw | Dr. Joan F. Godfrey |
| Dr. G. K. Thornton | Dr. M. Worlock |
| Dr. C. R. Steel | Dr. J. F. Paxton |
| Dr. A. C. Sommerville | Dr. G. F. M. Carnegie |
| Dr. E. G. Sibley | Dr. H. N. Hardy |
| Dr. B. C. Morton-Palmer | Dr. J. D. W. Hunter |
| Dr. E. J. Dennison | Dr. H. Bywater |
| Dr. J. O. Collin | Dr. R. L. Orcutt |
| Dr. P. H. Cardew | Dr. P. Steel |
| Dr. C. Palmer | Dr. R. Evans |
| Dr. F. B. Briggs | Dr. R. M. Lodge |

About 12 months ago a count was made of the National Health patients registered with the General Practitioners, and they totalled some 36,000. Allowing for some of these living on the fringe of the area who might on occasions be admitted to other hospitals and adding in those private patients who might not have registered under the Health Service, this figure of 36,000 probably represents fairly accurately the population served by the General Practitioner Unit, giving an average of 1.47 'acute' beds per 1,000 patients. The Ministry of Health,

* Resigned February 1963 — succeeded by Dr. C. E. Stroud.

in its new 'Hospital Plan' published recently, estimated the normal limit of acute beds required over the whole country as 3.3 per 1,000 of population, though this figure included a number of specialities such as Infectious Diseases, Radiotherapy, and Chest Diseases, which are not normally admitted to this Hospital. Even allowing for these there would seem on paper to be a rather large discrepancy here, and this is borne out by the fact, only too well known locally, that East Grinstead patients are sometimes unable to obtain admission to their own Hospital and are necessarily admitted to other Hospitals in the Group, and even sometimes outside it. Though the final plans for the development of this Hospital in the 'National Hospital Plan' are not at the moment available, it has been said that the Queen Victoria Hospital is scheduled to be upgraded to become a District General Hospital, with many more general beds available. Only time will show therefore and probably fairly soon, what the future holds for the General side of the Hospital. While the fame and glamour attaching to the Plastic Unit largely overshadows the General side of the Hospital, there is no harm in reminding ourselves that this side of the Hospital still exists and that it is doing a very important job for a very big local population who have largely paid for it in the first place, to a certain extent support it through the League of Friends, The Peanut Club and other voluntary activities, and for whom it remains, despite everything, their own local Hospital.

Included in the General Practitioner Unit, and situated in the main building, there is also the spacious new Casualty Department opened in September 1961. With Sister Shrimpton in charge, this Department is open constantly night and day and deals with some 5-600 patients every month. Casualties are normally attended in the first place by the General House Surgeon, and if admission is necessary, admitted either to the general wards under the General Practitioner whose duty week it may be and who also is on call for casualty relief duty, or to the Plastic Unit Wards if surgery or resuscitation is required. This is one of the points at which co-operation between the two sides of the Hospital reaches its highest level, for casualties may be admitted to either side, and the Plastic House Surgeon acts as relief Casualty Officer when the General House Surgeon is not available, while surgical advice at all levels is always freely available. The extent of this co-operation between the two sides of the Hospital is probably not sufficiently well realised by the local population, nor the degree to which they benefit by the presence of the Plastic Unit. East Grinstead Town has grown accustomed to receiving praise for the open-hearted reception it has always given to the Guinea Pigs and other plastic surgery patients during the war and since, but the goodwill generated thereby has paid handsome dividends. The relationship is essentially a happy one, with advantages accruing to both sides.

The Plastic Surgery and Jaw Injuries Unit, or more shortly, the Plastic Unit as it is commonly called, consists of 4 distinct parts: the General Plastic Surgery Unit, the Dental Department, the Corneo-Plastic Unit, and the McIndoe Research Laboratory. The General Plastic Surgery Unit with its 5 Consultant Plastic Surgeons, Mr. R. L. B. Beare, Mr. P. H. Jayes, Mr. C. R. McLaughlin, Mr. F. T. Moore, and Mr. J. H. Watson, its 136 beds, and its association with the Dental and Jaw Injuries and Corneo-plastic Units, its fine modern Surgical Block and extensive Post-graduate facilities, with the recent addition of the Blond Research Laboratories, is one of the leading Plastic Surgery centres in existence today. Officially the Plastic centre for the South-east Area of England, it receives large numbers of cases and in addition a constant stream of visiting surgeons from all over the world, and there are seldom fewer than 6-12 post-graduate trainees, many of them enabled to come here under the auspices of the British Council. Its popularity in this respect is largely because of its unique facilities for studying under one roof the whole modern field of plastic surgery. There are 2 Senior Registrars attached to the Unit, and a Resident House Surgeon. There is also for Nurses a Post-graduate course in Plastic Surgery nursing, with the McIndoe Prize awarded annually to the best nurse.

The Dental Department with Sir William Kelsey Fry and Professor B. Cohen as Honorary Consultants, and Mr. Terence G. Ward, C.B.E. in charge, assisted by Mr. G. E. Ryba, Consultant Dental Surgeon, and Mr. Dennis Glass, Ortho-dontist, is amongst the leading Post-graduate training centres in Oral Surgery in the world, apart from being the Regional

Jaw Injuries and Oral Surgery Unit for the South-east Metropolitan Region. Out of 3 Senior Dental Registrars in the whole of the South-east Region, 2 are attached to the Queen Victoria Hospital Dental Department, the third being at Guy's Hospital. In addition there is a Junior Registrar and a Resident Dental House Surgeon. The Unit has 23 beds at its disposal and is at present treating some 1,800 cases annually. The Services' Oral Surgeons and Technicians have all been trained here since the War, in addition to many Oral Surgeons from all over the world. There is a Nuffield Scholarship open to any oral surgeon in the Commonwealth tenable for one year at this training centre. The Department is at present carrying out research in co-operation with Professor Bertram Cohen of the Dental Department of the Royal College of Surgeons, on the drug treatment of jaw cancers. Mr. Ward was recently Chairman of the British Executive Committee of the First International Conference on Oral Surgery and during the Conference some 70 attending members visited the Department.

The Corneo-Plastic Unit and Regional Eye Bank, to give its full official title, under Sir Benjamin W. Rycroft, with Mr. A. W. Werb as his Chief Assistant, has 20 beds at its disposal and does more than 100 cases of corneal grafting annually. It is the leading clinic in this speciality in this country and again has an international reputation, attracting Post-graduate trainees from all over the world. There are 3 scholarships available, each given by a grateful patient of Sir Benjamin's, and, again owing to the generosity of grateful patients, a Corneo-Plastic Research Fund and, entirely separate, a Welfare Fund. The Unit also maintains the Regional Eyebank for the South-east area of England and, though its van is kept constantly busy collecting donor eyes from a wide area, there are never enough of them and the number of grafting operations could be considerably increased if more eyes were available. The Unit has 2 full-time Registrars, one of whom Mr. F. O. Muller is at present engaged in Research, under the Medical Research Council, into the long term preservation of grafts by freezing. There are in addition 4 part-time Registrars.

The Research Laboratory, the most recent addition to the Hospital, needs no further introduction than the plaque situated on the wall just inside the main doors with its simple inscription—

"This Research Unit commemorates the Pioneer Surgery of Sir Archibald McIndoe, F.R.C.S. Presented in his memory by Elaine and Neville Blond, 1960."

The Laboratory was designed specifically for research into the problems of tissue transplantation and is at present the only laboratory devoted solely to this purpose. The main theme of its work so far has been investigation into the various aspects of homo-grafting—the transfer of tissues from one individual to another—a problem which, with the exception of corneal grafting and the transfer of tissues between identical twins, remains at present largely unsolved. Hitherto it has been found that tissues thus transplanted have set up a reaction which resulted either in their own destruction, or on occasions in the death of the host, and it is the problem of these reactions between graft and host which forms the main line of investigation in these laboratories. There are known to be a number of ways in which mutual tolerance may be established, but at present they are largely impracticable in human beings. The techniques of investigation at present being followed involve the use of radioactive isotopes, X-irradiation and fluorescent microscopy, detailed descriptions of which would be out of place here, but it is reported that already some hitherto unrecorded and unexplained facts have come to light and are being actively investigated. Solution of these problems would not only save many lives, particularly of severely burned patients, but would revolutionise the entire practice of surgery; and this Hospital, with its special interest in surgical reconstruction, is particularly well placed to lead the field in these investigations.

The work of the Laboratory is carried out by a team of workers led by 41-year old Dr. Morten Simonsen, M.D. Copenhagen, and Fellowships granted by the Leverhulme Trust, the National Institute of Health of the United States of America, Messrs. Johnson and Johnson, and the World Health Organisation, have made it possible to enlarge the team to include 6 research specialists in addition to Dr. Simonsen, while 9 technicians are needed to keep the establishment running. As Mr. Blond expressed his hope at the opening of the Laboratory, this team may well "produce something of which we can tell the world".

The two main divisions of the Hospital briefly outlined above are linked and supported by the various ancillary services, chief amongst which is the Anaesthetic Department. The 4 American Theatres and the General (Rowntree Memorial) Theatre in the main building, are in almost constant daily use, so that there are frequently 5 surgical lists going at the same time. This naturally requires an extensive Anaesthetic Department and the large Anaesthetic Room with its 4 tables in the American Theatre Block is one of the busiest places in the Hospital. The anaesthetic team, headed by Dr. Russell M. Davies, consists in addition of Consultants Dr. Anthony Edridge, Dr. Hale Enderby and Dr. K. Chambers; 2 Registrars one Senior, one Junior—and a Resident House Anaesthetist. The annual number of anaesthetics given by them at present exceeds 4,000, and is increasing year by year. In 1955 the East Grinstead Anaesthetic Research Trust was formed in order to further research and post-graduate education in anaesthesia. The Department was recently visited by Professor J. Eckenhoff of Philadelphia who spent 12 months studying the special methods of anaesthesia used in this Hospital.

The X-ray Department, under Dr. William Campbell, with its 4 Radiographers, serves the entire Hospital and is at the moment X-raying over 7,000 cases annually. It is directly accessible by the 22 local general practitioners as well as the 6 local dentists, but it is in addition a specialised unit highly skilled in the investigation of eye and jaw conditions, as is bound to be the case in such a Hospital as this. The high technical standard of this Department, essential for the specialised work of the Plastic Unit, is far in excess of what would normally be expected in a small country General Hospital and is of course a tremendous advantage to the local population and their family doctors.

The Pathology Department likewise combines the specialised techniques necessary for the Plastic Unit with the functions of a general laboratory available to the local general practitioners. This Department, in charge of Dr. Albert Sachs, with its 5 technicians—of whom Miss Dorothy Fox has worked in it since

February 1948, Mr. Colin Streeter since August 1949, and Mr. Raymond Lloyd since 1952—is at the moment dealing with over 1,000 cases every month. Specialist work here also is done in connection with the Eye Department; a central sterile syringe service is run, and histology for the various surgical departments is carried out here, as is also the general pathology of the nearby Edenbridge Hospital. Approximately 100 post-mortem examinations annually are performed in the new enlarged Postmortem Room.

The Physiotherapy Department, under Miss Rosemary Wootton, with 3 assistant Physiotherapists, is treating well over 20,000 cases annually, both inpatients and outpatients, and is one of the busiest Departments in the Hospital being also accessible to the local general practitioners. Next door to it, the Occupational Therapy Department, with Miss C. G. Letcher* in charge and Technical Instructor Mr. Harrod to help her, accounts for an average of 7-800 attendances every month. The Pharmacy under Mr. Frank Summers, with 2 Assistant Pharmacists, one full-time, and a Dispenser, not only dispenses the drugs required for this and the Edenbridge Hospitals, but it undertakes rather more than simple dispensing in that it is responsible for the preparation of sterile solutions, injections, etc, which formerly were purchased.

The Almoner's Department also has grown since the day in 1940 when Captain Banham was told he must "carry out the duties usually performed by an almoner". Approximately 3,000 patients a year now pass through the hands of Miss V. Faith K. Gardiner, A.M.I.A., her 2 part-time assistants and 2 full-time secretaries. This Department has, like most of the others, its own problems peculiar to the dual nature of this Hospital. Patients coming from all over the world frequently have relatives who wish to stay in the area while they are under treatment, and finding accommodation not only for them, but also for post-graduate students and temporary overseas staff, is one of the extra tasks willingly shouldered, while closer liaison with the general practitioners leads frequently to easier following-up of local patients after their discharge from Hospital. The Photographic Department, with Mr. Gordon Clemetson in charge, takes some 12,000 photographs annually,

* Resigned January 1963 — succeeded by Miss M. Copeland.

and plays an essential part in the Plastic Surgery Unit. The Registration Department, with Mr. J. D. Crane as Records Officer in charge, with Miss E. Gain, Mrs. S. Sellwood and an Outpatient appointments Clerk to assist him, is responsible for all except emergency admissions and appointments, and keeps records going back to the opening of the Holtye Road Hospital in 1936. In addition it keeps a Diagnostic Index which is frequently useful for various research purposes. The nearby Outpatient Department, in charge of Sister Wood, runs up to 20 clinics every week and, like most of the other Departments, serves both sides of the Hospital.

The Hospital School, now in charge of Mrs. Beale, with Mrs. Ward to assist her, plays an important part in maintaining the morale of some of the younger patients. Maintained by the East Sussex Education Authority, it not only ensures that long-stay children between 5 and 16 years of age keep the continuity of their education going while under treatment, but it also sometimes provides an opportunity to give concentrated tuition to a child who may for some reason or other be backward in a particular subject. Indeed with classes averaging 10-12 pupils a day only, the tuition received here is frequently more individual than in some ordinary schools. The schoolroom is situated nearby the Children's Ward, and close co-operation between the teachers and the ward staff ensures that the best possible use is made of the school.

Oakleigh Annexe with its convalescent and male geriatric beds, in the care of Charge Nurse Mr. L. W. Jennings, is in the Lewes Road, some 2 miles distant from the main Hospital. Australia House and Engalee in the main London Road, are about the same distance, and Warrenside only some $\frac{3}{4}$ mile away; all of these have a twice daily shuttle service to and from the main Hospital by the Hospital's own transport in the charge of Mr. Frank Maynard and Mr. W. Payne.

The Catering Department, with Mr. Eland in charge and Miss V. Hardy to assist him, is responsible for feeding the entire Hospital including the outlying homes, and this means the serving of some 450 main meals every day of the year, in addition to the catering and provisioning for the subsidiary meals. Special problems occur in this Department too, for jaw injury patients frequently are splinted and unable to eat solid food, thus requiring, as do also severely shocked burns cases, an all liquid high-protein diet, the provision of which may occasionally require considerable ingenuity.

The annual expenditure of the Hospital is constantly increasing and is now running at the enormous figure of over £400,000, but even this figure is augmented not only by personal gifts, but also by the League of Friends and the Peanut Club. The League, with Mr. Peter Griffits as Chairman and Mr. Hugh Parratt as Secretary, has over the last 3 years spent no less than £1,850 on various amenities; this in addition to the £3,350 they provided to pay for the new Physiotherapy Department and the Canteen. The League is entirely separate from the Hospital administration except that its Chairman is on the House Committee. It has its own committee elected annually from its own members, who pay an annual subscription of 5s. It raises the money for all these benefactions by various means, of which the Annual Carnival is the chief. Film premieres, variety shows, flag days, and other voluntary collections make up the rest. Anybody who wishes to help the Hospital today can do so simply by joining the League or the Peanut Club, and it is of some interest to hear that new Peanut members are still being enrolled from all over the world at the rate of 1,000 per week. This Club, started and almost entirely run by Mrs. K. Clemetson, has raised a total of more than £100,000 for various Hospitals since it began, and still remains active in the interests of this Hospital. During the last year it has paid for the redecoration of the Peanut Ward and the Schoolroom, and has been largely responsible for the cost of the new Nurses' Swimming Pool, in addition to other minor benefactions.

Further big developments are already taking shape as the Queen Victoria Hospital prepares to celebrate its centenary. On Wednesday, June 5th, 1963 Her Majesty Queen Elizabeth the Queen Mother is to visit the Hospital to take part in the celebrations, and arrangements are being made for her to lay the foundation stone of a new £150,000 Burns Research Unit. This new building, a further memorial to the late Sir Archibald McIndoe, is being provided by the generosity once again of Mr. and Mrs. Neville Blond and their family, while the Peanut Club has undertaken to equip it at an estimated cost of £10,000.

After the Queen Mother's visit a play, "The Progress of Luke", specially written for the occasion by Miss Barbara Willard will be performed in the Assembly Hall, and numerous other events are planned to take place during this week, including a Hospital Open Day with exhibitions of the work going on in the various departments.

With the Burns Unit already under construction, and the proposed enlargement of the Hospital into a District General Hospital envisaged by the Ministry of Health's 'Hospital Plan for the Nation,' with continuing private benefactions, the Peanut Club, the League of Friends, and the many thousands of workers and wellwishers in the district behind it, one cannot help feeling that the future of this great Hospital shows every sign of being as glorious as its past.

# Early Changes

A committee had been formed to organise the Centenary Celebrations as early as May 1962, chaired by Mr. Mitchell and with members representing every department of the Hospital. It had met no fewer than eighteen times, so it is hardly surprising that the event passed off successfully and that in her introduction to the special Souvenir Centenary Brochure produced by the Courier Publishing Company, the Hospital's President, Gladys, Lady Kindersley, was able to offer her congratulations to everybody connected with the event.

The day itself, June 5th, 1963, was a lovely summer's day, warm and sunny. Our Patron, Her Majesty Queen Elizabeth the Queen Mother, arrived precisely at 3 o'clock, accompanied by her Lady-in-Waiting Lady Mary Harvey and her Equerry Sir Alistair Aird, and was welcomed by Lord Gage representing the Duke of Norfolk. She was introduced to the Chairman of the Management Committee, Mr. Mitchell, and other senior members of the staff, and a welcoming speech was made to her by the Honourable Philip Kindersley representing his father Lord Kindersley; both the Duke of Norfolk and Lord Kindersley were unable to be present on account of illness. In her reply Her Majesty spoke of her pleasure at being present at this Centenary Celebration and then officially declared the Celebration to be open. She went on to thank the donors of the new Burns Unit, Mr. and Mrs. Neville Blond and their family, together with the Peanut Club who were equipping it. Her Majesty then laid the foundation stone of the building, and the whole occasion and building were blessed at a short service taken by the Bishop of Chichester.

After the ceremony Sir Ivor Julian, Chairman of the Tunbridge Wells Group Hospital Management Committee, officially thanked Her Majesty for laying the stone and also again thanked the donors of the new building for their very generous gift. Her Majesty then toured a number of exhibitions that had been set up in various parts of the Hospital to demonstrate aspects of its work, and also visited the Peanut Children's Ward which had recently been enlarged to include a special unit for new admissions. After this there was a tea party in the large marquee especially erected for the occasion, during which the author was allowed to present Her Majesty with a specially bound copy of his history of the Hospital. Her Majesty left as arranged at 4.45 p.m. After her departure the exhibitions remained open to the public for a further two hours and they were open also during the afternoons of Thursday, Friday and Saturday. Performances of Barbara Willard's play took place at 8 p.m. on the following three evenings with a matinee on Saturday June 8th, and the celebrations were concluded on Sunday the 9th with a Civic Service of Thanksgiving for the foundation of the Hospital which was held at St. Swithuns, East Grinstead's Parish Church.

Once the excitement of the Centenary celebrations was over the Hospital had to think of more mundane things, and it is regrettable to have to report that the situation was not a very happy one. When the National Health Service began in July 1948, the Government had taken over the management of some 2,800 hospitals of all shapes and sizes and it is interesting to know that no less than 500 of them were General Practitioner Hospitals. It is fair to say that many of the smaller hospitals, and indeed also some of the larger ones, had in fact at that time been struggling to survive financially, and quite a few of them were relieved to be taken over by the Service which would presumably, everybody hoped, run them efficiently and economically.

Of course the Ministry soon found that the task of sorting them all out was going to be a very big one indeed, and not surprisingly it took them years to do it. This was the time when "biggest is best", and eventually some fifteen years later in 1963 a National Hospital Plan for the nation was presented by the then Minister of Health Mr. Enoch Powell. This was based mainly on the closure of some 1,100 hospitals; about 130 were to be redesigned; also 90 new ones were to be built and most of the smaller ones closed. The main unit then would be a District General Hospital with between 600-700 beds, which

217

would provide the top level of treatment in all medical and surgical specialities. Initially the Queen Victoria Hospital had been led to believe that it might become one of these District General Hospitals; this would have meant of course another big expansion and at first everybody was pleased, but gradually it became obvious that this plan would have to be modified. There just was not enough money available to carry it out, and as early as 1964 it began to become obvious that there would be no room in this situation for such a unique institution as the Queen Victoria Hospital with its two separate parts; in fact it seemed as though whether we became a District General Hospital or not, the General Practitioner side of the Hospital could possibly be closed. A few hospitals were closed but only a handful, and the reaction from their local communities was so intense that the authorities eventually took notice. It took then another six years to work out an alternative, as will be seen.

Despite all the political discussion as to the future of the small hospitals which was going on at Ministry level, the atmosphere at the Queen Victoria remained remarkably untouched by it. Few changes were being made; Mr. Mitchell was still Chairman of the House Committee with Mr. Peter Williams as his Deputy Chairman: a few members of staff both medical and nursing left their duties and were replaced; Miss Duncombe was still Matron with Miss Flunder as her Assistant, and Miss Dennis and Miss Page as Administrative Sisters; the Chief Administrative Officer was Mr. G. A. Johns with Mr. W. J. Moore as his Chief Assistant.

One part of the Hospital which was flourishing very successfully was the McIndoe Memorial Research Unit, familiarly known as the Blond Laboratories because they had been presented by Mr. and Mrs. Neville Blond. They had been opened in March 1962 by Mr. Enoch Powell, and of course later worked closely with the new Burns Unit, another planned memorial to Sir Archibald at the Hospital.

Meanwhile the Royal Air Force was paying its own tributes to the great man; on the 22nd September 1961, some few months after his death, they held a Memorial Service for him at St. Clement Danes Church in the Strand, popularly known as the Church of the Royal Air Force. The service was conducted by the R.A.F. Chaplain in Chief, The Venerable P. W. Cocks.

A chair was endowed by Archie's widow, always thought of as "Lady Connie"; it is made of dark oak and its general design blends beautifully with the decor of the Church. It bears the inscription "Archibald Hector McIndoe, Knight, C.B.E., F.R.C.S., M.S., F.A.C.S., 1900 to 1960". Above the inscription the Chair carries the emblem in gold of the Guinea Pig Club, and a cushion worked in petit point reproduces in colours the four foreign Orders of Chivalry bestowed on Archie during the War; namely, the White Lion of Czechoslovakia, the Eagle of Poland, the Dutch Order of Orange and Nassau, and the French Legion of Honour. Archdeacon Cocks preached the sermon and referred to a "very gifted man whom the R.A.F. held in special affection". Lady McIndoe and members of Archie's family were present at this Service, and a contingent of Guinea Pigs, plus representatives of all ranks of the Royal Air Force, were among the congregation; altogether it was a most memorable and moving Service. At the same time Archie's ashes were interred within the Church—an honour awarded to no other civilian. This Chair makes a very fitting memorial to a great man and is well worth visiting if any readers find themselves at any time in the vicinity of the Church.

Also during 1962 the Royal Air Force Association founded a biennial lecture in memory of Sir Archibald, the subject to be Plastic Surgery or any allied subject based on the lecturer's experiences in that field. The lecturer was to be nominated by the President and Secretary of the British Association of Plastic Surgeons, and in 1964 the lecture was given by one of our own Consultant Surgeons Mr. Percy Jayes.

Arrangements had been made to provide a measure of reciprocity between our Laboratory and the Royal College of Surgeons' Laboratory in order to allow workers in this field of research to communicate as much as possible. The College honoured Dr. Simonsen the Director of our Laboratory by appointing him Professor in Transplantation. In addition to this the Medical Research Council had provided £6,000 to support the Laboratory; a similar reciprocal arrangement was made with the M.R.C.'s Laboratory at Porton, and they sent two of their Scientists and three Technicians to our Laboratory here. Johnson & Johnson also provided a Fellowship. The Laboratory became a very popular place to visit for other people involved in the same sort of work, who began to arrive from all over the world when they heard of the kind of work that was being done here. There was a Research Fellowship also from the Leverhulme Research Unit and this was financed by Mr. and Mrs. Terence Kennedy—Mrs. Kennedy being Mrs. Blond's sister. So thanks to all this nationwide co-operation and generous grants from various people including the Peanut Club, the Laboratory was able to work so that there was no involvement by the National Health Service Authority in any way financially. Mrs. Blond's daughter and her husband Mr. and Mrs. David Susman had also made a generous gift towards the cost of its building.

During 1964 we have to record that Mrs. Kennedy died, and also that her and Mrs. Blond's brother, Lord Marks, died round about the same time. They had both been very generous to the Laboratory, and had established what became known as the Marks Fellowships for training young Plastic Surgeons both in this country and from overseas. Also in 1964, Dr. Douglas Robertson retired, having been our Consultant Physician since 1946, when he returned from war service in the R.A.F. He had worked as our Honorary Cardiologist briefly before his war service. He was succeeded by Dr. David Pyke from Kings College Hospital.

The Burns Unit, of which the Queen Mother had laid the foundation stone in the centenary year 1963, became operational eighteen months later in January 1965 with twelve beds, and on July 8th the building was formally opened by Her Royal Highness Princess Marina of Kent. She was greeted by Mr. J. H. Mitchell, Chairman of the House Committee, and welcomed in a speech by Sir Ivor Julian. Mr. Blond was unfortunately unwell at this time and unable to attend the ceremony, but his wife acting on behalf of them both handed over the building officially to the Ministry of Health. Princess Marina in a speech paying tribute to Mr. and Mrs. Blond said it was very heartening to hear of generosity on such a grand scale. She unveiled a plaque commemorating the event and then toured the area. The building itself was something of a novelty in that there was not at that time in the whole world another building which was designed entirely for the treatment of burns; it had been designed largely by John Watson and others from the

Plastic Surgery Department, and they had done a lot of research into alternative designs for such a specialised unit. Sterility was of course of paramount importance and there was the strictest discipline as to who entered the building and their procedure within it. Another novelty was that it had its own helicopter landing area beside it. Research in the Unit was made possible by the Rayne Foundation, which promised £8,000 per annum over a period of ten years for the formation of a Burns Research Team which would work in co-operation with the Research Laboratory already established. Mr. T. D. Cochrane was appointed the first Rayne Research Fellow in 1966. He had been a Marks Fellow in 1965, and was again in 1967, and he specialised in long-term preservation of skin. He was subsequently appointed Honorary Plastic Surgeon to the Guinea Pigs, which he remains to this day.

In June 1965 it had become obvious that enlargement of the Research Laboratory was necessary, and the Wolfson Foundation offered to meet the cost of building and equipping it. Owing to this enlargement, it had been decided to create the new post of Treasurer to the Trust, and Mr. T. D. Lawrence was elected to the Committee for this purpose.

In September 1965 Mr. M. D. Awty, having been Senior Registrar in the Dental Department for the previous two years, was appointed Consultant in that Department, in succession to Mr. G. E. Ryba, who retired on account of ill-health. Dr. H. B. Shaw retired during this year, and his place on the Hospital staff was taken by Dr. Bryan Christopher. Mention should also be made here of the very specialised work that Mr. John Cobbett was doing at this time on the subject of Small Blood Vessel Anastomosis, in co-operation of course with the Research Unit; it was towards the end of this year that he addressed the Winter Meeting of the British Association of Plastic Surgeons on this his specialised subject. Mr. Cobbett had been a Marks Fellow in 1963-64 and at this time was working in the Plastic Surgery Unit as a Senior Registrar. He became a Consultant Surgeon at the end of 1967.

The League of Friends should be mentioned here; founded in April 1949 it had built itself up into a formidable organisation and it had continuously benefited the Hospital in many different ways of which we shall hear mention later on. Here it is necessary to mention merely that their President was Lady Kindersley, Vice-Presidents Lady McIndoe and Mr. L. W. E. Dungey, who had been a founder member and previous President. The Chairman was Mr. P. J. Griffits and Vice-Chairman Mr. E. J. Dakin, Secretary Mrs. Hodges, Treasurer Mr. H. R. Hall and Registrar Miss M. E. Curtis. On the general committee there were a number of local people well known in the Town and Hospital, particularly including Mr. H. G. Powell, Mr. D. M. Renshaw, Mrs. Ann Standen and Miss Rosemary Wootton; their meetings were of course attended by Mr. Johns the Administrator.

On November 5th, 1965 the Hospital was honoured by a private visit from His Royal Highness Prince Philip Duke of Edinburgh, who came to inspect both the Research Laboratory and the new Burns Unit. Following the tour, refreshments were served in the Stern Hall and after a speech of thanks from Mr. Neville Blond, Prince Philip left, having spent an hour and a half in the Hospital.

Early in 1966 it was beginning to become more obvious that the Hospital Plan for the nation was not being as successful as had been hoped, and the Minister of Health Mr. Kenneth Robinson set up a committee jointly with the British Medical Association Joint Consultants Committee, six members from each side, and they were "to consider what developments in the hospital service are desirable in order to promote efficiency in the organisation of medical work". This was an example of Ministry of Health co-operation with the medical profession designed to improve the hospital services, which was both welcome and long lasting. The Committee made three Reports at various times, one in 1967, one in 1972, and a third in 1974, and because it was thought that their separate recommendations were intended to fit in with each other, they came to be known as the Cogwheel Committee. It was the second, and by no means the last, of Governmental efforts to improve the hospital services, for over the next 30 years there were to be numerous other committees, White Papers, Royal Commissions and Working Parties with the same object in view. The first Cogwheel Report defined the Committee's official opinion of the problem. One of their observations was that the development of modern scientific medicine and growth of hospital teams which had ocurred had not been accompanied by corresponding development of an appropriate administrative structure, and that the present advisory machinery was not suitable to meet modern requirements. They said also that, to date, there had been an unfortunate lack of coordination and communication between the three component groups of the National Health Service, hospitals, general practice and public health. This was of course very true, and they were perfectly right to draw attention to it, as also to their further remark that the hospital service was by far the most complex sector of medical services. In any large scale enterprise, they said, the problem of management has many facets and the hospital service is no exception. Opportunities for failure of communication abound in such situations and many clinicians fail to appreciate fully the importance of their own role in management; this Committee therefore recommended that there should be training for medical administration, and furthermore continuous post graduate training for those involved.

On the 29th March Sir Benjamin Rycroft died while still on the Hospital's staff. He had been appointed to the Hospital early in 1949 so had been with us nearly twenty years and had built up his Department from ten beds to twenty. He had established the Regional Eye Bank for south-east England at the Hospital, having been heavily involved in the introduction of corneal grafting in 1952, shortly after which he received a knighthood for this work. Assisting him he had at first Mr. Giles Romanes from 1951 to 1957, and thereafter Mr A. W. Werb. Sir Benjamin of course brought tremendous renown to the Queen Victoria Hospital. He was succeeded after an interval of a few months by Mr. Tom Casey who continued the work of corneal grafting. It was also in 1966 that Dr. Timothy Taylor from the Lingfield General Practice was appointed to the General Practitioner staff.

Early in 1967 there is more about the Memorial Research Laboratory. Sir Arthur Porritt, who was one of the Trustees, had been appointed Governor General of New Zealand and Sir Max Rayne took his place on the Committee. Professor Simonsen, who had been organising research since the Trust's foundation, left us on September 1st having resigned to become Director of the Institute of Experimental Immunology in the University of Copenhagen, after being with us for six years. He was succeeded by Professor J. R. Batchelor who had been doing similar work at Guys Hospital before coming to us. Also in November of this year the new wing of the Laboratory, which was the gift of the Wolfson Foundation, was formally opened by Sir Hedley Atkins, President of the Royal College of Surgeons. The Medical Research Council was still providing continuing financial support for the Laboratory and for Consultant Plastic Surgeons Robin Beare, John Watson, John Cobbett and Tom Cochrane, who were travelling all over the world to visit other organisations engaged in similar work, so well had the work at Queen Victoria Hospital become recognised. Mr. Cobbett also read a paper on Small Vessel Surgery in which he was specialising, at an international meeting of the American Society for Plastic Surgery. Dr. Arnold Sanderson, who had been here for several years as second in command since the opening of the Laboratory, was officially appointed as Assistant Director to Professor Batchelor. Mr. Peter Williams had become Chairman of the Hospital House Committee, and Dr. G. K. Thornton from the Forest Row General Practice had retired, being replaced by Dr. Michael Hall. The League of Friends had undertaken to build a Day Room at the end of Dewar Ward and the Hospital had undertaken to furnish it; also at this time the League of Friends were given permission to convert the reception hut on the left of the drive into a shop, which would be open every afternoon from 2.30 to 7.30 p.m. This shop has been a great success and is still functioning nearly 30 years later. In 1966 comes more news of Mr. Cobbett who achieved a world first operation of replacing a badly damaged thumb by using the patient's great toe, using of course his by now world famous microvascular surgical technique. Surgeons had been sewing back severed fingers for a year or more, and this was shortly to be followed by the operation of sewing back severed hands. All this work was helped by the tissue typing research carried out by our Research Laboratory, as later on was the operation of corneal grafting.

At the League of Friends' meeting on the 22nd January, 1968 the Chairman of the Committee, Mr. Griffits, asked the members to stand in silence in memory of Gladys, Lady Kindersley, President of the League of Friends, who had died on the 17th

January. It is impossible to exaggerate the good influence that Lady Kindersley had on the Queen Victoria Hospital; she and her husband Lord Kindersley became associated with it way back in the 1930s and had been continuously generous in many different ways, and they are very high on our list of benefactors. At the following meeting of the League in March, Mrs. Blond was elected President to succeed Lady Kindersley. Dr. B. C. Morton-Palmer retired on the 1st April, 1968, having joined the General Practitioner staff in 1937. The Annual General Meeting of the League of Friends was addressed by Peter Williams, Chairman of the Hospital House Committee, who thanked them for all they had done and pointed out that since there was no sign of the Hospital's finances improving for some time, we were therefore depending more and more on the League. By May 1968 there had been formed in London a National Association of Leagues of Hospital Friends, chaired by Lady Monckton, which of course our League joined. By 1968 the total number of National Health Service Hospitals had fallen by 300 to 2,500 but it was still felt by the Department of Health that many fewer hospitals were required. Dr. J. F. Paxton retired from our G.P. staff and also from the Lingfield Practice on health grounds, and Dr. Joan Godfrey also retired from her Felbridge Practice in October 1968, having been on the staff since February 1952. The McIndoe Memorial Lecture this year was given by one of our former Consultants Mr. Fenton Braithwaite, O.B.E.

On April 8th, 1969 the new Dewar Day Room was officially handed over by the League of Friends to the House Committee and it was named after Mr. Griffits. During the previous twelve months numerous small items had been donated by the League, including such things as television sets, cubicle curtains, trolleys, carpets, lamp shades, hairdryers, flower vases, and a number of other items. At the League's Annual General Meeting on the 19th May, Mrs. Blond's appointment as President was confirmed and they also elected as Vice-Presidents Lady McIndoe, Mr. Dungey, and Miss Helen Beale, Mr. Griffits remaining Chairman. At the next meeting of the League held in September the Committee stood in memory of the late Mr. Alfred Wagg, who had been Vice-President when the League first started; he had also been on the Hospital House Committee for very many years, and had contributed very generously to the general welfare of the Hospital.

By the middle of 1969 it was well known that Mr. Powell's National Hospital Plan was in difficulties, and every hospital wondered whether it was going to be next on the list of closures; nobody of course works their best under such conditions, and the whole hospital system throughout the country, including the Queen Victoria, entered a period of depression which was destined to last for many years. Mr. C. R. McLaughlin retired towards the end of September 1969, having been Consultant in Plastic Surgery since November 1946, and having taken particular responsibility for the Medway Towns and Canterbury. At this time also two General Practitioners were appointed to the staff, Dr. A. R. Del Mar from Forest Row and Dr. Elizabeth Robinson from the Crawley Down Practice.

From this general mood of depression there were occasional spells of relative relief. One of these came unexpectedly in November 1969, due to two separate and totally unrelated events. Firstly, the Oxford Regional Board, having considered the area for which they were responsible, decided there was not a single hospital in that area which would fulfil the necessary criteria to become a District General Hospital, and they independently decided on a policy of decentralisation. This would mean the establishment of what were to be given the name of Community Hospitals, considerably smaller, with 100–300 beds each. This decision was of considerable political importance and provoked much discussion, both in the media and in the medical profession, and relieved some of the depression. The next thing that happened, three weeks later, was a meeting of General Practitioners which was convened by Dr. Meyrick Emrys-Roberts, a General Practitioner from Walton-on-Thames and a member of the staff of his local General Practitioner hospital; this meeting in Exeter decided to form what was called the Association of General Practitioner Hospitals. Dr. Horace Swete would have been delighted, for 99 years previously he had written "it would greatly help if some central society were formed—a national association for instance for the promotion of Cottage Hospitals". A year or two before, this same Dr. Emrys-Roberts had written a letter to The Times pointing out that not all General Practitioner Hospitals were uneconomic and that in fact they formed in general an outer defence for the inner central specialised hospitals. This Association was immediately successful and Dr. Emrys-Roberts played a central role in its formation: he will go down in history as having played a major part in contributing to the general survival of such hospitals, for which we should all be very grateful to him. The Queen Victoria, which was one of the earliest Cottage Hospitals in the country, had, owing to the arrival of the Plastic Surgery Unit in 1939, grown to such an extent that in 1943 the House Committee altered its name from the Queen Victoria Cottage Hospital to the Queen Victoria Hospital, East Grinstead, so we were ineligible to join this Association. Within a few years it had some 500 or so members, and it is interesting to note that it is still in operation and very active 25 years later. But for these two almost simultaneous developments, the General Practitioner Hospitals might well have disappeared.

However, 1970 started off with a rumour circulating that the Hospital was to be re-zoned, and might be turned into a Specialist Geriatric Unit, so this period of relief did not last very long. And early in the year came the news that the House Committee was to be disbanded, not immediately, but some time in the future. In April Mr. Don Attwater, who had been nursing in the Recovery Ward where he had made a very good reputation for himself, was appointed our first male Assistant Matron. We shall hear more about him, because shortly afterwards he was appointed Matron, and subsequently Senior Nursing Officer, and had several very successful years in this position. Also in 1970 Dr. E. G. Sibley from the Forest Row Practice retired, to be replaced by Dr. O. Jones who had been House Surgeon to the General Practitioner side of the Hospital; he joined the practice in September and joined the General Practitioner staff of the Hospital at the same time. Sir Terence Ward retired from directing the Dental Department; Mr. Michael Awty became Senior Consultant in the Department in his place, and Mr. P. Banks joined the Department as Junior Consultant. The McIndoe Memorial Lecture was given this year by Mr. John Watson.

In May 1970 our Pathologist Major General Dr. Albert Sachs retired; he had been with us ever since he left the Army in 1956 so he was here for some fourteen years. He had had a distinguished military career; born in South Africa, he was one-time Honorary Physician to the late King George VI and the Queen Mother when she was Queen. In 1952 he was made a Commander of the Order of the British Empire, and a Companion of the Bath in 1955, while in 1964 he was made Commandant of the Royal Army Medical Corps. He was a much loved character, always cheerful and a very good colleague, willing to give advice and discuss patients; apparently he had unlimited time to spend with everybody. A very remarkable man and one who brought considerable distinction both to his job and to the Hospital itself. He was replaced by Dr. Peter Stevens who also came to us with a considerable personal reputation, having been in the Royal Air Force, and we shall hear more of him later.

In 1970 Dr. G. J. D. Moore joined the Lingfield Practice and was appointed to the General Practitioner staff in Dr. Paxton's place; he later went on to become Chairman of the British Leprosy Mission while maintaining his place on the Queen Victoria staff. Also in 1970 Dr. Peter Cardew left his practice in Dormansland and the staff of the Hospital; he went to Canada and joined a practice in Nova Scotia, where he stayed for ten years or so, before eventually returning to the United Kingdom. He was replaced shortly afterwards by Dr. A. J. Robertson (a nephew of Dr. Douglas Robertson, our recent Consultant Cardiologist and General Physician) who joined the Lingfield Practice about this time, and who now works one day a week in our Anaesthetic Department as a Hospital Practitioner.

On August 3rd, 1970 the Research Trust, and indeed the Hospital also, sustained a devastating blow with the death of Mr. Neville Blond; he had been Chairman of the Trustees since 1959 and had interested himself in all aspects of their work; he had also been one of the most generous benefactors of this Hospital in all its history, and not only this Hospital but very many other charities and individuals have cause to remember his generosity, including the Royal College of Surgeons, who recognised their gratitude by electing him an Honorary Fellow of the College in 1969; he died knowing that the Laboratory which he had been instrumental in founding in 1961, was flourishing. At the following meeting of the Trustees his widow Mrs. Elaine Blond was unanimously elected to take his place as Chairman, and his son Mr. Peter Blond was elected as an extra

Financial Adviser to deal particularly with the Charity Commissioners. Also in this year the Laboratory was enlarged again; Mrs. Susman, Elaine Blond's daughter by a previous marriage, and her husband gave a generous donation from which it was possible to build an expansion to the Animal House. The Laboratory at this time was doing research mainly in the field of tissue typing, useful of course to all kinds of replacement surgery, kidneys, livers, hearts, and in the field of corneal grafting.

Early in 1971 Don Attwater, the Acting Matron, became Senior Nursing Officer, Miss Duncombe the Matron having left in January, so this was the point at which the title "Matron" disappeared. Many people thought and some still do think that this should never have happened and they may well be right, but it was in fact inevitable. Round about this time there was a worldwide movement against discipline of all kinds; freedom to do what one wanted was all that mattered, and Matrons, whatever else they were, were firm disciplinarians, some possibly too firm. One of their jobs in most hospitals was what was known as "Matron's Round" which took place every morning and took precedence over everything else in the hospital. She made a tour of the entire hospital every morning, which sometimes took an hour or so, and some may have thought it a waste of time—perhaps possibly it sometimes was—but at the end of it she knew exactly what was happening in every nook and cranny of the hospital and why. She knew why the patient in bed number two was taking so long to recover, and that there was no soap in the Domestic Staff Washroom. It was her job to keep the whole place running smoothly and happily, and most Matrons did this, but with the prevailing worldwide obsession they did not have a chance and had to go. Round about the same time Mr. Johns, who had been Secretary for several years, changed his title to that of "Administrator". These changes came about largely as a result of the second Cogwheel Report which had recommended that hospitals' administrators should learn to communicate with other branches of the Health Service and with other hospitals; the Committee also mentioned that they were conscious of the impending reorganisation of the National Health Service, which was to come about in the next year or two.

Sadly about this time the Marks Fellowships, which had been

started in 1947, came to an end. This scheme had been outstandingly successful not only for the work of the Hospital, but in that no fewer than 17 of the 22 holders over the years went on from the Queen Victoria to become Consultant Plastic Surgeons elsewhere. One became a successful E.N.T. Surgeon and four actually stayed on here and were appointed Consultants, as follows:—John Watson, the first to be appointed in 1947; John Cobbett, who held his Fellowship for two years in 1963 and 1964; Tom Cochrane, who also held his Fellowship for two years in 1965 and 1967, and John Bennett, appointed in 1969. Each of these made his own individual contribution to the work of the Hospital and we shall hear more about them all later.

Meanwhile the Research Laboratory was being very successful and another Research Fellowship in Burns was appointed. Dr. Pamela Hinton was already internationally known for her work in this field and she took up her duties in February 1972. The South East Regional Hospital Board agreed to finance her salary for a period of three years; this was of some importance as it was the first time any of our Research appointments was financed from the Department of Health funds. Unfortunately though Dr. Hinton died after a short illness in Kings College Hospital after only a year in her appointment. Her death was a great loss to Burns Research.

Another matter which may be mentioned at this point is a reminder of Richard Hillary's publication of a book called 'The Last Enemy' in 1942. In it he talked frequently about the Queen Victoria Hospital; he was treated here and was largely cured of his injuries, but later in the War went back to flying and was subsequently killed in an aircrash. Soon after his death his family set up a Trust to establish funds which could be used to encourage creative and imaginative writing. This book had become one of the most popular books of the Second World War and in 1972 this family Trust was taken over by Trinity College Oxford, who managed it so successfully that it flourished and we will hear more about it later on.

Moving on to October 1973, there was another sad loss to the Hospital when our Surgeon Sir Edward Muir died suddenly and unexpectedly. Appointed to the staff of Kings College Hospital before the War, he had left to do service in the

R.A.M.C. for five years and then returned to Kings. He was appointed to the Queen Victoria Hospital in 1946 and had served us very well for 27 years. He soon built himself up a very good reputation as a highly skilled surgeon, and in 1954 he was appointed Surgeon to the Royal Household and ten years later, in 1964, Surgeon to Her Majesty the Queen, and was knighted in 1970. He had been on the Council of the Royal College of Surgeons and had been appointed Vice-President in 1972 and became President in 1973, so he did in fact die while President of the Royal College. One of his Obituary Notices remarked that the Queen Victoria Hospital had had a number of great men on its staff but Edward Muir was among its greatest. Incidentally it is quite a remarkable thing that such a small country hospital should have had on its staff one President, Edward Muir, and also Archie McIndoe who some years before had been Vice-President of the College. It may be mentioned here that Mr. Muir's colleague John Peel, also from Kings College Hospital, had been appointed to the Queen Victoria soon after the War ended and was an outstanding member of our staff; he had been our Consultant Obstetrician and Gynae-cologist and stayed with us for many years. He was appointed Surgeon Gynaecologist to Her Majesty the Queen. He also was knighted and became President of the Royal College of Obste-tricians and Gynaecologists, so we had on our staff two Presidents and one Vice-President of Royal Colleges. Quite a remarkable trio.

In March 1973 Dr. David Bainbridge had joined Dr. Collin's practice in the town; he was shortly afterwards appointed as a Hospital Practitioner in General Surgery, a post which he currently holds 22 years later. Percy Jayes retired at the end of 1973 having completed 33 years with us; he had been ap-pointed early in the War as Resident Surgical Officer and he was appointed Consultant Plastic Surgeon on the 5th July, 1948 along with Mr. Fenton Braithwaite, Mr. C. R. McLaughlin and Mr. F. T. Moore. Percy Jayes made himself a popular member of the staff and was commemorated by having the hut in which he lived called after him. The Resident Medical Officers for many years to come lived in what came to be familiarly known as Percy Lodge. He had also been Consultant Plastic Surgeon at St. Bartholomews Hospital in London. At the end of 1973 Dr. Michael Hall from the Forest Row practice resigned from his appointment on the staff of the Queen Victoria, and was replaced by Dr. D. A. Martin. Early in 1974 sadly there occurred the death at the age of 39 years of Dr. David Godwin, a partner in the Judges Close practice; he died on March 2nd having been ill for several months with a cerebral tumour. He had joined the staff in 1963 so had had approximately ten years with us. He was replaced by Dr. R. J. R. Dunstan.

1974 was quite an eventful year one way and another; first of all we welcomed back Lord Porritt from his session as the Governor of New Zealand and he rejoined the Research Laboratory Trust Committee. About the same time Mrs. Simone Prendergast—Mrs. Blond's daughter—who had been a member of the Committee for some time became one of the Trustees of this body. It was about this time that the Medical Research Council arranged a special Conference given by our Research Laboratory which was very well attended by scientific researchers from all over the country. The Director of the Unit at this time was Professor Richard Batchelor, with his Deputy Dr. Arnold Sanderson, and under these two the Laboratory had achieved the position of being accepted as one of the foremost Research Centres for transplantation biology in the world.

Early in the year the Queen Victoria Hospital's own Medical Council set up a Working Party to consider development of the Hospital. It seems that the reorganisation which had taken place in 1973 had not been as successful as had been hoped, and the Working Party amongst other things discussed what was described as the new Integrated Health Service which was to come into force on the 1st April. Chairman of this Committee was Mr. P. Banks from the Dental Department. One of the big changes recommended by the Ministry of Health Integrated Health Service was that our House Committee in common with other House Committees all over the country was to come to an end on the 1st April, 1974; they had managed the Hospital since 1888 and had managed it extremely well as has been seen, so this was a big blow. This Working Party amongst other things recommended an extra 25 male beds on the Plastic Surgery side and an extra fifteen beds on the General Practitioner side plus an enlargement of the Outpatient facilities. The Outpatients Department was indeed enlarged but the extra beds never materialised. The Working Party also pointed out the mutual advantages to the two sides of the Hospital of working together. The local public benefited from having far better supporting services such as pathology and radiology than most G. P. hospitals, but there were also advantages on the Plastic side in that their technicians, nurses, and anaesthetists whose work was so highly specialised occasionally had the advantage that they could provided services for the associated General Practitioner Hospital with its more broadly based needs.

The Working Party also recommended expansion of the X-ray Department, with a third X-ray theatre with changing rooms, which they said was a high priority. They mentioned also the value of the Casualty Department both to the public for general emergencies and its value as an assessment area for acute burns and plastic surgery admissions, thus stressing its value to both sides of the Hospital. And they recommended an increase in the establishment of Consultant Plastic Surgeons to a minimum of six full-time staff over the next few years. All these enlargements and improvements would of course involve quite a considerable amount of new building and modification of the existing buildings; and further accommodation for the extra nurses would also be required.

Among other important events during 1974, there was the retirement of Aunt Agatha (Mrs. Clemetson) from her appointment as Editor of the Kent and Sussex Courier which she had held for many years; it was of course she who founded the Peanut Club, and altogether over the years she had been a great benefactor to, and a very popular member of, the community and the Hospital. Another retirement during this year was that of Dr. Russell M. Davies, our Chief Anaesthetist since 1959. He had played a major part in the establishment of anaesthetic research and had instituted the Recovery Ward—one of the first in the country at that time—and we owe him our thanks for his devoted work as a Trustee of the Research Laboratory; he sat on most of the Hospital committees at various times, and for a considerable time also he was our representative on the Tunbridge Wells Health Authority's Executive Committee, so he was a very busy worker for, and benefactor of, the Queen Victoria. He was also Chief Liaison Officer to the Guinea Pig Club and was energetic in helping Guinea Pigs to re-establish themselves in business

233

and private life.

It was also in this year that Sir Terence Ward, formerly in charge of our Dental Department, gave the annual McIndoe Memorial Lecture. Another thing that should be mentioned here was that Group Captain Douglas Bader conducted a B.B.C. Charitable Appeal for the Laboratory which was very successful in raising several thousand pounds. And towards the end of the year Dr. A. C. Sommerville retired from the General Practitioner staff; he had played a large part in the successful running of the Hospital as a dual organisation during the War. In November 1974, Dr. H. Patel was appointed Consultant Anaesthetist to the Hospital and at the same time in December Mr. F. T. Moore O.B.E. resigned his appointment as a Consultant Surgeon, having been in that position and having held an appointment also to Kings College Hospital for more than twenty years.

On the 1st January, 1975, Dr. Peter Harborow was appointed to the General Practitioner staff; he was to replace Dr. E. J. Dennison who retired in 1977.

The League of Friends had recently extended its voluntary services to include both St. Leonards Hospital, the geriatric establishment in Railway Approach, and also Oakleigh our convalescent annexe in Lewes Road. As in previous years they gave a Christmas present to each patient in both hospitals, and in addition birthday gifts were made to all geriatric patients and Easter eggs to every child in the Peanut Ward. They also collect used stamps from letters received at the Hospital and sell them to various charities and receive additional income towards their expenses from their sale. They assist in the staffing of the Outpatients Reception Office and keep the Hospital well supplied with flower arrangements; magazines are distributed and read to patients and they also visit patients. All these services have been largely in the charge of Mrs. Ann Standen, Henry Standen's wife, a loyal and faithful friend of the Hospital, she is still doing most of these things in 1995. The Hospital Shop has also been a great success; it is open daily from 2 p.m. till 7.30 p.m. including Sundays for the sale of most essentials for patients, and all profits go to the League funds which during the last year had amounted to £2,000. It might perhaps be mentioned that membership of the League consists mostly of local people but there are also grateful patients from over a very wide area who become members of the League when they leave. At this time there is the first mention that the League intended to provide a radio service for the patients. Early in December there was the usual official handing over of Christmas gifts to every patient by Mr. Peter Griffits the Chairman. Don Attwater thanked them on behalf of the nursing staff and Anaesthetist Dr. Hale Enderby thanked them on behalf of the medical staff. Mr. Johns, the Administrator, officially received the gifts and in his speech he referred to the Community Health Council, thanking them for their help, but, he said, "the close personal contacts with the Hospital have disappeared with reorganisation. It is difficult for Health Council members to take such a personal interest in individual hospitals as the former Management Committees did. Fortunately, however, this Hospital has never wanted for friends and I do not know how we would have managed to survive without the support of our League Friends".

In June 1975 Mr. J. P. Bennett, who had been a Marks Fellow in 1969, was appointed as a Consultant Plastic Surgeon in succession to Mr. F. T. Moore. Another retirement towards the end of the year was that of General Practitioner Dr. Jones from the Forest Row practice, and Dr. Hamish Aitken was appointed to the Hospital staff in his place.

The most important event in 1976 was the appointment on the 19th May of the Royal Commission, chaired by Sir Alec Merrison, "to consider both in the interests of patients and those who work in the National Health Service the best use and management of the financial and manpower resources of the National Health Service". They started off by noting that they had been appointed at a time when there was widespread concern about the National Health Service. There had been a complete reorganisation of the Service throughout the United Kingdom in 1973 and 1974, which few had accepted as an unqualified success. The Service had suffered a number of industrial disputes, accompanied in some cases by a partial withdrawal of labour by ambulance men and ancilliary staff and some hospital doctors and dentists, and in addition to all this the Service was of course suffering from the country's generally chill economic climate in the 1970s. This Commission had 35 meetings altogether including five large conferences and they visited each of the four constituent parts of the United Kingdom. They took oral evidence in Edinburgh, Cardiff, and Belfast as well as London, and they also travelled to and held discussions with officials and individuals in Canada, the U.S.A., West Germany, France, Holland, Sweden, Denmark, Yugoslavia and the U.S.S.R. Not surprisingly all this took a little time and their final Report was not issued until the middle of 1979. The findings were then, however, very interesting and worth reporting at this juncture. They confirmed of course that recently the Health Service in general had been under-financed, and this was why all workers in the Service had for the last few years received such small pay increases. They stated also that in their opinion the Health Service was so vast an organisation that its finances were bound to be complex. "There is no quick answer to this", they said, "that will produce immediate results, but the position must be watched carefully and constantly in the future". At the same time however they did point out that the Service had in its life-time achieved a great deal, that it still embodied aspirations and ideals of great value, and that further advances would only be brought about by constant application and vigilance.

One of their minor recommendations was that all hospitals should provide explanatory booklets for the patients before they came into hospital—this the Queen Victoria Hospital did quickly. They went on to say that although they were quite satisfied with the general approach to providing specialist services, they had no doubts that more flexibility was plainly required. There was still dispute over the best use of the many small hospitals which were not part of the general hospital system. It was clear, they thought, that the community hospital approach was not at that time acceptable, and they were relieved to hear that the Ministry of Health was rethinking its present policies. They thought there was plenty of room for experiment in this as in so many other parts of the Service and they would deplore too rigid an approach. They also recommended that the role of Hospital Administrator at unit level should be expanded, and that there should be one management level only between regions and units. This meant of course that the Tunbridge Wells Health Authority along with others would disappear, as it eventually did in April 1994.

Towards the end of 1976 there was a reorganisation of the Burns Centre. Mr. John Bennett agreed to take over complete charge of all patients admitted to the Unit; this was to prove most helpful in providing a greater measure of continuity of both treatment and research in the face of inevitable changes in junior staff. The McIndoe Memorial Lecture this year was given by our former Chief Anaesthetist, Dr. Russell M. Davies. Dr Ingrid Fisher was appointed to the General Practitioner staff on the 1st October.

It was in 1977 that the Ministry of Health, evidently not satisfied with the slow progress of the Royal Commission, produced its own White Paper entitled 'The Way Forward' putting forward their own current views on hospital management. In it they proposed that small local hospitals would in future be called Community Hospitals, thus in effect admitting that the National Hospital Plan had been abandoned. This was a relief to hospitals generally, and not least to the Queen Victoria. In February the Queen Mother, who had been Patron of the Hospital since shortly after the War ended, had extended her patronage specifically to the Research Laboratory, so that it would now have its own patron separately from the Hospital. This would of course assist them in their efforts to become independent of the National Health Service, towards which end they had been successfully building up their own capital investments; they had doubts apparently then as to the Hospital's future and wanted to survive if necessary independently on their own. There was much reference at this time to the use being made of our tissue typing facilities by hospitals and other organisations all over the country; in this respect there was special mention of the Kidney Transplant Unit at Guys Hospital, the Liver Unit at Kings College Hospital, and the Institute of Neurology in Queens Square, London, with their studies for multiple sclerosis. In June 1977 the third International Corneo Plastic Congress organised by Mr. Tom Casey was held at the Festival Hall. It was opened by Lord Porritt and Papers were presented by our own Professor Batchelor, Mr. Robin Beare, Mr. J. Bowen, a former Burns Research Fellow, Mr. Tom Cochrane, Mr. A. Werb, and Mr. Michael Awty from our Dental Department. During that year also there was an International Congress of Ophthalmology held in Japan, at which Papers were given on Corneal Graft Rejection by Mr. Casey, Dr. T. Gibbs and Professor Batchelor. It was during this year that Sir Max Rayne was honoured by becoming Lord Rayne; and also Lady McIndoe joined the Committee of the Research Trust. John Watson had resigned from the National Health Service but remained Secretary to the Trust. On the 1st March, 1977, Don Attwater became a Grade 1 Senior Nursing Officer. And mention should be made here of the retirement of a very popular member of staff—Mrs. Gladys King, after 27 years working as a nurse at the Hospital. She was a sister of ex-Matron Caroline Hall and Cherry Hall who had worked here during the War. These three were part of a family of nine girls, all in the nursing profession. Her constantly smiling cheerful face would be sadly missed from the Hospital.

The League of Friends at this time were busy arranging the extension to the Physiotherapy Department, which was to cost some £19,000 to £20,000. Over the years the League has accumulated quite a lot of capital from bequests. At their Annual General Meeting in the summer the Chairman made special mention of Mr. Peter Bateman who had been in charge of the League's publicity for some years; he had maintained excellent contacts with the Press and helped the League generally. At the end of the year Dr. E. J. Dennison retired from the General Practitioner staff having been elected in September 1938, so having completed some 39 years on the staff. He was elected an Honorary Life Member of the staff by the Tunbridge Wells Health Authority at the request of our own Medical Council, in recognition of having written the Hospital's history.

In May 1978, the League of Friends deleted St. Leonards Hospital from their title; there had been talk of its closure for some months, and this marked its final closing down. During 1977 the League had given gifts to both Queen Victoria and St. Leonards Hospitals amounting to over £20,000. They also announced that the former hospital canteen was closing because of heavy running costs but would soon re-open after some very necessary redecoration as a new venture called the Coffee Lounge; this is the Coffee Lounge which is still in being in 1995 and it is a very popular part of the Hospital amenities. It was in 1978 also that Mr. Frank Summers, who had been our Pharmacist for some years, left, and his place was taken by Mr. Ian Smith.

In October 1978 the first Study Course in Plastic Surgery was held at the Hospital. This Course had originally been proposed by Mr. J. P. Bennett and in fact turned out to be a far reaching proposal. Research and clinical applications in the treatment of burns were flourishing so extensively at this time, and Mr. Bennett realised that teaching was also important, so he suggested it should be developed on an international scale, to encourage the dissemination of knowledge between young surgeons from all over the world. It was decided that up to 40 students might attend these Courses, the duration of which would be six days, and that a Course would be held annually. It had originally been thought that the Lecture Theatre of the American Wing would be adequate for the purposes of this Course, but it had in fact needed redecoration, the installation of modern equipment for slide presentation etc., and an examination couch. It was Mr. Bennett who had also suggested the foundation of a Museum. The Queen Victoria Hospital had evolved, he said, out of personalities and achievement, and there was no adequate record of this. A display of photographs, instruments, books and anything relating to the people who had contributed to the Hospital, should be made a focal point to show visitors. This he thought should be tackled as a matter of some urgency, before any more material could be lost or discarded, and would become a tangible part of our tradition. This suggestion was made in 1978 but in fact it took a little time to arrange and the Museum was eventually opened in 1994, as we shall see.

We are fortunate in having a list of the Consultant Staff in 1978. Some of their dates of appointment and retirement are not available, owing to the Hospital Authorities having had an official policy of destroying records during the 1970s and 1980s. "Retain for two years—then destroy" is written on a few that did survive, and in spite of multiple and exhaustive searches, the House and Management Committee Minute Books for the period 1963 to 1983 are simply not available. But this list was one of the survivors:—

| | |
|---|---|
| *General Surgery:* | L. T. Cotton. |
| *General Medicine:* | D. A. Pyke. |
| *Plastic Surgery:* | R. L. B. Beare, J. P. Bennett, |
| | J. R. Bowen, J. R. Cobbett, |
| | T. D. Cochrane. |

| | |
|---|---|
| *Gynaecology & Obstetrics:* | J. G. Hill, J. M. Brudenell, |
| *Orthopaedics:* | D. A. Reynolds, K. W. R. Tuson. |
| *Ear, Nose & Throat:* | J. B. Musgrove. |
| *Ophthalmology:* | H. Cheng. |
| *Corneo-plastic Surgery:* | T. A. Casey. |
| *Dental Surgery:* | D. E. Poswillo, M. D. Awty, |
| | P. Banks, H. G. Lewis. |
| *Anaesthetics:* | A. W. Edridge, G. E. H. Enderby, |
| | J. M. Brown, H. Patel. |
| *Dermatology:* | P. A. J. Smith. |
| *Geriatrics:* | C. W. J. Ussher. |
| *Chest Diseases:* | H. C. May. |
| *Radiology:* | W. Campbell. |
| *Pathology:* | P. J. Stevens. |
| *Psychiatry:* | J. A. Stewart. |

It is interesting to compare this list with the position in 1963; only seven names out of the original 30 are the same, one General Surgeon, one Plastic Surgeon, two Anaesthetists, the Radiologist, the E.N.T. Surgeon, and the Dermatologist. Two new Specialities have been introduced, Corneo-plastic Surgery and Geriatrics. And three, Paediatrics, Urology, and Physical Medicine, have disappeared, hopefully only temporarily. The official count of beds is given as 266, down by 50 since 1963, owing to the closure of Oakleigh.

At the end of the year Professor Richard Batchelor resigned from his position as Director of the Research Laboratory, to take up a new post at the Hammersmith Hospital. He was replaced on January 1st, 1979 by Professor Page Faulk who was also elected Honorary Professor of Transplantation, which meant that skin grafting research at the Burns Unit at the Hospital would now come under his charge, and would be expected to go ahead steadily. It was about then the Research Trust Committee elected two further members to join them; one was Mr. Tom Casey, our Ophthalmological Corneal Grafting Surgeon, and the other was the President ex-officio of the Royal College of Surgeons.

Work on an extension to the Physiotherapy Department began in March 1979, Also in March, Mr. Dakin, Deputy Chairman of the League of Friends, attended a ceremony to receive a

The McIndoe Memorial Chair

Don Attwater
Nurse – Sister – Matron 1954-1971
Senior Nursing Officer 1971-1982
Director of Nursing 1982-1987

Dr. Christopher Sommerville
General Practitioner 1936-1974

Dr. Russell M. Davies
Consultant Anaesthetist 1940-1974

certificate on behalf of the League to celebrate their 30 years' membership of the National Leagues of Friends and it was decided that the certificate should be framed and hung in the Coffee Lounge, which incidentally was proving to be a great success, having made a profit of £1,000 during the previous year. At the League's Annual General Meeting Mrs. Leach was elected to be the new Secretary, and we hear at the end of the year that the League has given during the year gifts worth altogether £14,500 to the Hospital.

The second East Grinstead Study Course in Plastic Surgery took place in October 1979, and it was reported that 26 doctors from ten different countries attended it. The Course had been made possible by a grant from the Marks & Spencer Charitable Trust.

The Annual Reunion Weekend of the Guinea Pig Club took place as usual at the end of September, and it was marked this year by a special ceremony of the unveiling of a commemorative plaque to hang on the wall of Ward Three where the Guinea Pig Club had originally been born in 1941, 38 years previously. This plaque was unveiled by our former Anaesthetist Dr. Russell Davies.

In November the Royal Commission which had been set up three years earlier reported. Mrs. Thatcher had become Prime Minister in May, and she lost no time in visiting the Department of Health & Social Security, as there was much to do in the Health Service before all its resources could be used more efficiently. This visit of hers, she reckoned, planted seeds that later grew into the Griffiths Report on N.H.S. management, and later still to the internal market reforms of the Health Service which came into being in 1990.

On March 10th, 1980 the Physiotherapy extension was opened by Lady McLeod, who was Chairman of the National Association of Leagues of Hospital Friends; and some 70 people were present including members of the League, Joe Dakin, Lady McIndoe, Mrs. Blond, and Mr Griffits their Chairman, and the building was received on behalf of the Hospital by Mr. John Bennett and Miss Rosemary Wootton, the Superintendent of the Department. This was the second time the Physiotherapy Department had been expanded, the first one being in 1960, and that also had been paid for by the League of Friends. Lady

McLeod unveiled a plaque commemorating the event. Among other events that took place during 1980, John Watson retired from being Secretary to the Research Trust and handed over this position to Mr. John Bennett, although he remained as a Trustee for several years. Edna Storey retired in June from the X-ray Department, in which she had been Senior Radiographer for 23 years; she was another popular figure who had contributed much to the work on both sides of the Hospital since she joined the staff in 1957. She was replaced by Miss Janet Rhodes. And in December 1980, it was decided to sell the old Nurses' Homes —Australia House, Engalee, and Warrenside—in order to build a purpose built Nurses' Home within the Hospital grounds. As it seemed unlikely that Oakleigh would ever re-open, it was decided that it too should be sold and the money put towards the Nurses' Home.

In January 1981 the Sector Planning Group held a meeting to discuss several important planning projects under discussion at the time, perhaps the most important of which was the provision of a new Day Hospital; Dr. Ussher had recently stressed his need for this and Dr. Hunter reminded the meeting of its urgency because a total of 69 geriatric beds had been lost since the closure of St. Leonards and Oakleigh. Another important proposal was to install a new main kitchen together with dining room and staff rest room facilities. Lady McIndoe made a most successful B.B.C. Appeal for funds for the Laboratory, and Marks & Spencer gave a fashion show, while Mrs. Standen and colleagues continued their successful efforts in raising money locally.

On 1st January Dr. Anthony Enskat from the Judges Close practice was elected to the General Practitioner staff. At the January meeting of the League of Friends it was mentioned that Mr. Jack Mitchell had recently died; he had been Senior Partner of Messrs. Turner Rudge & Turner, and he had given nearly 40 years of voluntary service to the Hospital; he had been Chairman of the House Committee for many years, including the year 1963 our centenary year. He would be remembered as one of the most keen and efficient workers for the Hospital we had ever had. One of the League's future projects was to be the provision of new changing rooms for the American Wing theatre staff at a cost of some £13,000. Mr. John Bennett also

242

spoke at this meeting, and one interesting thing that he recalled was that his senior colleague, Consultant Plastic Surgeon Mr. Robin Beare who had recently retired had been the last Surgeon actually to have had contact with and worked with Sir Archibald. Mr. Beare had joined the staff as early as 1957 and so had been with us for some 24 years ,during which time he had also had the appointment of Consultant Plastic Surgeon to St. Marys Hospital, Paddington. Mr. Bennett mentioned again the possibility of assembling a Museum at some time in the future, and referring to the economic state of the Hospital, he said it could in no way afford the amenities it had without the help of the League and thanked them for their continued support.

In May 1981 a very popular member of the staff, our Maintenance Foreman Mr. James Draper, retired—he had been working for the Hospital for 35 years, as over the years have so many other members of staff in various Departments. In June Miss Frankie Wilde, secretary to the Pathology Department, retired, having been here very nearly 25 years. She had been a most popular member of the staff who had contributed much to the efficiency and pleasant atmosphere of the Pathology Department. Together with her two bosses, initially Dr. Sachs and subsequently Dr. Stevens, she worked, as did Dr. Campbell and his staff in the X-ray Department, for both sides of the Hospital.

It cannot be too strongly stressed that these supporting services, Radiology and Pathology, plus Physiotherapy, Outpatients, Casualty, Occupational Therapy, Speech Therapy, Kitchens, Catering, and Maintenance Departments together provide the operational strength that keeps the Hospital going, and between them keep the other two Departments, General Practitioners and Plastic Surgeons, working happily together, as they do; how fortunate we have always been in the strong support they have given us.

Also in June occurred the death of another great benefactor to the Hospital, Dr. Christopher Sommerville; he had come to East Grinstead in 1936 and retired in 1974, making him one of the longest serving members ever of the staff. Unable for health reasons to join the Services, he remained in practice in East Grinstead throughout the Second World War; this was a very busy time for all those like him who were also looking after the patients of younger colleagues who had been called into the Services in addition to his own practice. His Obituary Notice in the British Medical Journal had the following to say—"He also fought energetically for the Queen Victoria Hospital's survival as the local Cottage Hospital against an attempted takeover by the Emergency Medical Service as a major Burns Unit. Happily both survive today in amity, thanks to his efforts". A word of explanation about this seems necessary. It should be noted that in 1939 when Mr. McIndoe arrived to take over the Hospital, there had been some misgivings in the minds of the House Committee as to what precisely this meant, and these misgivings were in no way reduced when early on the Ministry decided that they wanted the Children's Ward as an Operating Theatre. This meant that local children needing hospital admission had either to be admitted to adult wards or sent elsewhere, which was inconvenient to say the least, but was accepted by the House Committee as a necessity. But when further requests were made for further beds it was Dr. Sommerville who cried "Enough"; he strongly supported the House Committee in refusing to hand over any more beds and this was eventually accepted by the Ministry. Had this not happened, local resentment at the taking over of any more of the Hospital by the Plastic Surgery Unit would have been so great that it would have been irretrievable and the present happy relationship between the two sides of the Hospital and the public would never have come into being. Mr. McIndoe, as he then was, knew what he was doing when at this point early in the War, he made a speech at a public meeting asking the local people to accept him and his Unit and to invite his mobile patients into their homes and do their best to make them welcome and be generally friendly. This the local people did willingly and very successfully and the whole Hospital has benefited from it ever since. The local people have much to thank Chris Sommerville for. He had also served for 25 years as Coroner for East Sussex and some of his cases attracted national attention. He was a great personality and had undoubtedly done more than any other General Practitioner before him or since for the Hospital. Donations to the League of Friends from his friends and family in memory of his life, amounted to £300, and Mrs. Sommerville requested that this money should be used for the Peanut Ward; it was agreed that a cot be purchased and it would be called the Sommerville Cot. Another General Practitioner who had done a lot for the Hospital was Dr. J. O. Collin who retired during this year. He had been Chairman of the Medical Council for some years, and always supported the cause of the General side whenever necessary. His place on the staff was taken by Dr. J. J. Vevers who had joined his Practice the previous year.

In September 1981 came the weekend celebration of the 40th anniversary of the founding of the Guinea Pig Club, rather a special occasion; it is worth noting at this point that out of some 900 of the original members of the Club, 170 of them were Canadians. The Toronto Sun newspaper reported that 30 of the Canadian Guinea Pigs, led by their Surgeon Mr. Ross Tilley, who had been in charge of the Canadian Wing of the Hospital during the latter years of the War, had attended this celebration, and they understood that the Canadian Government had paid for their flight and made all the arrangements. The Weekend was also marked by having a Spitfire fighter plane, one of the great symbols of World War Two, standing proudly in the forecourt of the Felbridge Hotel; it had a 24 hour guard placed on it by the local ATC Cadets. After the trauma they had all suffered, the Guinea Pigs retained a strong spirit of comradeship; their common experience of suffering severe burns, and then undergoing restorative surgery at the brilliant hands of pioneer Plastic Surgeon Sir Archibald McIndoe, created a bond which still does not weaken. The Guest of Honour at the Annual Dinner this year was Lord Porritt, who spoke of the wonderful work being done by the Club in finding jobs and generally giving relief to Guinea Pigs in many practical ways. The Weekend ended with the Club hanging a portrait of Mrs. Blond in the Boardroom of the Burns Research Unit alongside that of her husband. A packed gathering of Guinea Pigs was told by Mr. John Bennett that Mrs. Blond was one of the greatest benefactors of the Hospital of all time, and incidentally of the medical profession generally. Lord Porritt recalled that when the Laboratory opened it had been named the Blond McIndoe Research Centre and that Mr. Neville Blond had been its first Chairman, being succeeded on his death by his wife. Mrs. Blond herself was of course present and thanked the Trustees and the staff for their presentation of her portrait and for their achievement generally, singling out Mr. J. E. (Blackie) Blacksell, who was the Resettlement Officer of the Club, for his part in arranging the gift. During 1982 major changes took place in the layout of the Hospital. For some years the Outpatient Department had been grossly overcrowded, while at the same time there were bed vacancies in McIndoe and Kelsey Fry Wards, which were not being fully used. This latter surprising situation had arisen in many other hospitals, and was due to a number of causes. Traditionally, hospitals have expanded and multiplied to keep up with the increase in population. Between 1963 and 1982 the Census figures showed a National average of some 6% increase in population, while the figure for East Grinstead was around 30%, several big estates having been built during these years. So the Queen Victoria might well have needed many more beds during this time, as was indeed recommended by our own Working Party as recently as 1974.

But other factors were at work. Firstly, superb pharmaceutical and clinical research had led to Keyhole Surgery, Day Surgery and Day Centres, dramatically changing the treatment of common surgical conditions such as hernias and cataracts; in 1963, patients with either of these conditions spent two weeks in bed recovering from their operations; today both operations are being carried out as day cases, and the same tendency applies to many other conditions. Add to this the proliferation of Hospices, Rest Homes, Private Hospitals, Community Care, Home visiting and Community Physiotherapy, and it easy to see how overcrowding due to extra population is counterbalanced by these modern innovations, resulting in more patients being treated more quickly in fewer beds.

These two problems, overcrowding in Outpatients and empty beds in some wards, were solved when it became known that the Tunbridge Wells District Management Team had decided to convert Wards Three and Four, the eye wards, to a 20-place Geriatric Day Hospital, at an estimated cost of £75,000. The eye patients were to be reaccommodated, together with eye outpatients, in McIndoe Ward, which thus became the Eye Department; the few Plastic Surgery patients from McIndoe Ward were moved to Kelsey Fry, as were also the Plastic Surgery outpatients, so both these wards were now full and the original Outpatient

Department considerably less crowded. These changes resulted in a net decrease of some 30 beds officially available, which taken together with the loss of 50 beds from the closure of Oakleigh, brought the total number of beds available at the Queen Victoria down to 236.

The new Geriatric Day Hospital was to be under the charge of Dr. C. W. J. Ussher and could give a full day hospital service for up to 50 patients a week. Physiotherapy, Occupational Therapy, Speech Therapy, Chiropody, Social Services, would all be available, as well as Hairdressing, Catering and Recreational facilities. Another change at this time was that what used to be called the Dental Department, but is now known as the Maxillo-Facial Unit, was upgraded and expanded to accommodate Maxillo-Facial surgery, and now covered double the area that it used to. The completed new building was officially handed over to the Hospital Authority on January 19th.

The other major event in this year was the retirement of Dr. William Campbell from the X-ray Department at the age of 65. He had joined the Hospital early in 1947, and had run the Department very successfully for 35 years, so it was a matter of great regret when he announced his retirement. He was the first full time Radiologist the Hospital had ever had, and he brought the Unit into widespread renown, not only by his work for the local population, but also in dealing with facial injury cases from the whole of the South East region. He became an acknowledged authority in this field in which he published books and Papers. Everybody was delighted to hear that he was to remain as Honorary Consultant to the Hospital. In accordance with the Hospital's usual custom on these occasions, he was given a farewell party, which a large number of his colleagues attended. He was succeeded by Dr. N. B. Bowley. Mrs. Elaine Blond received a well deserved O.B.E. in the Birthday Honours List.

In July Professor Faulk gave up his Directorship of the Research Unit to take up an appointment at the Immunology Department at the University of Nice. The period of his Directorship had been very fruitful, especially his investigation of aspects of maternal-foetal relationship, and his work has since had clinical applications in many fields including leukemia and breast cancer. He was succeeded as Director by Professor John Fabre who took up his post in July; he had worked in the Blond

Centre in 1973 and 1974 and then moved to the University of Oxford for the next eight years where he worked in the Department of Biochemistry at the Radcliffe Hospital.

Also in July the Canadian Wing of the Guinea Pig Club held a reunion in Calgary, and this was attended by the Chief Guinea Pig Tom Gleave C.B.E., and his wife, who met some 35 Canadian members of the Club, including of course Mr. and Mrs. Ross Tilley. A rather special feature of the Guinea Pigs' Weekend at the end of September this year was that it was attended by some of the men who had been wounded in the recent Falklands War. Don Attwater became Director of Nursing in September.

The year 1983 started off with an M.B.E. in the New Year Honours List for one of the General Practitioner staff. Dr. Peter Steel had joined his father Dr. C. R. Steel in practice at Hartfield and had worked at the Hospital since 1955. This was the first and only time in our history that any member of the G.P. staff had been so honoured. He claims to have received it "just for being a General Practitioner", for he knows of no other reason for it.

On 23rd January, Henry Standen died. He was one of the important people in the running of the Guinea Pig Club, in that having been a Guinea Pig himself, in addition to his normal job with B.P. in the City, he became Editor of the Guinea Pig magazine in 1947, a job which he held for the next 35 years until shortly before his death; living locally, he and his wife, Ann, who also worked at the Hospital, gave much of their time to helping the Guinea Pigs. Some six months or so after his death there was a moving Service held at the local St. Swithuns Church, East Grinstead, at which a stained glass window, made specially for the occasion, was unveiled. One of the panels of the Window commemorated the Guinea Pig Club in general and Henry Standen in particular; he had received an M.B.E. in the Birthday Honours in June 1982. Henry had been ill for some eighteen months before his death, having survived a serious operation in the summer of 1981. He had also been honoured by the East Grinstead Town Council when in 1976 they named one of the roads of the new Ashplatts Estate after him, and in 1978 he had been elected a Freeman of the City of London. The Memorial Service was taken by the Vicar of St. Swithuns, the Reverend Roger Brown; the Lesson was read by Tom Gleave and the

Service was attended by a large number of Guinea Pigs. After Henry's death, Ann Standen went on with her work for the Club in arranging their Annual Weekend.

Another way in which the Guinea Pigs had contributed to the life of East Grinstead was the donation in 1949 of a seat in the High Street as an expression of the gratitude of their members for kindness shown to them and for assistance given by the people of the Town in their rehabilitation. The condition of this seat had deteriorated in the intervening years, but in 1983 a new seat was given to replace it, with a plaque expressing their gratitude.

Mr. George Johns, Hospital Secretary for many years but recently renamed the Administrator, left, also in January. He had joined us in 1952, having previously worked for the Tunbridge Wells Health Authority, and had been with us for over 30 years; he was succeeded by Mr. Peter Turner. In January 1983 Mr. Turner attended a meeting of the League of Friends and proposed a policy whereby all requests for funding made to the League should be submitted through him; he would examine them, and where possible delete them as not being applicable to the League; this proposition was agreed to by the Meeting. At their Annual General Meeting in May, the League was told that Mr. Joe Dakin had died; he had joined the League in its early days and had been a very effective Chairman of the Amenities Committee; he had also recently served as the League's Vice-Chairman. It was proposed that Mrs. Ann Standen should take over as Chairman of the Amenities Committee, and she, in her speech of acceptance, said that after having been an active member of the League for 35 years she would feel privileged to accept the office. Gifts to the Hospital by the League during the previous twelve months had amounted to over £21,000. and their Capital Account now amounted to something over £43,000. It was in this year that Mr. John Brown joined the Committee; he was later to become its Chairman.

On the 14th April, 1983, the new Day Hospital was officially opened by Dr. R. E. Irvine, the then current President of the British Geriatric Society. Meanwhile the Memorial Research Laboratory was also flourishing. Sir Miles Clifford, who had been one of the original Trustees of the Unit, had retired. He had been instrumental in securing the first grant for the initial building, ensuring that the Laboratory would be built, and he had helped the Laboratory in many ways with his enthusiasm and drive in furthering its reputation. He is also one of the few distinguished laymen who were awarded Honorary Fellowship of the Royal College of Surgeons, along with our own Chairman Neville Blond. Sir Miles was replaced as a Trustee by Mrs. Simone Prendergast, Mrs. Blond's daughter by her first marriage. John Watson, who it will be remembered had also been instrumental in the building of the Laboratory, had retired from the National Health Service in 1977 and from his position as Honorary Secretary of the Trust in 1980, but stayed on and was still a Trustee, having had altogether some 25 years to do with the Trust. In 1983 the work of this Laboratory had become so important that the B.B.C. devoted a whole programme to its work, entitled 'Medicine Now'.

# 12

# The Pace Quickens

In spite of all the changes that had taken place as a result of the Cogwheel Reports in the 1970s, hospitals generally had so far been comparatively little affected. The changes that had been made such as the title of Matron becoming Senior Nursing Officer, the Secretary becoming Administrator, and the House Committee becoming the Board of Management, were comparatively superficial. Now in the early 1980s the pace of change markedly accelerated, and in fact has been doing so, in some form or another, ever since.

It began in February 1983, when Mr. Norman Fowler, the Minister of Health, asked Mr. Roy Griffiths, the Managing Director of Sainsbury's, to chair an enquiry team to give advice on the effective use of management manpower and resources in the National Health Service. This he agreed to do, and the other members of the team were Mr. Michael Bett of United Biscuits, Mr. Jim Blyth of British Telecom, and Sir Brian Bailey of South West Television; these four leading business executives carried out the most thorough investigation of the N.H.S. structure ever undertaken. They started by recognising that doctors as a general rule are not concerned with business matters; a successful business man is concerned with making a profit—a successful doctor is not in any way concerned with making a profit, and this was the premise from which the Griffiths Committee worked. Of all the committees which have studied the working of our hospitals, the Griffiths Committee was certainly the clearest and one of the quickest—they reported in October of the same year. They had visited various hospitals and individual doctors and organisations all over the country, and they had been appalled by what they found. The National Health Service, they said, was the biggest employer of labour in Europe, but barely knew how many people it employed, let alone who was in charge of what. It was very difficult to see how policy at the top

251

was translated into action on the front line. They recommended that there should be a more dynamic management organisation at the top and furthermore that the country should be divided into regions, regions into districts, and that the districts would be responsible for the ultimate management units. They considered it essential to efficient management that doctors themselves should be closely involved, and that this was critical to its effectiveness at local level. Having recognised that there were differences in the approach of businessmen and the medical profession, they also recognised that in the medical profession there were other vital factors which could not be measured. They dealt with these differences in detail. Among other recommendations was that responsibility should be pushed as far down the line as possible, and that each hospital should have its own budget and general manager. The National Health Service, they said, requires enormous resources. Its role is very politically sensitive and it demands top class management, the introduction of which is urgent and should be begun straight away. At the same time they recalled that in 1944 when the National Health Service was first being worked out, the Government declared at that time that "There is a danger of over organisation, of letting the machine designed to ensure a better service itself stifle the chances of getting one". They also said again that they could not over stress the importance of doctors being concerned with management at all levels.

After publication of this Report, the Ministry of Health expressed its acceptance of its general ideas, and wrote to Authority chairmen to invite their views on them, as a matter of priority; in December 1983 the Minister set up a Social Services Committee to undertake the sifting of reactions from the various Bodies they had consulted, which of course were very varied, some in favour and some very strongly against, and in fact the whole process took another year or two before very much could be done about it. After publication Mr. Griffiths became a member of the Health Services Supervisory Board and was knighted in 1985 for his services to the N.H.S., and a year later he was appointed Supervisor to the Government on the Health Service. He was not unmindful of the problems of unwarranted growth in the management in the Service, but later on expressed his regret that his 1983 recommendations for decentralising of responsibility were not acted upon until 1991. He died in March 1994 aged 67.

Margaret Thatcher in her book "The Downing Street Years" on page 47, said:—

"In 1983 the Griffiths Report was the basis for the introduction of general management in the National Health Service, without which the latter internal market reforms of the Service would not have been possible".

The Social Services Committee came up with the idea that all hospitals could be contracted out to privatisation and that this would loosen control of the hospital service from the centre; this is the first mention publicly of the reforms such as Independent Status that were introduced in the 1990s.

1983 was also notable for the foundation of the McIndoe Burns Support Group. This very worthy organisation provides support to patients and relatives of patients, providing friendship and reassurance and counselling to patients at any time; one of their activities is to arrange for ex-patients to come and talk to and reassure current patients in the Wards. There were a number of Guinea Pigs present at the inaugural meeting, the main idea for which appears to have come from Mr. Turner who had recently succeeded Mr. Johns as Administrator. Mr. Brent Tanner was the first Patron of the Group, assisted by Mrs. Anita Harrison, Mrs. Audrey Allen and Yvonne Kennard. They now cover the South East region, which is covered by our Plastic Surgery Unit.

In November 1983 the Research Unit was honoured by their Patron Queen Elizabeth the Queen Mother, who came to a reception held at New Zealand House. The Trustees of the Committee and many distinguished guests were all introduced to Her Majesty; an exhibition of photographs was a feature of the reception and a short video film was shown illustrating the work of the Trust, after which Lord Porritt proposed a vote of thanks to Her Majesty.

In January 1984 Mrs. Blond was admitted to the Court of Patrons of the Royal College of Surgeons, the highest honour the College can bestow on a layperson; this was a very appropriate recognition of her inestimable contribution to the alleviation of

253

human suffering through her dedication to the cause of medical research. Early in the year the Radiotherapy Unit at Pembury Hospital had to close, and all Queen Victoria patients needing this treatment had now to go as far as Maidstone. Needless to say there were many objections to this decision but, having come from the Regional Board, it had to be accepted. Recently the new Seat Belt Law had come into force, and our Plastic Surgeons found that the number of cases of severe facial injuries admitted to the Hospital fell dramatically following its introduction. In May Mr. Turner, who was an enthusiastic long distance runner, had the excellent idea of inviting local entrants in the forthcoming London Marathon to take part in a fifteen mile run on the previous Sunday starting and finishing at the Hospital. In March the new Day Room at the end of Kindersley Ward was opened, named as a memorial to Mr. Joe Dakin, who had been Deputy Chairman of the League of Friends for some years, and had run the League's Shop. This was a tribute to the many years of hard work that he had given to the Hospital.

In April 1984 a sad moment in the Hospital's history occurred, namely the retirement after 36 years of Miss Rosemary Wootton from managing the Physiotherapy Department. She had come here in 1948 and became Head of the Department in 1949, and during her time here there had been two extensions to the Department, both of which were paid for by the League of Friends. Her retirement was marked by a large party, well attended, at which John Bennett presented her with gifts of garden furniture on behalf of her colleagues. In thanking him for these presents she said "It would have been impossible to do this sort of work if we didn't get on; we have to work very much as a team. I am very lucky that I have worked with some wonderful people". The Courier reporting this event described her as "The very much loved and respected Superintendent of the Hospital's Physiotherapy Department", and so she was. Her Department, along with the X-ray and Pathology Departments, Anaesthetics and the Peanut and Recovery Wards, had always been shared between both the General Practitioners and the Plastic Surgery Specialists, and both benefited greatly therefrom. Working always with equal facility with both General Practitioners and Specialists, these parts of the Hospital together play a large part in keeping the two sides together, making as it were a firm foundation on which they both have been able to build, thus welding the Hospital into a homogeneous and contented whole, and we cannot thank them enough.

In May there took place an interesting football match between the Brighton & Hove Albion Football Club who came to East Grinstead to play the East Grinstead Football Club for the Richards Hospital Charity Rosebowl. This trophy, founded in 1938, has been held every year and the proceeds are donated to the Hospital. The 1984 match raised £700, and Brighton won by three goals to nil. In July there is a note that the new Day Hospital for the elderly was being well used and that there was a waiting list for its services. Also in July Dr. A. A. J. Mackenzie, the new partner in the Field Cottage practice in the Town, was appointed to the staff. The League of Friends frequently received funds from many different sources, but two unusual events occurred during the summer of 1984; the first was that a young man of 22 made a sponsored cycle ride from East Grinstead to Dorset and back and following it presented £500 to the League; and the other was when some naval ratings from the Patrol Vessel 'Endurance' hauled a bobsleigh 70 miles from Portsmouth and collected £183 for the League.

In August there was an announcement that as a result of the Griffiths Report, a general manager would be appointed sometime during 1985 and would be referred to as the Unit General Manager. We hear also in September that enlargement and redecoration of the Surgeons' Mess was now completed, and also that Radio Queen Vic was to be a 4-Channel service. In September there was the usual Guinea Pig Weekend, and the Dinner was held this year at the Copthorne Hotel, there having been a serious fire at the Old Felbridge Hotel at which they usually had the Dinner. This Weekend was marked especially by a Spitfire from the Battle of Britain Memorial Flight being flown over the Hospital by Flight Lieutenant Peter Bouch during the lunch hour on Sunday; as it dipped its wings in salute it was a most nostalgic moment for all the Guinea Pigs who were present.

In November Mr. Peter Turner, our Administrator, was admitted to the Hammersmith Hospital in London and he unfortunately died there shortly afterwards. He had been at the Hospital for two years and it was reported that Mr. W. J. Moore, his Deputy, would be taking over from him; Mr. Moore had of course already been at the Hospital for very many years and had been promoted to Acting Administrator.

In May 1985 the work on the Canadian Wing upgrading was going ahead and it was hoped to be finally finished in another few months. Dr. Bryan Christopher was elected to be the General Practitioner representative on the Board of Management. In October there was a gift of £1,000 for the Peanut Ward from a Mr. Hill who had run in the London Marathon for the last three years, during which time he had raised £3,500 through sponsoring. In October of this year Dr. D. G. M. Powell joined Dr. Worlock's practice, and was elected to the Hospital General Practitioner staff.

In November 1985 came the sad news of the sudden death of Mrs. Elaine Blond. She had had over 40 years connection with the Hospital and, together with her husband Neville, was known for her many benefactions during this time, especially the founding of the Memorial Research Laboratory and the building of the specialised Burns Unit. Some years before at the opening of the Laboratory extensions, Sir Ivor Julian, Chairman of the Regional Hospital Board, had said in a speech that in his opinion the Hospital had never had any greater friends than Mr. and Mrs. Blond. Their work was to be continued however by Mrs. Blond's daughter, Mrs Simone Prendergast, who was elected to take her place as Chairman of the Trustees of the Research Unit, with Mr. Peter Blond, Mr. Blond's elder son by a previous marriage, as Vice-Chairman.

In December 1985 there was a list published of the General Consultants at the Hospital as follows:—

| | |
|---|---|
| *Gynaecologists:* | Mr. J. M. Brudenell, Mr. J. G. Hill |
| *Ophthalmologist:* | Mr. H. F. Harper |
| *General Surgeons:* | Mr. J. Bull, Mr. B. Jackson, |
| | Mr. J. A. C. Neely |
| *Orthopaedic Surgeons:* | Mr. K. W. R. Tuson, |
| | Mr. D. A. Reynolds |
| *Paediatrician:* | Dr. J. E. Meyer |
| *Ear, Nose and Throat* | |
| *Surgeon:* | Mr. R. J. Sargeant |
| *General Physician:* | Dr. David Pyke |

Remember with honour and gratitude HENRY STANDEN M.B.E and the other members of the Guinea Pig Club who as severely burned aircrew in the war years 1939-1945 underwent pioneering plastic surgery at the Queen Victoria Hospital East Grinstead

Henry Standen and Guinea Pigs Memorial Plaque
in St. Swithuns Parish Church, East Grinstead

Mr. John Watson
tant Plastic Surgeon 1950-1977

Mrs. Kaye Clemetson
"Aunt Agatha" 1939-1989

Mrs. Ann Standen
has worked continuously for the Hospital for 54 years

Mr. John P. Bennett
Consultant Plastic Surgeon 1975-1994

Mrs. Lorraine Clifton
Chief Executive since January

*Dermatologist:*          Dr. P. A. J. Smith (appointed 1959)
*Haemotologist:*       Dr. C. G. Taylor

Only one of these Consultants, Dr. P. A. J. Smith, had been on the staff in 1963, but owing to the decision of the Board of Management round about this time to destroy Management Committee notes after two years, we have no records of when these Consultants were appointed.

The year 1986 begins with the retirement of Dr. David Pyke in February. He had taken the place of Dr. Douglas Robertson in 1964 so had been on our staff for over twenty years, during which time he had also been Consultant Physician at Kings College Hospital in London; he had come down to us once a week and on other occasions and also to see emergencies. He had been a most popular member of the staff and we were sorry to lose him. He was succeeded in this post by Dr. R. C. King from the Kent & Sussex Hospital. About this time there was another report that the Health Authority was in financial difficulties and their deficit was substantially worse than had been originally anticipated; as a direct result of this there was discussed for the first time the closure at nights of our Casualty Department, of which we shall hear more later. It was also in 1986 that a committee was formed to organise the new radio service for the Hospital, initiated by Mr. Malcolm Powell and financially supported by the League of Friends. The committee advertised for a Manager and received eighteen applicants for the job. It made its first broadcast in the middle of October, at first broadcasting for only two hours on Tuesday and Thursday evenings and all these broadcasts came from a cramped cellar adjacent to the Boiler Room. But gradually things improved and we shall have further news of its growth and great success later on. It had been officially recognised by the name of 'Radio Queen Vic'.

In April the Hospital was asked to nominate four members of the staff to attend the Queen Mother's Garden Party at Buckingham Palace, and Sister Jean England, Sister McGowan, and Mr. and Mrs. Bob Marchant, attended this ceremony. Also in April there was a report that the Kitchen/Dining Room complex was to be reorganised. And in April the Hospital had advertised for the new appointment of Unit General Manager; interviews were due to take place for this job early in May, and in due course Miss S. C. L. Borlase was appointed to the job during June. During May the League of Friends held its Annual General Meeting which saw the last appearance as Chairman of Mr. Peter Griffits; in his farewell speech he referred to the fact that this was the 28th time that he had made the speech; when he joined the Committee 34 years earlier, help for the Hospital was not more than a few thousand pounds a year, but in the past year the League had made gifts to the value of nearly £43,000. Mr. Griffits was at the same time invited to be President of the League in the place of Mrs. Blond who had recently died. Mr. H. Gwynne Powell was elected in his place as Chairman.

The question of closing the Casualty Department at night was discussed by the Medical Council, of which the Chairman at the time was Dr. Francis Briggs, who strongly protested. As a result of this the matter was discussed by an urgent Working Party within the Hospital consisting of the Unit General Manager Miss Borlase, the Director of Nursing Services, the Financial Director, and Dr. Christopher; it was further discussed by Tunbridge Wells Health Authority and also the new District Health Authority later in the year.

On 1st July, 1986 came the retirement of Dr. G. F. M. Carnegie from the General Practitioner staff. He was succeeded on the staff by Dr. Katherine Brooks, who had recently taken his place in the Judges Close practice in the Town. He was succeeded as Hospital Practitioner in Geriatrics by Dr. A. R. Enskat. At the same time Dr. Hugh Hardy from Forest Row also retired from the G. P. staff and was replaced by Dr. Steven Miller. And Mr. A. Werb retired during September; he had been Clinical Assistant in the Eye Department since the middle of 1959, so had had 27 years on our staff.

The Guinea Pig Reunion this year was once again treated to a fly past on the Sunday morning, this time by three planes, a Spitfire, a Mustang, and a Kittyhawk.

The District Health Authority was discussing the future and the long term role of the Queen Victoria Hospital and its services to the community, with special reference to what they called the Regional Specialities, meaning of course the Plastic Surgery Unit. This was the beginning of a particularly unpleasant period of the Hospital's history, which lasted for several years during which we did not know whether we would survive at all. Amongst other things we heard that the Regional Health Authority was reconsidering the criteria for specialities in the region, particularly the de-classification of oral surgery and corneo plastic surgery within this district. But to finish the year on a happier note it had been the 25th anniversary of the founding of the Research Laboratory and an Anniversary Dinner was held at the Royal Society of Medicine in London, at which Mrs. Prendergast the Committee Chairman presided and the guests were entertained after dinner by Ronnie Corbett.

The year 1987 opened with Mrs. Prendergast being made a Dame of the British Empire in the New Year's Honours List. She had also recently been elected, like her mother before her, to the Court of Patrons of the Royal College of Surgeons. Early in the year Wing Commander Page, a founder member of the Guinea Pig Club was elected a member of the Research Laboratory's Advisory Committee. Mr. Adrian Percy retired from being Appeals Director and was succeeded by Mr. Alasdair Campbell. Also in January Mr. Peter Broadberry, who had been in charge of the Photographic Department for some years since the retirement of Mr. Clemetson, retired; he was succeeded by Mr. Trevor Hill. In February came the retirement of Mr. W. J. Moore, who had been Assistant Secretary to Mr. Johns for many years since he joined us in 1957, so he had had 30 years service with the Hospital. He had been responsible largely for the administration of our finances and our Joint Consultative Committee offered him their sincere thanks for his contribution to the Hospital over a period of so many years. He was sadly missed by many friends around the Hospital. Another retirement about this time was that of Consultant Plastic Surgeon Mr. Bowen who had succeeded Percy Jayes early in 1974.

On 18th May, 1987 Mr. Gwynne Powell chaired the Annual General Meeting of the League of Friends, his first A.G.M. as Chairman. In his speech, one item of interest was that the League had recently hosted an evening of light entertainment 'Say 99' by Colin Davis and Hugh Hardy which had been a great success and Mr. Powell had written to them to offer the League's sincere thanks. Also in May, the psychiatric services provided by the Mid Downs Health Authority were apparently considered inadequate and there was some discussion as to how to provide a better service, the result of which was that Dr. J. R. D. Stevens from Haywards Heath's Princess Royal Hospital would take up his post in the autumn. Another appointment at this time was that of Dr. Mary Northen to the General Practitioner staff; she had recently joined the Lingfield general practice.

On 20th May there was news of Mr. Don Attwater's retirement; he had come to the Hospital on January 1st, 1952 and had worked in the Recovery Ward; in April 1970 he had become assistant to Matron Miss Duncombe, and Acting Matron from 1st January, 1971. In April 1971 his title had changed to Senior Nursing Officer and in September 1982 he became Director of Nursing. He had been at the Hospital altogether for some 35 years and had taken a big part in various changes that had taken place during this time, and the Unit Executive Committee recorded their sincere thanks to him and said that he had made a valuable contribution to the Hospital. He was succeeded as Nursing Services Manager by Mrs. Blomfield. Meanwhile Miss Borlase had taken up her post as Unit General Manager, and Anaesthetist Dr. C. J. Barham had joined them as the Consultant representative on the Unit Executive Committee, with Dr. A. R. Enskat representing the General Practitioners. Dr Charles Palmer from the general practice in Crawley Down retired in July having worked at the Hospital since 1948, very nearly 40 years. He was recommended by the Medical Committee to become an Honorary Member of Staff; Dr. Palmer in addition for many years had been a member of the British Medical Association General Medical Services Committee, and in 1966 had been elected Chairman of the Brighton branch of the British Medical Association.

To add to the gloom concerning the de-classification and possible re-siting of the Plastic Surgery Unit an even more disturbing piece of news came from the Tunbridge Wells Health Authority during July; it had been considering a strategic plan for their Area for the next ten years and said of the Queen Victoria Hospital "The implications for the Queen Victoria Hospital as a result of their appraisal will need to be identified for all general practitioner facilities"; this information was generally interpreted as being a threat to the future of the General Practitioner Unit. In September the news became even more gloomy and depressing, when Miss Borlase reported that all theatres at the Hospital were currently closed and approximately a third of the Hospital's beds were also closed. The Unit Accountant confirmed that the Hospital was now considerably overspent and that he would have to curtail expenditure in order to bring the budget into line. Options to be considered were the closure of Wagg Ward, consideration of the closure of McIndoe Ward, closure of the Night Casualty Service, and also the closure of ten beds on the Peanut Ward. If these measures were not sufficient to achieve their object, it would be necessary to consider the closure of Kindersley Ward as well. Wagg Ward was actually closed in October, and there was a reorganisation of the General Office and the Supplies Department both of which suffered a reduction in manpower. In November the Unit Board of Management was even more depressing, saying that every department at the Hospital must be subject to immediate financial scrutiny, and the Hospital was told that it must cut its expenditure by £90,000 for the following twelve months and £180,000 for the year after that. A Working Party was set up within the Hospital to try and achieve these savings, and one of their suggestions was that both Kindersley and Dewar Wards should be closed. Naturally the General Practitioner Medical Committee, led by Dr. Bryan Christopher, were very alarmed by all this, and wrote a strongly worded letter to Miss Borlase stating that these changes were totally unacceptable to them, and that any further closures would seriously affect the services that could be given to the local public.

Meanwhile the League of Friends had been struggling manfully on; they had agreed amongst other things to upgrade the American Wing Lecture Theatre at a cost of some £14,000, and altogether during 1987 their gifts to the Hospital had totalled £24,637. On the whole though, 1987 was not a happy year for the Hospital.

In 1988 the Research Unit's Scientific Advisers were Professor J. R. Batchelor, Professor L. Brent, and Professor Sir Roy Calne, the latter having taken the place of Sir Peter Medawar who, having been Scientific Adviser to the Laboratory from the beginning, had recently died. The Consultant Plastic Surgeons in order of appointment at this time were Mr. J. R. Cobbett, Mr. T. D. Cochrane, Mr. J. P. Bennett, Mr. B. J. Mayou, and Mr. N. S. Brent Tanner. Both John Cobbett and Tom Cochrane had served as Honorary Secretary to the British Association of

Plastic Surgeons, and Mr. Cochrane as Honorary Treasurer of the same body.

In January fears for the closing of the Hospital came from as far away as Canada. A Canadian TV company had been over here filming the grounds and wards of the Hospital, obviously paying special attention to the Canadian Wing built by the people of Canada during the Second World War. This documentary had been shown all over Canada and a tremendous interest resulted, in the shape of hundreds of letters from all over Canada, not a few of them enclosing financial contributions. Also at this time, on the matter of economies, the management re-stated that further economies would probably have to be made, and one of the suggestions was even the complete closure of the Hospital for a period of, say, two months every year. The Medical Council again protested vigorously at these suggestions and their Chairman Dr. Christopher said they would result in such a drastic reduction in services to patients that the Medical Council could not possibly support them. The Unit Board of Management at this moment consisted of Mr. D. C. Bennett as Secretary, Miss Borlase as Unit General Manager, Dr. Christopher, Mr. J. N. Gibson, Mr. Jones the Finance Officer, Mr. J. Lowe Chairman, Mrs. Rowe, Mrs. Blomfield the Chief Nursing Officer, Mr. C. Smith and Mr. A. R. Thom.

Wagg Ward did actually re-open on 25th April but with only six beds. In February the Finance Officer had announced that the money realised from the sale of Australia House and Warrenside came to a figure of £1,500,000. Most of this money had been spent on various capital projects, for instance Meridian Way £600,000, new telephone switchboard £80,000, Canadian Wing upgrading £300,000, and an energy management system which had cost £80,000, and there was still talk of further developments, a new Day Hospital, and also the new Kitchen and Dining Room.

In June we had to say goodbye to one of the most popular members of our staff, namely Sister Jean England who had been on the staff for 35 years, for several years latterly as Sister of Kindersley Ward. She was a hard worker and always noted for being cheerful, and a party was given for her at which in her speech she remarked "I have had such good friends here over the years, it really has been a wonderful place to work". Of course she was sadly missed. In July there was another sad good-bye to Dr. J. D. W. Hunter from the G.P. Staff who was retiring after 35 years on the Hospital staff. He had contributed a lot to the running of the Hospital during these years, having been amongst other things first of all Secretary and a few years later Chairman of the Medical Council. He also was given a party and in his speech of thanks said "It has always been a particular thing of mine that the Hospital should not be split between the specialist Plastic Surgery Department and the normally prac-tising General Practitioner. I have always liked to think that the Hospital was of one entity", a sentiment with which most of us would agree.

In July came the first serious mention of the funding problems in regard to keeping the Burns Unit operational, and it was thought that it would only be possible to do so for another two years; this information of course caused considerable concern. In August Mr. Jack Lowe, District General Manager of the Tunbridge Wells Health Authority wrote a letter to one of the local papers stating "In a previous letter I said that the TWHA is proud to be associated with the Queen Victoria Hospital, and I repeat that statement now without reservation; we shall con-tinue to do our best by the Hospital as far as we are able within the financial constraints which apply to all our activities". In spite of his reassurances, in August came another official report on the future of the specialist side of the Hospital from the team of Regional and District Health Officers, who had been dis-cussing the reorganisation of the whole Region, and who were now considering moving the Plastic Surgery Department to Maidstone. In October we hear that Mr. Fermer who came as locum Unit General Manager between Mr. Turner's death and Miss Borlase's appointment, returned to his post with the Tunbridge Wells Health Authority. Also in August seven beds on Kelsey Fry Ward were closed due to staffing problems and Kindersley Ward was also closed over the Bank Holiday weekend in order to make more nursing staff available in the Casualty Ward; it was also reported that no further progress had been made at the moment towards the re-opening of the remaining beds in Wagg Ward. In August Mr. R. W. Norris was appointed Consultant Plastic Surgeon in place of Mr. Bowen who had recently left. Mr. Jones the Unit Accountant resigned his post on promotion to another Authority. In September we heard that the enlargement of the X-ray Department had been completed and that it was now being furnished.

Not surprisingly all these threats of closure of the Hospital brought about a tremendous storm of protest from East Grinstead residents, and a special petition was sent to our Member of Parliament and also to the local Health Authority. Family Doctors were particularly concerned and were doing their best to influence the future of the hospital services in the area, as was also the local branch of the Pensioners Association, who asked the Mid Downs Community Health Council to stop the closure of the Town's Casualty services at night. A local paper had the headline 'Closing the Queen Victoria Hospital by stealth'; apparently a lot of people thought that the closing of Casualty was maybe the first step to the closure of the entire Hospital. Another change supporting this point of view was that the responsibility for medical services for the Town had now been transferred from the Tunbridge Wells Health Authority to the Mid Downs Health Authority, and there were rumours that the G.P. side of the Hospital would be similarly transferred. There were rumours also that the Tunbridge Wells Health Authority was trying to close the G.P. side anyway, and this prompted another letter from Mr. Lowe, the Manager of the Tunbridge Wells Authority, to the local press asking the people of East Grinstead to accept that the Tunbridge Wells Health Authority were definitely not trying to close the Hospital.

So it can be seen that 1988 was another year of depression over the future of the Hospital, and we heard again towards the end of the year that decisions about these matters had been postponed for twelve months, and would be made during 1989. This statement in itself did not relieve the general anxiety.

Dr. Roger Orcutt retired officially at the beginning of 1989, and was made an Honorary Member of staff because he was doing locums for his old practice. He had been appointed in 1961, so had served the Hospital for 28 years. On April 28th came the good news that Casualty Department would from now on be remaining open at night; and it was noted that the Department would now remain open 24 hours a day, seven days a week, but this only became financially possible because the East Grinstead Family Doctors had agreed that their call-out payments

264

would be cancelled. It was a sacrifice made to produce a welcome result and we were grateful to them.

In May 1989 the subject of the Hospital being granted Independent Trust Status arose for the first time. A White Paper had been issued by the Ministry of Health entitled "Working for Patients" in which it expressed its ideas as to how hospitals should in future be managed. The Hospital set up a Working Party consisting of the Acting Unit General Manager Mr. D. C. Bennett, Mr. J. P. Bennett, Senior Plastic Surgery Consultant, Dr. Bryan Christopher, Chairman of the Medical Council, and the East Grinstead Town Clerk, with a representative from the Mid Downs Authority and the Unit Accountant, to consider and advise on this very important matter. Somebody mentioned at the time that this approach might take four or five years, and in fact this was a very accurate prediction, because it was made in the year 1989 and in fact the event actually took place on 1st April, 1994. The Unit Board of Management discussed the matter also of course, and expressed a unanimous opinion that they generally endorsed the view that the two sides of the Hospital must operate as one unit if the Hospital overall were to succeed as a long term proposition.

At the end of May 1989 Dr. Peter Stevens retired from being in charge of the General Pathology Department, to which post he had been appointed in 1970, succeeding Dr. Sachs. Having been a Wing Commander in the R.A.F. Medical Service, he had on his appointment just published a book called 'Fatal Civil Aircraft Accidents, their Medical and Pathological Investigations'. The first book to be published about these matters, it had a large circulation, and was to be followed by two others of which he was co-author—'Investigations of Mass Disasters', and 'Unexpected Death due to Natural Diseases'. He became Treasurer and later President of the British Association of Forensic Medicine, for which he received an O.B.E. He had been the Consultant Representative on the Tunbridge Wells District Management Team for several years. He had also been Senior Lecturer in the Forensic Medicine Department of the London Hospital. Like his predecessor, he was a fine colleague with whom to work, and a well loved character with time for everybody. He was to be sadly missed.

A few other changes took place round about this time; Miss

Borlase had resigned from her position as Unit General Manager on her secondment to duties connected with the White Paper at the Regional Health Authority. She was warmly thanked for her work at the Hospital during the last three years and Mr. David Bennett was appointed part-time Acting Unit General Manager in her place. In the League of Friends Mr. Gwynne Powell, Chairman of the League for the last three years, announced that he would not be seeking re-nomination for the office and thanked everyone for their help during his term of office; he was thanked for his services by Mr. Peter Griffits and was elected a Vice-President of the League. Mr. John Brown was elected Chairman in his place. An interesting change occurred in June 1989, when the Management decided to alter the name of the Recovery Ward and call it instead the 'Russell Davies Ward'; this of course being in honour of the recent Head of our Anaesthetic Department who had originally designed the Ward and over the years had made it an essential and extremely efficient part of the Hospital. On 1st July Dr. Antony Fulford-Smith was elected to the staff of the Hospital, having recently joined the Judges Close practice in the Town. On the 6th July, 1989, the upgraded and enlarged X-ray Department was officially handed over.

At the League of Friends' meeting on 25th July the new Chairman John Brown introduced John and Anne Myson, new members at their first meeting of the General Committee. Mr. Myson had worked all his life in the Health Service both at the Regional Authority and also at Tunbridge Wells Health Authority and then retired to live locally in Dormansland; he was therefore a very useful person to have on the Committee since he knew something about every branch of medical management, and in view of all this was elected to the vacant office of Honorary Secretary of the League. Shortly after this he was also elected to represent West Sussex on the National Committee of Leagues of Friends, a position which he still holds to this day. This year incidentally was the 40th anniversary of the founding of our own League of Friends and also of the National League itself, and there was a party at Tunbridge Wells to celebrate it.

1989 saw the 50th anniversary of Mr. McIndoe's arrival at the Hospital at the end of August 1939, and the Hospital celebrated the occasion very suitably; in fact they devoted two whole days to it. On Wednesday 20th September a Scientific Congress took place, which was attended by surgeons from all over the world. One of the messages carried away from this meeting was a lesson to be learned particularly from this Hospital that there is a need to carry treatment beyond simple surgical repair, and on to rehabilitation of patients into society. This was something on which Mr. McIndoe had always insisted. One of his ex-patients spoke at the meeting and said "He (McIndoe) always used to say to us patients 'Your problems if you are going to have any will start the day you leave the Hospital'; but he made sure that we were surrounded by attractive nurses and enjoyed a great social life; we were never allowed to feel sorry for ourselves, and so when the day came that we had to depart from the Hospital we were well prepared to meet the outside world". Another speaker was Cyril Jones, the Chief Technician working in the American Theatre and, at that time one of the only two members of the staff in the Theatre who had actually worked with Mr. McIndoe; he drew attention to the fact that the surgery done 50 years ago was very different to that which was being done today, and that McIndoe had laid the foundations. "Fantastic things are being done today", he said, "like nerve grafts, and it is all thanks to McIndoe sowing the seed". The following day the 21st, the celebration was joined by the Duchess of Kent who spent two and a half hours touring the Hospital, talked to many patients and autographed the plaster of one small boy's fractured hand, Stephen Webb. She toured the Burns Centre and unveiled a painting commissioned by the surgeons at the Hospital celebrating the unbreakable link between the Queen Victoria and the hundreds of brave pilots who fought in the Second World War; and she pulled a cracker with one of the elderly patients, at the Day Centre. She had been met on arrival by Sir John Grugeon, Chairman of the T.W.H.A., and also by the Health Minister, David Mellor, who was paying his first visit to the Hospital. During her visit luncheon was served at which a number of senior Guinea Pigs were present, and Mr. John Bennett made a speech of thanks to her.

In September came news of the resignation of the Plastic Surgeon Mr. B. Mayou, and in October the resignation also of Dr. F. B. Briggs who had been appointed in 1952, and so had nearly 38 years on the staff. Around this same time some senior members of the Hospital Management Committee attended a

Department of Health Conference on Self-Government. 1989 also marked the 45th anniversary of the opening of the Canadian Wing in 1944 and this was celebrated by the Canadian Wing of the Club in June at Gwelph, Ontario. This Canadian Wing had its own Friends of the Guinea Pig Club, many of whose members attended, together with Guinea Pigs from all over Canada and a strong contingent from the United Kingdom which included Mr. and Mrs. Tom Gleave, and of course Mr. Ross Tilley was present.

On Saturday 23rd September the Guinea Pigs held their 48th Annual Reunion Dinner at the Old Felbridge Hotel again—they had been meeting for several years at the Copthorne Hotel due to the large fire at the Felbridge Hotel but this year they were able to return to it. On the following day the Guinea Pigs were treated to a flyover during their Sunday morning party round the pool of the Hospital, this time by two biplanes from another era—one of them flown by Mr. Nicholas Parkhouse, one of our Plastic Surgery Registrars, and the other by one of his friends Mr. Jonathan Elwes, a very fine nostalgic gesture by the two young pilots which was much appreciated by the members.

This year also the League of Friends celebrated its 40th Anniversary, with a meeting at which Mr. John Bennett the Senior Plastic Surgeon recalled the wonders that the League had achieved in its 40 years; in seven years 1981 to 1988 alone the League had committed to the Hospital over £250,000. "The Health Service is being reorganised once again", he said, "which is always a time of anxiety and worry, but as long as the Hospital and the League of Friends keep working together all will be well". On this special occasion no fewer than 200 guests attended.

It was rumoured at this time that the land at the back of the Hospital was to be sold for building; apparently the South East Thames Regional Health Authority had actually submitted Outline Plans for development on this land, but Planning Permission had been turned down by the East Grinstead Town Council. In the end the Tunbridge Wells Health Authority issued a statement that the land would not be sold and that the Hospital's future was assured, and the Mid Sussex District Council also turned down these building plans. So the year having been a rather anxious one finished on a slightly happier

268

note, and the Courier, wishing its readers a Happy New Year, said "The past year has been hectic and prosperous for East Grinstead people and there have been some political successes, and several Royal visits have brought sparkle to the local people", and it ended up by saying "The Hospital is safe for now".

One of the first events in 1990 was the opening by Lady Grugeon of the new Day Hospital. It is not generally known that at this time the names of Wagg and Kirkhope Ward were interchanged. Both were situated opposite what had been the eye wards, originally wards three and four, and which had recently accommodated the Day Hospital; Kirkhope had been the first on the right of the corridor and Wagg beyond it, the second on the right. The names being changed meant that Wagg became the first on the right, and Kirkhope the second. It was to the new Wagg Ward that the Day Hospital was transferred. Kirkhope, further along the corridor was now given over to Geriatric patients, who have a much quicker turn-round than they used to. Both Wards had accommodated Geriatric patients in 1963, but now only one of them did and this of course accounted for more of the loss in the total number of beds at the Hospital. It means day patients instead of long stay patients and this is very much in line with modern methods. Also early in this year a suggestion was made for a crèche to accommodate the children of Hospital staff to be organised by Mrs. Julie Jones of Dormans Park; she and her colleagues already ran other successful crèches locally.

On March 1st the Hospital had to face another item of bad news; apparently a cash crisis had forced the Management to close the Queen Victoria Hospital to all except emergency cases until the beginning of April, that is for one month. In effect this meant that 50 operations had to be cancelled in order to save cash and balance the books. Not unnaturally this news caused very great concern to everybody concerned with the Hospital and both local papers. The Observer had an article saying that all these temporary money-saving measures at the Hospital might become permanent and The Courier had a headline "Anger Mounts Over Ward Closure and Cuts at the Queen Victoria Hospital", and they also said that these temporary closures were becoming so regular that they were in danger of becoming permanent. There was a meeting between the Unit Management Committee and the Tunbridge Wells Health Authority which did nothing to allay the public concern. The District General Manager, Mr. Jack Lowe, at this meeting said that they were currently negotiating with the Regional Officers the level of funding of services for next year, but he told the meeting that he could give no reassurances of resumption even on April 1st this year, nor about last year's budget. Mr. David Bennett, who was part-time Acting Unit General Manager, said that these cuts had been unpalatable but necessary, and a repeat of the year's closures would only be avoided through careful budgeting, and that this was a very difficult thing to do when there were patients needing care, but only set levels of money to meet the expense. In the middle of May the local Press interviewed Mr. Bennett as Secretary to the Tunbridge Wells Health Authority, and he said "We know there is public concern about the Hospital, I want to dispel that by saying quite categorically that so long as this Authority is associated with the Hospital it will continue to do all in its power to consolidate the outstanding work the Hospital does both locally and internationally and prepare it for the changes which are coming in the National Health Service". "There are changes", he said, "but this Hospital is one place which will challenge the changes. It has a strong team and looks forward with confidence to the future".

In May we received a visit from television crews filming the Hospital as part of the film 'A Perfect Hero' in which Nigel Havers played the part of a World War Two pilot who suffered terrible burns. The Hospital was not actually named; it had however been mentioned by the Royal Air Force Benevolent Fund which had been celebrating the Battle of Britain's 50th Anniversary Appeal. In May also the childrens' crèche was opened, aimed principally at pre-school children of Hospital staff but with vacancies for other children aged four months to five years. There was news also of a massive million pound plan which was due to start in the autumn to replace the Hospital Kitchen, and was being financed partly by the South West Thames Regional Health Authority. The recent transfer of the Day Hospital from its original site on the left of the corridor over to the new Wagg Ward on the right, had left a large unoccupied area, and the new kitchen was to be built on this site. In June there was an announcement that the Unit General Manager's post, recently vacated by Miss Borlase, was being advertised. There were 70 applications for the job and five shortlisted candidates visited the Hospital. In due course Mr. Richard Farnfield was appointed to be the new Unit General Manager. He was a Naval Officer who retired with the rank of Captain, and had spent a large part of his naval career in submarines. Unfortunately he was unable to take up this post until the end of the year, but in the meantime Mr. D. C. Bennett was to continue acting as part-time General Manager until his arrival. There are two retirements to be recorded; at the end of March Dr. Christopher Bywater retired from the General Practitioner staff, having been appointed in 1959 and had 31 years at the Hospital, he was replaced both in the practice and on the Hospital staff by Dr. P. H. Cliffe. Also John Cobbett retired from the Plastic Surgery Department in May; he had been with us since the middle of 1963 so this was another 27 year's appointment in various capacities. He had of course brought renown to the Hospital as already noted, by his work on micro-surgery; he had been a popular member of the staff and we were sorry to lose him. During the summer Dr. J. Allen was appointed Consultant Histo-pathologist to the Hospital.

At the beginning of August came the Queen Mother's 90th birthday, and a group of 27 members of the Queen Victoria Hospital staff were included amongst others to march along the Horse Guards Parade past Her Majesty. Amongst those in this party was Mrs. Sheila Averill who is still with us today. The Hospital held a party in Kelsey Fry Ward to celebrate this auspicious occasion on the 4th August. Her Majesty had of course been our Patron since the end of the War and a very popular and successful one too, having visited us on several occasions, and always taken a very great interest in our affairs, and at the moment of writing is still our Patron.

During September Sothebys auctioned a Spitfire and a Hurricane amongst nearly 700 lots at the R.A.F. Station Hendon, and the Guinea Pig Club together with the R.A.F. Benevolent Fund and our own Research Laboratory shared in the proceeds of their sale. Also in September there was more trouble about the Hospital finances. Once again our services were being cut because of a cash crisis and this meant surgeons having to reduce the number of operations until more money was available. This was of course a misfortune that the Queen Victoria shared with N.H.S. hospitals all over the country and many people felt that if the National Health Service was so starved of cash, the Health Minister should be looking at how it was funded instead of asking staff to cut services. This was a generally agreed feeling around this area, and was not a very happy state to be in, but there was the news of the rebuilding of the Catering complex to cheer us up; it was to start soon but would probably take a year to complete; there was also the news that we had got extra funding from the Government for an additional Plastic Surgeon as well; he was to be Mr. R. W. Smith and the appointment dated from the 1st November.

At the end of the summer there was news of a sad occasion when Mrs. Kay Clemetson died. She was of course Aunt Agatha of the Peanut Club; she had done magnificent work for many years for our Hospital, and as well as her main job as Editor of the Kent and Sussex Courier, she had also given time to her profession—she was for seven years a member of the Press Council and also had become President of the Guild of Editors early on in her career. She was a remarkable person, a very strong character, and in 1948 when the National Health Service wanted to take over the Peanut Club funds she had raised, she fought back with Archibald McIndoe and finally agreed only to give up the money provided that the Ministry promised to build a new Childrens' Ward. She is reported as having said at a public meeting held as a protest against this move, "I have a duty to those who subscribed this money, and I will not sign it away under any circumstances". She did a great deal for our Hospital, and it was a sad day when she died.

During the summer of 1990 there was a reorganisation of the Research Laboratory. It had been originally organised in order to research clinical surgical work on burns and had worked intimately with the Special Burns Unit. In fact they had been so successful over the years that they had become world famous for immunological research, and the Committee felt that since the funding was now going to general immunology rather than to specific burns and plastic surgical research, this work on immunology could be better conducted in other larger organisations. Professor John Fabre's appointment terminated and Dr. Colin

Green was appointed to guide the Unit in the new direction, upon which the Trustees and Committee had decided.

At the end of the year came Mr. David Bennett's last meeting as Acting Unit General Manager, and the Chairman thanked him for his magnificent work on behalf of the Hospital and the hard work that he had put in generally during his time here. During this year the League of Friends had actually spent over £50,000 on the Hospital. Its membership at this time was around 1,200 members.

In January 1991 we received instructions to prepare the Hospital and particularly the Plastic Surgery Unit once again for its original purpose, for treating war casualties, in this case from the Gulf War; "Financial considerations are to be put aside in dealing with Gulf casualties", we were told. This was interesting because only a few months previously the Burns Unit faced an all-time low point in its existence with temporary closure for a few months in response to the serious cuts in funding. People began asking the question—has the Gulf War saved our Burns Unit? In the end the Gulf War was over so quickly, and in fact no such casualties were received in this Hospital. While on this subject, an interesting point was that the television series 'A Perfect Hero', which had been filmed at the Queen Victoria last May had its showing postponed until after the war, it being felt that showing pictures of badly burned servicemen would not be appropriate at this time.

Also in January Dr. Michael Worlock retired from the General Practitioner staff; he had been appointed in 1953 so he had given 38 years of service to the Hospital, for some of this time having been a Clinical Practitioner Assistant in charge of geriatric beds. Early in January 1991 Dr. Stephen Bellamy was appointed to the General Practitioner staff having joined the Field Cottage practice in the Town at the same time; Dr. Bellamy shortly after his appointment was appointed Clinical Hospital Practitioner in General Medicine. On Saturday the 23rd March Radio Queen Vic was formally opened by B.B.C. Radio Sussex; it had been operating since 1986 but with not very comfortable quarters, but they had now extended their broadcasting hours since what they called the 'early cellar' days and from an initial membership of about eight, it now had 50 members or volunteers, and they had elected Vince Hill to be their Patron.

In April a very depressing rumour went around that the Mid Downs Health Authority had said that as a result of a newly built General District Hospital being opened in Haywards Heath, which had surplus capacity, it was felt that patients could well be directed there instead of to the Queen Victoria, which could easily result in the demise of the Queen Victoria; fortunately this has not happened.

About this time early in 1991 the whole country was preparing for the new arrangements of the National Health Service, namely Trust Status for hospitals and Fund Holding for General Practitioners, and this Hospital had a very well attended meeting of its Medical Council to discuss this. With Dr. Bryan Christopher as Chairman and Mr. Farnfield as new Unit General Manager attending, there were eighteen representatives from all over the Hospital. We were one of the 111 first-time bidders for Trust Status, but in our case the matter was complicated by the fact that the Hospital was funded by Tunbridge Wells Health Authority while the General Practitioners were funded by the Mid Downs Health Authority. In May we heard that only 56 of the first-time bidders were to be granted Trust Status during 1991 and we were not amongst them. A month or two later it was decided that there was no time to prepare a proper application for 1992 and so it was decided that we would apply for the third wave to come into operation in 1993.

Also in May Mr. Michael Awty left; he had been in charge of the Dental Department since Sir Terence Ward had retired but had worked previously in the Department, altogether giving service for nearly 30 years; he was well liked and a popular member of the staff and in his speech at the party he was given he made the remark, "When I came here in 1963 I was immediately struck by what a friendly place it was". The new Catering Department which incorporated a spacious canteen together with a new and up-to-date kitchen, on the site of the old Day Hospital, was opened in June by our M.P. Mr. Timothy Renton.

1991 saw the 50th anniversary of the founding of the Guinea Pig Club and it celebrated the event by holding a Buffet Dance at the Old Felbridge Hotel on Friday October 3rd at which it was estimated there were 400 people present. The cabaret, arranged as usual by Mrs. Ann Standen, was given by Dame Vera Lynn one of the favourites of the Second World War, and she was given a standing ovation at the end of it. In her speech of thanks she referred to the first time she had visited the Club at the Hospital and again later when some members of the Club came to her dressing room at her London shows. The Duke of Edinburgh was present at the usual Dinner held on the Saturday, along with over 100 Guinea Pig members and senior members of the Royal Air Force, and Lady McIndoe was there. An interesting aside to this Dinner was that one of the founder members of the Club, Mr. Jackie Mann, who had been one of the hostages held in the Middle East and had only recently been released, telephoned to say he wished he could be with them, but he was not yet physically able to be. The message was recorded and replayed over the Hotel's loudspeaker system during the Dinner. The original Club had been formed in 1941 with 400 members of the Royal Air Force and an additional 300 from twelve other nationalities. On the Sunday morning the usual Service of Thanksgiving was held at St. Swithuns Church and was well attended. The Chief Guinea Pig, Mr. Tom Gleave, spoke and gave thanks for the gift of human friendship and spirit of fellow suffering that had kept the Club together for such a long time.

In October the Casualty Department was moved, to work in the Assembly Hall for approximately eight weeks while its rebuilding took place. It happened that the League of Friends had recently been left some £63,000, and the Committee felt that, as the donor, Mr. Todd, was a local resident this money should be devoted to a project which would benefit the local people; they had discovered that the Casualty Department expansion was going to cost just about that sum, so it can be said that Mr. Todd through the League had entirely paid for it. The League incidentally had some 1,200 members, of whom 300 or more donated their time in various ways to the Hospital.

Another large benefaction to the Hospital had come from the Peanut Club, now run as a Trust under the chairmanship of Mr. Peter Williams; they had organised a special Gulf Appeal and collected nearly £30,000, of which the bulk was given to our Anaesthetic Department towards the cost of special monitoring equipment. Another major contribution from the Peanut Club had been the nurses' swimming pool within the Hospital grounds, and they have of course been responsible for much of the development of the grounds. During the year Dr. Peter Venn had joined the Anaesthetic staff, and Mr. K. W. Cullen had become a Consultant in Plastic Surgery. Also in October Dr. J. H. Clarke from the Moatfield practice had joined the General Practitioner staff, and currently now at the time of writing has a Clinical Assistantship appointment in Geriatrics.

Towards the end of the year the Unit Management Committee held a special meeting to discuss the matter of application for Trust Status; this was attended by a representative from the Regional Hospital Authority who was responsible for Trust applications for this Region. He told the Committee what acquiring Trust Status involved; firstly he said the Hospital would remain within the National Health Service and although all staff would transfer their existing employment to the Queen Victoria Hospital Trust, they would still remain N.H.S. employees. The Trust would be run by a Board consisting of a Chairman and ten Directors, and they would be directly responsible to the National Health Service Management Executive of the Ministry of Health, thus missing out the current Management Committee middlemen of the Health Authority and Regional Board. Since the Trust would be run by locally elected members it would have much greater freedom and flexibility to take its own decisions, which included the ability to acquire, own, and dispose of their own assets. They would receive funds from the Health Authorities for treating their patients, from General Practice Fund Holders for treating theirs, and also from the private sector as at present. One of the advantages of a Trust was that the Unit could retain its monetary surpluses, whereas under the then current regime any surplus belonged to the District Health Authority. Mr. Farnfield wrote a letter to the League of Friends which they published in their Bulletin No. 22 at the end of the year, setting out the position. At the same time he invited all members of the League to attend a briefing to be given in the Barclay Club at the end of January 1992. At this meeting Mr. D. C. Bennett, now Secretary to the Tunbridge Wells Health Authority, presented his last secretarial report to this Hospital.

We had heard rumours of a new Burns Unit being built, and now the rumour was confirmed. Building finally commenced early in 1993 and took a year to complete. The original Unit had been the first of its kind when it was built in 1964 and had recently outgrown its use, its techniques having become obsolete, and the new Unit will keep the Queen Victoria Hospital in the forefront of burns treatment.

In the middle of October 1991 we had sadly to report the death of one of the Hospital's greatest benefactors, a former member of our Anaesthetic staff, Dr. Russell M. Davies, who had come to the Hospital during the War and was appointed Consultant Anaesthetist to help out Dr. John Hunter, in which post he remained from 1948 until 1974. He had taken over running the Anaesthetic Department after Dr. Hunter left and built it up over the years to a highly efficient Department with four Anaesthetists; he also founded the Recovery Ward, one of the earliest in the country. Along with John Watson he had organised the foundation of the Research Laboratory. He was a founder member of the Guinea Pig Club, and had helped many of its members with their financial affairs and in obtaining jobs. He had helped to turn the Queen Victoria Hospital into a mecca for doctors, and surgeons, and his Department into a centre for post graduate training, a rare distinction outside a London teaching hospital. He had served on the Tunbridge Wells District Health Committee for a number of years, and in short had given an enormous amount of his time and skills to various aspects of the Hospital; as one of his Obituary Notices commented, the Queen Victoria had been lucky to have working for them somebody of his calibre.

Towards the end of the year the Chest, Heart and Stroke Association set up a new Advice Centre for stroke patients, to be held in the Barclay Club three days a week, offering guidance on the various problems connected with strokes, and a comprehensive information service.

Another death to be reported in October was that of Sir Terence Ward. He had taken over the Dental Department in 1945 at a time when it was rather depleted and not in very good shape generally, but it was not long before he had a new Dental Department built; he had been demobilised from the Air Force where he had been a Squadron Leader in charge of a Maxillo Facial Unit. The development of this Department in the succeeding years, assisted from 1947 onwards by Mr. G. E. Ryba, was dramatically successful; he had received a C.B.E. in 1961, followed in 1971 by a Knighthood, not only for this work but also for his work with the British Association of Oral Surgeons, of which he became President, and for being Secretary General and later President of the International Association of Oral Surgeons. He was also Consultant Adviser in Oral Surgery to the Ministry of Health, the Army, and the Royal Air Force. He had specified in his Will that there was to be no funeral or memorial service for him.

We cannot leave 1991 without recording a very special anniversary. In 1941 Ann Standen came as a young nurse to what was still then known as the Queen Victoria Cottage Hospital. She married Henry Standen, a founder member of the Guinea Pig Club, and they settled in the centre of East Grinstead town. Henry died in 1983, but Ann had continued her connection with the Hospital, both by her work for the Club and also for the League of Friends. Many members of staff have achieved 30-35 years service to the Hospital in various capacities; a few have made it to 40 years, but Ann is the only person in the history of the Hospital to be recorded as having served it for 50 years. Needless to say the anniversary was celebrated with a well attended party.

On 16th January, 1992, the refurbished Casualty Department was officially opened by Sir John Grugeon. The work had been started the previous September and in the interval the Department had been housed in the Assembly Hall. Sir John in his speech thanked the League of Friends for its generosity. He also remarked that he thought the newly enlarged Casualty Department combined with the works shortly to be started on the new Burns Unit in a few months time showed that the Queen Victoria Hospital was here to stay. This was incidentally one of Sir John's last tasks connected with this Hospital, as he was due to resign at the end of March having been Chairman of the Tunbridge Wells Health Authority for eight years.

Meanwhile the League had been busy in other ways. Mrs. Anne Myson took over the task of managing the League's shop, and at its Annual General Meeting the Chairman also thanked Mrs. Standen for the time she devoted to handling requests for amenities, and for her management of the Coffee Lounge. He went on to say, "although the Hospital has recently applied for Trust Status, this will not in any way alter the League's task. We shall still need to raise money to ensure that our Hospital remains the country's best". He also referred to the fact that the League was financing the Radio Queen Vic, which was in the process of improving the bedside radio reception.

On the 1st February, 1992 Dr. Veronique A. L. Foulger, who had recently joined the Moatfield practice, was appointed to the Queen Victoria General Practitioner staff, and on the 31st March Dr. R. M. Lodge retired; he had been elected to the staff in June 1961 so was another person to have had 30 years service with us. He was succeeded by Dr. J. D. Hill.

In April Mr. William Waldegrave, then Minister of Health, happening to be in the area, visited the Hospital and spent an hour or two touring and talking to patients. He commented when he left "They're carrying out so much pioneering work here and also providing a first class service for the Town" and he added "It is a remarkable Hospital". Another event that has to be mentioned at this time was the departure of our Unit General Manager Mr. Richard Farnfield. He had had only some eighteen months in the post, and his departure was a matter of considerable regret throughout the Hospital. Mrs. Blomfield took over as Deputy Unit General Manager, until a new Manager could be appointed, and the Tunbridge Wells Health Authority continued to be in overall charge of the running of the Hospital. The Occupational Therapy Unit was joined by Miss Sarah Mee, who is at present in charge.

In September the Guinea Pigs held their Annual Weekend celebrating their 51st Anniversary, and this celebration was remarkable for the fact that Mr. Jackie Mann, who last year was not well enough to attend the Weekend, was this year able to do so. He had been a founder member of the Club and had been shot down six times during the War before he came to the Hospital. He said in his short speech "It was my bottle of sherry that helped start the Guinea Pig Club". Norman Wisdom was the entertainer on this occasion. In December a leading article in the Courier referred to the fact that the Hospital had been dealt a double blow earlier in the year with the departure of its General Manager Mr. Farnfield, and the Government rejection of its application to become a Trust.

The year 1993 started off with the arrival of our new Unit General Manager Mrs. Lorraine Clifton on the 1st January. She had had no previous experience of working in the Health Service,

279

but having graduated from St. Hugh's College, Oxford in 1979, she soon found herself working with B.P. in their London office. Some twelve years later, still with B.P., she was selected to take part in their Senior Managers' Development Programme, and there acquired her managerial skills. She had married a doctor, who had recently been appointed Consultant Neuro-Radiologist at Atkinson Morley's Hospital in Wimbledon. With this medical connection and her own interest in management, it was hardly surprising that the recently created vocation of Hospital Management attracted her. Finding that the Tunbridge Wells Health Authority was advertising the job of Unit General Manager at the Queen Victoria Hospital, she applied for it and was appointed.

Mrs. Clifton's first task on arrival at the Hospital was to try and lift the morale of the staff. They had been living under the threat of closure for very nearly 30 years, and nobody can be expected to work happily under these conditions. Morale round about this time was at an all-time low, not only in the Hospital but with the outside staff, the public, and all who had its wellbeing in their thoughts; and it was through no fault of hers that there was to be a further threat of closure in the coming months. It came in the form of a recommendation contained in the Report of the Plastic Surgery and Burns Services Review Group, published on the 23rd June, and was as follows:—

"Serious consideration be given to relocating services from Queen Victoria Hospital East Grinstead to two Acute Hospital sites in the South East which would improve the accessibility of services for the population of Kent and Sussex".

Needless to say there was tremendous public reaction against this news; the local Town Council led a local campaign to resist it and the League of Friends organised considerable resistance in the shape of a special letter from its Chairman Mr. John Brown to all members asking them to write immediately to the Secretary of State for Health objecting strongly to the Review Group's proposal. Apparently this proposal was part of a shake-up of London's health services and the final decision on the recommendation was to be made by Mrs. Bottomley. There was a Public Meeting in the Town to which nearly 400 members of the public came, which was both positive and constructive and reflected well on those present, particularly on Mrs. Clifton herself and her senior hospital colleagues who gave a polished presentation and thorough answers to many questions asked of them. Mrs. Clifton said "The Queen Victoria Hospital is not a small District Hospital, it is a mixture of Regional Speciality Units and a well respected Community Hospital. It is something quite unusual in the National Health Service and it works well".

The East Grinstead Observer joined in the fray by having copies of a petition at various points in the Town and begged all its readers to sign the petition objecting to the possible closure of the Hospital. Letters of objection came in from all sorts of places, and it is understood there was a letter from Clarence House from where our Patron, Queen Elizabeth the Queen Mother, requested information on any closure proposals; letters of protest also came from all across the country to Mrs. Bottomley. No less than 200 members of the League of Friends wrote individual letters, including Lady McIndoe who wrote personally to Mrs. Bottomley and a copy of her letter was published in The Observer. Dame Simone Prendergast also spoke out against this threat and some 28,000 people signed The Observer's petition against it. In due course the petition was presented to No. 10 Downing Street by Lady McIndoe and Dame Simone Prendergast and others; questions were also asked in the House of Commons, as our M.P. Mr. Timothy Renton tried to find out from the Ministry how much truth there was in the rumour, and a delegation consisting of Mr. Renton, the Mayor of the Town Mr. David Clark, and also the Town Clerk, had a meeting with the Junior Health Minister, Mr. Tom Sackville, to discuss the future, so there was in fact huge public support against closure. The result of this was that the Ministry, in an official communication to Mrs. Clifton in August, said "The Burns Unit at the Queen Victoria Hospital provides a first class service to its patients, and Ministers are aware of the excellent results it obtains. No suggestion has been made that its very special services should be discontinued; the Plastic Burns Review Team has merely suggested that consideration be given to relocating these services". So this appeared to be the end of the matter, but it had produced quite a stir within a large area while it lasted.

Early in January 1993 Lady McIndoe was Guest of Honour at

a ceremony to mark the start of work on the new Burns Unit, and she personally turned the first spadeful of earth on the site where it was to be built; this was quite an occasion for her, she pointed out in her speech, for of course she was still very much associated with the Hospital both through the Guinea Pigs, the League of Friends, and the Research Trust. Also during January the League of Friends elected its Secretary John Myson for a further three year term as constituency member for East Sussex of the National Association of Leagues of Friends. And, again in January, there was a report of a special lecture being given at Oxford by Professor Burden, a Fellow in English at the University, to commemorate the 50th anniversary of Richard Hillary's death. It will be remembered that he wrote the book 'The Last Enemy', and the Trust which had been formed by his family to encourage creative and imaginative writing had been taken over by the University. Professor Burden talking about Hillary's connection with Oxford said, "Although 'The Last Enemy' is now 50 years away, I would still say that that book is one of the most moving and influential works that I have ever read". In February Dr. Barbara Turk joined the Forest Row general practice and at the same time was elected to the Hospital's General Practitioner staff. In February Mr. Tom Casey, our Ophthalmologist and Corneo Plastic Surgery Specialist died after a short illness; he had worked up to the end of December and this was a very big blow to the Eye Department. He had been appointed to the Hospital in August 1967 and had been a member of the Research Unit Committee. Towards the end of March there was a further piece of bad news in that the Radio Queen Vic team suffered a surfeit of operational problems, which resulted in their activities being considerably curtailed for a while.

Mrs. Clifton's next and very important task in 1993 was to supervise the second application for Trust Status, which had to be sent in during May, so during the first few months of her appointment there was a lot of hard work to be done before such an application could properly be made. Amongst other things a very competent glossy brochure of nearly 60 pages was produced and widely distributed, giving an account of the Hospital down to the smallest detail, and very well printed on expensive paper and with many coloured photographs; altogether it was a most impressive document. It started off by saying "The proposal, and the details set out in this document, will be considered for approval by the Secretary of State for Health after a three month consultation period with local people and interested organisations. The South East Thames Regional Health Authority is carrying out this consultation and would welcome your views, which will be forwarded to the Secretary of State for Health to assist her in making her decision", and it went on to give names and addresses to which people could address their personal views. If this application was successful it would mean that our Hospital would take over responsibility for administering its own services in April 1994. In May 1993 Dr. Bryan Christopher retired from being Chairman of the Medical Council, and was succeeded in this post by Dr. Alan Del Mar, Senior Partner in the Forest Row practice.

In June the Chief Guinea Pig Tom Gleave died aged 84. He had been Chief Guinea Pig for over 30 years and the Club felt his death very deeply. Also in June the National Association of Hospital Leagues of Friends held a most successful Regional meeting at the Copthorne Hotel which was attended by our representative Mr. Myson, and over 100 delegates from the South East of England. There was another interesting occurrence at this point, in that a team from the Hospital consisting of Plastic Surgeon Roger Smith, and Anaesthetist Dr. Keith Judkins, and Theatre Sister Orchard, went to Russia, where they had been asked by the British Embassy to help treat the victims of a very nasty road accident in which a petrol tanker had exploded; our Burns Unit being recognised as one of the best in the world was called upon to treat the victims.

In August the League of Friends Committee decided to change its name from being 'The Committee' to being 'The Committee of Trustees'; this was to reflect the impact of the revised Charity Law. In his speech at its Annual General Meeting the League's Chairman, Mr. J. H. Brown, drew attention to the fact that during the previous twelve months the League had subscribed £33,000 to the Hospital, and he said they were committed to a further £45,000 to enhance security within the Hospital and its surroundings. This work was now in progress and amongst other things meant exterior lighting in corridors, car parks, and in the vicinity of the League's shop. "Now we must look to the future" he said "it is an unfortunate fact that several Hospital Leagues of Friends have closed down over the last few years as they could not attract sufficient support. We are fortunate that our Hospital has always been the core centre of the Town, and I'm sure that the League will continue to enjoy strong support in the future as it has done in the past". Its membership at this time was around 1,200, fairly constant over the years. The League had recently taken under its wing the long established McIndoe Supporters Burns Group, together with a new group being formed to give support to patients who had undergone major plastic surgery at the Hospital. Their Secretary John Myson, said "It means taking on a new role of befriending former patients in keeping with the new trend of shorter stays in hospital and care in the community". The Chairman of the Unit Management Committee thanked the League for its magnificent donations to the Hospital, and said "It is quite clear now that the Queen Victoria really does have a good future".

On October 1st one of the most popular members of the staff, Cyril Jones, Senior Theatre Orderly in the American Wing Theatre, died. He had first come to the Hospital in the early days of the War; he was aged 72. He had been awarded the Queens Jubilee Medal in 1977, and was only the third non-professional person to receive the Pask award of the Association of Anaesthetists of Great Britain and Ireland; throughout his life here he had helped to organise many fund raising events for the Hospital, and been made President of the East Grinstead Snooker League. He had worked personally with Sir Archibald McIndoe, and it was a very great loss to us all when he died. Plastic Surgeon Mr. Bill Norris retired on October 1st, and was replaced by Mr. H. R. Belcher.

At last in the middle of October 1993, came the welcome news that the Hospital had been granted Independent Trust Status. Mrs. Clifton wrote a letter to the local press expressing gratitude from herself and everybody at the Hospital for the overwhelming level of support they had been given by the people of East Grinstead and the Town Council. She thought the magnitude of this support had been a considerable surprise to the Authorities and the National Health Service, and had had a significant influence in our obtaining Trust Status. "Now that this exists" she said "we must go on to take advantage of the opportunity to build a locally managed hospital which is very responsive to the needs of its patients, and in this way I am sure we will be able clearly to demonstrate that all the services we provide here are valuable and should remain here". At a December meeting of the League of Friends Mr. Brown the Chairman mentioned again the granting of Trust Status which he thought was a sign of the Minister's and the Regional Health Authority's confidence in the Hospital's future, but he added that this future could only be secured by providing services of the right quality at the right price; fortunately there was every sign that the Hospital could secure its future in this way. Also in December the League received a very generous donation of £25,000 from Mr. Jeff Frederik, Chairman and owner of a local business, which was to be put towards new equipment for the Hospital; and there was a mention also by the General Manager that the League in the last ten years had given over £500,000 to the Hospital.

The first few months of 1994 were taken up with the introduction of the Trust Status on the 1st April. Trust Status for hospitals was a comparatively new idea and there was little experience to draw upon; every hospital had its own problems, and the Queen Victoria, owing to its unusual constitution, probably had more than most, so there was a tremendous amount of planning to be done between October and April. Individual contracts with local Health Authorities and with local General Practitioner practices had to negotiated and new jobs allocated, and all this in addition to keeping the Hospital running smoothly meanwhile. It had all proved to be a very big task indeed; that it has been successful is a very big tribute to all those who were involved in getting it off the ground.

Meanwhile, however, a few other things were happening. Firstly, in the middle of January there had been another attempt by the South East Thames Region to sell the vacant land at the back of the Hospital for building. The Planning Application, this time for only 24 houses instead of the 44 they had asked for the previous time, was also rejected by the local Town Council.

On March 25th the Museum, the idea for which had first come from Consultant Surgeon Mr. John Bennett sixteen years previously, finally came to fruition. The opening ceremony was well attended by Consultants and former patients and the actual opening was done by John Bennett himself; in his speech he said

"This is a memory of past work which will take us into the future; it is our aim to build on the past, and we have to know upon what we are building". Funds for the Museum, which is situated on the first floor of the American Wing, had been raised by the Guinea Pig Club and League of Friends, and had been augmented by a large donation given in memory of Cyril Jones by his widow Vi, who had also worked for many years in the American Wing Theatre. The room is dominated by a large and very excellent portrait of Sir Archibald McIndoe and also contains instruments, photographs, paintings, etc., including the original Case Book of Dr. Rogers the Hospital's founder; the old instruments illustrate the various changes in surgical technology which have taken place over the past hundred years. Mr. Bennett had been largely helped in getting it together by Mr. Bob Marchant, now Senior Surgical Technician in the American Theatre in which he has worked for 38 years, and who is now the longest working member of the staff at the Hospital. Mr. Bennett himself, who had been Senior Plastic Surgeon for some years, retired on the 1st April, 1994, as also did Dr. Evans who retired from the Practitioner side of the Hospital, having been in practice at Hartfield for some 30 years or so, and was succeeded by Dr. P. Furneaux. Mr. Bennett, in addition to his appointment here, had also been Consultant Plastic Surgeon to Kings College Hospital, where he was elected Sub-Dean of their Medical School. He was replaced as Consultant Surgeon by Mr. J. N. Parkhouse.

On April 1st, 1994 the Queen Victoria Hospital became an Independent Trust, and a new Trust Board was formed, with Mr. Jeffery Park as its chairman. In May the new Burns Unit became functional; it had been financed entirely by the National Health Service as a special building project, and it is attached both to the American Wing Theatre and to the Children's Ward.

On July 1st Lady McIndoe was awarded an O.B.E. in the Birthday Honours. In addition to her long-standing commitments to the Queen Victoria Hospital, she had also worked for years for the Marsden Hospital, through its League of Friends, and had been associated with the R.A.F. Benevolent Fund since as long ago as 1960, so this honour was richly deserved. Dr. H. Patel retired from the Anaesthetic Department in July, he had been here since 1975, so had served the Hospital for nearly twenty years. And in October comes the announcement of the appointment as new Director of Nursing, of Mr. David Monkman, who had previously been Director of Nursing at Bradford.

Towards the end of the year came news of a new procedure whereby local people would be invited twice a year to meet the Executives and Directors so that they could ask questions and put forward their own views. The first of these meetings took place on November 24th, 1994. One of the views expressed at this meeting was that the Hospital was being made rather top heavy by having too many administrators, and Mr. Park was able to announce that the number of administrative staff had been reduced by two in the last six months since Trust Status had been granted. While on this subject it is worth remembering that in 1963 Matron Duncombe had an Assistant Matron plus two administrative Sisters; Mr. Johns the Secretary had an Assistant Finance Officer, and the Almoner Miss Jardine had two part-time Assistants, making eight people in the administration category, and they were only responsible for part of the administration of the Hospital. Large areas such as Catering, Personnel and Maintenance were administered directly by Tunbridge Wells Health Authority, say another seven to eight individuals, making fifteen to sixteen in all. Nowadays all these important matters are dealt with under one roof. Obviously under modern conditions there are more administrative personnel per patient than there used to be, but not as many more as is sometimes thought.

There was a letter in The Courier in November 1994 from a present Consultant Maxillo Facial Surgeon saying, "Since I first came to the Queen Victoria Hospital in 1960, it has never been better managed, and the present Trust Board had much of the flavour and incentives of the former House Committee". Mrs. Clifton added her own contribution to this discussion at the meeting by saying that of course there had been a number of changes since Trust Status was granted and there was bound to be a lot of uncertainty throughout the whole community about what is happening, but she also added that "Statistics prove that the Hospital's future is secure". At the same meeting Dr. Bryan Christopher representing the local General Practitioners said "We have so much support from the community, for which we are deeply grateful". It was in the last few months of 1994 that the decision was made on economic grounds, and as an experiment, to establish mixed wards, for male and female patients, and simultaneously to close Dewar Ward; the reason for this together with other closures on the Canadian and American side of the Hospital have already been explained. Dr. Elizabeth Robinson retired from the G.P. staff at the end of the year, and was replaced by Dr. Ann Berkovitch.

At the end of March 1995 Dr. Tim Taylor from Lingfield retired from the General Practitioner staff; he had been on it since 1966, and was replaced by Dr. James Gardner, both in the practice and on the Hospital staff. On the 30th May the League of Friends held its Annual General Meeting and Chairman Mr. John Brown's report is interesting; "All the functions which were until now the responsibility of the Tunbridge Wells Health Authority are now handled 'in house' which had understandably meant an increase in local management. I can assure you that our excellent specialist services will be preserved and enhanced, and much thought has been given to that part of the Hospital which serves the Town's needs and I'm sure results will soon be seen". He mentioned that after twenty years as a Trustee and many of them as Treasurer, Mr. Derek Dyer had left the Committee and his sound advice would be greatly missed; he mentioned also that Mr. John Beardall, Mrs. Maureen Hull, Mr. Derek Pocock, and Mr. Brian Rugg, had been co-opted on to the Committee of Trustees. He then went on to say that "On the 30th May I shall be relinquishing the Chair and I would like to take this opportunity of thanking all the many volunteers who have helped us throughout my Chairmanship as also of course every member of the staff for their friendship and help". At the meeting, Mr. D. W. Pocock was elected to take his place as
Chairman, with
Mrs. Ann Standen as Vice-Chairman,
Mr. B. Rugg as Treasurer, and
Mr. Myson was re-elected as Secretary,
Mrs. Boyd as Registrar, and
Miss Wootton as Liaison Officer;
the following were elected to the Committee of Trustees:—

| | |
|---|---|
| Mr. J. L. Beardall | Mrs. J. A. Evans |
| Mrs. A. Goldsmith | Mrs. M. Hull |
| Mrs. Y. Kennard | Mr. K. Knapp |
| Mr. R. B. Marchant | Mrs. A. Myson |
| Mrs. S. Ramble | |

On the 6th July, the Peanut Ward celebrated the 40th anniversary of its opening in 1955 by Her Majesty Queen Elizabeth the Queen Mother, with a garden and teaparty, which was well attended. In July also the local press reported that the Hospital had received top markings in N.H.S. performance tables recently issued. It had received fourteen Five Star ratings in matters such as waiting lists, assessing casualty patients, and other items.

But the most important event that has so far taken place in 1995 was that on February 23rd the new Burns Unit was officially opened by the Duke of Edinburgh. Arriving at 10.20 a.m. His Royal Highness was accompanied by the Vice Lord Lieutenant of West Sussex and Mr. Jim Sandeman Allen of the Guinea Pig Club. It should be remembered that Prince Philip is the current President of the Club. The Vice Lord Lieutenant presented the welcoming party consisting of amongst others Mr. Jeffery Park, Chairman of the Board of Management, and Mrs. Lorraine Clifton, our Chief Executive, and representatives of the Burns Centre and Plastic Unit. His Royal Highness was shown round the Centre by senior medical and nursing staff. The Unit has eight beds and its own Operating Theatre and is expected to admit around 300 patients a year, of whom 50 per cent will be children. Following his visit to the Burns Centre, Prince Philip visited the display prepared by the McIndoe Burns Support Group, meeting Yvonne Kennard, Audrey Allen, and Anita Harrison. This Group had been formed in 1983 and provides valuable support to patients throughout the Hospital. He next visited the new Museum and was guided round it by Mr. Bob Marchant the Curator; he also met a number of Guinea Pig Club members together with Mr. John Brown, Chairman of the League of Friends. He then proceeded to the Lecture Theatre adjoining the Museum where representatives of the commissioning Health Authorities and medical staff were presented. He talked individually to and shook hands with some 30 people here and wanted to know all about the new Trust Status and how it was affecting us. He then signed the Visitors Book and departed at midday. Altogether it was a most successful and popular visit, with an almost informal atmosphere. Following his departure quite a lot of spectators and visitors toured the Museum. During the afternoon the Burns Ward held open house for visitors and staff.

Speaking afterwards the Hospital's Chairman, Mr. Jeffery Park, said "The official opening marks an important stage in the development of the Hospital. The combination of superb facilities and the appointment of Mr. Parkhouse as Director of the Centre ensures that we will remain one of the leading providers of specialist treatment for burns patients in the country, serving over 3,500,000 people in Kent, Sussex, and part of London. It also strengthens our future as an essential local hospital for 60,000 East Grinstead residents". A few days after, the Duke of Edinburgh wrote to Mr. Sandeman Allen saying how much he had enjoyed his visit to the Hospital; and he added that "he had thought its atmosphere was absolutely first class where both staff and patients were concerned and he very much enjoyed the chance to see round it himself". The new Unit had been largely designed by a team, led by Mr. Ron Holmes, Chief Engineer at Tunbridge Wells, and including two of the Plastic Surgeons, Mr. John Bennett and Mr. Roger Smith, together with our Anaesthetist at that time Dr. Judkins, who has since left, all of whom had of course specialist knowledge of the techniques which were required to make it an especially modern addition to the Hospital.

This would seem to be the appropriate point at which to end this updated edition of the Hospital's history. It had started in 1963 with the Royal occasion of the Queen Mother laying the foundation stone of the original Burns Unit, which, when it was opened by Princess Marina in 1965, had all the most modern facilities current at that time in the treatment of burns. That was however over 30 years ago, and burns treatment, like all medicine and surgery, has undergone many technological advances during this time. Some ten years ago, about 1985, there was a report that the Unit's roof was leaking, and only temporary repair work, not fundamental refurbishment, was done. On more than one occasion it had become infected and had to be closed during disinfection. Over the next few years it became apparent that it should be replaced by a more modern unit, and in 1993 building began. There was this time no generous donor to finance it, but fortunately the Ministry of Health was sufficiently concerned to pay for it. This in itself is of some significance, as showing one of the big changes that has come over the Hospital scene during these years.

The first edition of this book ended by mentioning as far as possible everybody currently working in and for the Hospital. Of them all, five are still doing so today and deserve special mention. Ann Standen first came to the Hospital as a nurse in 1941, and has by far the longest record, 54 years, of service to the Hospital. She married a leading Guinea Pig and quickly became involved in the Club's affairs, making her own special mark by making herself responsible for its annual September meetings, and still does this in 1995. She also became involved with the League of Friends as a tireless worker in its affairs, and is at present its Vice-Chairman. Connie became Lady McIndoe in 1954, and has worked indefatigably for the Hospital ever since, and is still doing so, 41 years later. Her special interests are the Guinea Pigs, the Research Laboratory and the League of Friends. Peter Williams was elected to the House Committee in 1955, and became its Chairman in 1967. Since Mrs. Clemetson's death he has looked after the Peanut Club, and still continues to do so. Bob Marchant, currently Senior Surgical Technician in the American Wing Theatre, joined the staff in 1957, and is in fact the only remaining staff member who worked with Sir Archibald McIndoe. He is Curator of the recently opened Museum, and has given many years service to the League of Friends and the Guinea Pigs. And Liz Hodgson was one of Rosemary Wootton's three Assistant Physiotherapists, having joined the staff early in 1963; since Rosemary's retirement in 1989, she has been Senior Physiotherapist in charge. Altogether these five have given 205 years of active service to the Hospital.

The Queen Victoria Hospital today is an Independent Trust and is administered by a Trust Board, the Chairman of which is Mr. Jeffrey Park. Mr. Park, aged 52 and a university graduate with multiple business interests, was appointed by the Secretary of State for Health in October 1993 soon after we were granted Independent Status; he played a big part in setting-up the Trust, and, when it officially came into being on April 1st, 1994 became its Chairman. At the same time the old Management Board, chaired by Mr. J. Lowe the District General Manager, and with twelve members, disappeared, and the only two members of the old Board to be transferred to the new Trust Board were Mrs. Lorraine Clifton, our Chief Executive since January 1993, and Dr. C. J. Barham, then and now our Senior Anaesthetist. The five Executive Directors are now Mrs. Lorraine Clifton, Mr. Peter Banks, who took Dr. Barham's place on May 1st, 1995, Mr. David Monkman, Director of Nursing who also acts as Deputy Chief Executive and takes Mrs. Clifton's place when she is not available, Mr. Mike Schofield our Director of Finance, and Mr. Kyn Aizlewood, Director of Business Development. The five Non-Executive Directors, appointed by the Secretary of State are Mr. Andrew de Candole, Mrs. Teri Hawksworth, Mrs. Veronica Horman, Mr. Chris Russell, and Mr. Mike Stubbs; as has been said earlier they have 'much of the flavour and incentives of the old House Committee'. They have all, in other words, successfully made their mark in some way in the local community. Mrs. Horman has been Mayor of East Grinstead and has served on the Mid-Sussex District Council; she is currently a J.P. and Chairman of the South East Advisory Committee on Education. Mr. Russell is Senior Partner in a local firm of Solicitors, as was Mr. Peter Williams in the old days. Mrs. Hawksworth is Director of Human Resources for I.C.C. Information Group, Mr. de Candole manages Kennet Properties and is Managing Director of the Pathfinder Group of Companies, and Mr. Stubbs is a Management Consultant with multiple interests.

In addition to the Trust Board, there is the Operational Management Group, representing all branches of the Hospital employees and administration, corresponding largely to the old Joint Staff Consultative Committee. There is also the Medical Council, the present Chairman of which is Dr. Alan Del Mar, and the General Practitioners Committee which used to meet in their own surgeries, now meets at the Hospital. And there is the Working Assembly for Local and Regional Unit Survival, known familiarly as the 'Walrus Committee'. Each of these bodies can bring up with the Management any subject that they think should be discussed.

The General Practitioners on the staff, in order of their appointment, are:—

| | |
|---|---|
| Dr. P. Steel | Dr. B. W. Christopher |
| Dr. A. R. Del Mar | Dr. G. J. D. Moore |
| Dr. A. J. Robertson | Dr. D. R. Bainbridge |
| Dr. R. J. R. Dunstan | Dr. D. A. Martin |
| Dr. P. C. Harborow | Dr. H. W. Aitken |

| | |
|---|---|
| Dr. N. J. Clemens | Dr. J. J. Vevers |
| Dr. A. R. Enskat | Dr. Lesley Croucher |
| Dr. A. Mackenzie | Dr. D. G. Powell |
| Dr. Kathryn Brooks | Dr. S. A. Miller |
| Dr. Mary E. Northen | Dr. A. Clifford |
| Dr. A. Fulford-Smith | Dr. P. Cliffe |
| Dr. S. Bellamy | Dr. J. Clarke |
| Dr. Veronique Foulger | Dr. J. D. Hill |
| Dr. Barbara K. Turk | Dr. D. Jefferies |
| Dr. P. Furneaux | Dr. Ann P. Berkovitch |
| Dr. J. Gardner | |

31 of them as against 22 in 1963, when they were last listed, reflecting merely the increase in local population during this period.

The Consultant Plastic Surgeons, in order of their appointment, are:—

| | |
|---|---|
| Mr. N. S. B. Tanner | Mr. R. W. Smith |
| Mr. K. W. Cullen | Mr. J. G. Boorman |
| Mr. H. R. Belcher | Mr. N. Parkhouse |
| Mr. P. Arnstein | |

and the Consultant Maxillo-Facial Surgeons:—

| | |
|---|---|
| Mr. P. Banks | Mr. K. P. T. Lavery |
| Mr. A. E. Brown | Mr. P. P. Ward Booth |

with Mr. O. R. Thom and Miss L. Winchester as Orthodontic Consultants. Mr. S. Daya is the Corneo-Plastic Consultant (assisted by Mr. W. K. C. Hoe).

They have the following mainstream Consultants to advise them:—

| | |
|---|---|
| *General Surgeons:* | Mr. J. C. Bull |
| | Mr. B. T. Jackson |
| *General Physicians:* | Dr. D. E. Jewitt |
| | Dr. W. Shattles |
| *Chest Physician:* | Dr. R. A. Banks |
| *Geriatric Physician:* | Dr. A. Martin |
| *Gynaecological Surgeons:* | Mr. F. G. Lawton |
| | Mr. B. McKenzie-Gray |
| *Orthopaedic Surgeons:* | Mr. D. A. Reynolds |
| | Mr. E. J. Parnell |
| *E.N.T. Surgeons:* | Mr. R. J. Sergeant |
| | Miss C. Milton |

| | |
|---|---|
| *Urological Surgeon:* | Mr. M. G. Royle |
| *Paediatric Physician:* | Dr. K. Greenaway |
| *Dermatological Physician:* | Dr. A. MacDonald |

And the so-called 'Supporting Services' which in fact are the very heart of the Hospital; the Anaesthetic Department is one of the busiest and most important in the whole Hospital, and has the following Consultants:—

| | |
|---|---|
| Dr. C. J. Barham | Dr. S. J. Squires |
| Dr. J. M. Brown | Dr. P. J. Venn |
| Dr. P. Jones | |

plus Hospital Practitioner Dr. A. J. Robertson and three Registrars. The X-ray Department is presided over by Dr. N. B. Bowley, who was appointed in 1982; the Department has been greatly enlarged since 1963 and now has three Radiology Theatres, and facilities for a visiting Radiotherapy Consultant Dr. D. M. Barrett. The Pathology Department now has the following specialist Consultants:—

| | |
|---|---|
| Dr. J. Allen | Histopathology |
| Dr. E. Baylis | Chemical Pathology |
| Dr. D. Gillett | Haematology |
| Dr. D. Gladstone | Microbiology |
| Dr. G. Martin | Histopathology |
| Dr. G. Russell | Histopathology |
| Dr. C. G. Taylor | Haematology |

The Physiotherapy Department, led by Miss Elizabeth Hodgson, now has six Assistants and is of course very busy in the Day Hospital. The Occupational Therapist is Miss Sarah Mee, and the Speech Therapist is Denise Dive. All of these Supporting Services, support and serve both the Plastic Unit and the General Practitioners with equal success.

Of the above medical and dental staff, the only ones to have survived from the 1978 list are Orthopaedic Surgeon Mr. D. A. Reynolds, Maxillo-Facial (Dental) Surgeon Mr. Peter Banks, and Anaesthetist Dr. J. M. Brown.

But the best news of all is that during the summer of 1995 the Board has issued a brochure entitled 'The Changing Face of the Queen Victoria Hospital National Health Service Trust—a Strategy for the next Five Years'. It opens by saying that "The Queen Victoria Hospital is a unique hospital combining local hospital services for the community of East Grinstead with the work of a highly specialised regional centre offering care to patients living throughout the South East of England. Success has come and will continue to come through the enthusiasm and skills of our staff. After a period of uncertainty we are rebuilding the Q.V.H. to provide a quality of services unmatched within the region. Through partnership between management and clinicians the Trust has secured financial stability for the Hospital. A largely new team of Consultants is reaffirming the clinical reputation of the Hospital. By effectively involving clinicians in management, we seek to harness innovation in a partnership which will take the Q.V.H., as a market leader, into the next century. In setting our stall for the future we have defined our mission, which is as follows: -- to provide the highest quality service to both our regional speciality and to general hospital patients and to strive continually to improve both the scope and the effectiveness of our services". The brochure then goes on to explain various ways in which they propose to improve the service, and mentioning particularly that they plan to build a new Day Surgery Theatre for plastic day surgery patients with its own recovery room, and one of our main buildings is to be opened as an overnight stay ward for patients who are unable to return home the same day but will be expected to do so the next. This building will be adjacent to the main American Wing Theatre suite, and will of course be a major capital investment of the Trust itself. It is scheduled to be opened in January 1996.

Bearing in mind the constant anxieties of the last 30 years, it would be foolish to make any specific predictions as to the future of the Queen Victoria Hospital. In common with most other hospitals in the National Health Service, we have recently undergone many changes, both in our constitution and in our staffing arrangements, so let us hope there may now be a period of constancy in order to allow us to adjust ourselves and achieve some degree of stability. But what can be said is that the Queen Victoria Hospital is at the present time an efficiently managed and thoroughly modernised Hospital, and that it should be able with reasonable confidence to look forward to an assured and successful future.

# Index

Madden, Admiral Sir Charles, 63, 74
Maggs, Dr. Ronald, 166, 206
Mann, Mr. Jackie, 275, 279
Maplesden, Mr. F. C., 121
Mappin, Major and Mrs., 90, 94, 97
Marchant, Mr. Bob, 257, 286, 288, 289, 291
Margary, Major, 28
Marks Fellowships, 131, 220, 229-30
Marks, Lord, 131, 191, 220
Marks & Spencer Charitable Trust, 241
Marshall, Dr. W. H., 48, 52, 70, 169, 172, 184, 188
Martin, Dr. A., 293
Martin, Dr. D. A., 232, 292
Martin, Dr. G., 294
Martin, Miss I. G. E., 158
Maternity Beds, 111, 119, 139, 169, 170, 174
Maternity Patient, 76
Matron, Appointment of, 27, 35, 37-8, 46, 75, 154, 180, 193
Matron, Appointment of Assistant, 88, 158
Matthews, Mr. H. E., 40, 45
Maxillo-Facial Unit, 86, 90, 96, 247
Maxillonian Club, 97, 100
May, Dr. H. C., 240
Maynard, Mr. Frank, 213
Maynard, Mr. Fred, 173
Mayou, Mr. B. J., 261, 267
Medawar, Professor P. B., 195, 200
Medawar, Sir Peter, 261
Medical Committee, 92, 97-8, 122-3, 125, 132, 154, 161, 180
Medical Council, 180, 185, 197, 232, 274, 292
Medical Research Council, 224, 232
Medical Society, 132
Mee, Miss Sarah, 279, 294
Mellor, Mr. David, 267
Meridian Way, 262
Merrison, Sir Alec, 235
Metric System, introduction of, 198
Meyer, Dr. J. E., 256
Mid-Downs Health Authority, 259, 269, 274
Mid Sussex District Council, 268
Millar, Mr. R. H. J., 95, 113, 183
Miller, Lt.-Gen. Sir Euan, 185, 193, 195, 200, 203
Miller, Mr. E. J., 46, 48, 57
Miller, Dr. S. A., 258, 293
Mills, Miss Naomi, 130
Milton, Miss C., 293
Ministry of Health, 82, 118, 125, 128, 131, 133, 156
Minor, Mr. D. Clark, 103, 126
Mitchell, Mr. J. H., 69, 99, 123, 137, 141-2, 148, 152, 161-2, 175-6, 181, 195, 201, 203-4, 216, 218, 220, 242
Mixed Wards, 287
Moat Road Clinic, 24

Monckton, Lady, 225
Monk, Mrs., 175, 184
Monkman, Mr. David, 286, 287, 292
Monteath, Miss A. T., 180, 184, 193
Moore, Mr. F. T., 108, 132, 141, 161, 192, 208, 231, 234-5
Moore, Dr. G. J. D., 228, 292
Moore, Mr. W. J., 184, 204, 218, 255-6, 259
Morton, Miss, 38
Morton Palmer, Dr. B. C., 76, 87, 121, 155, 206, 225
Mortuary, 170, 187
Motton, Miss Sheila, 147, 185
Moyle, Dr. R. D., 126, 187
Muir, Mr. E. G., 125, 206
Muir, Sir Edward, 230-231
Mullins, Sister Jill, 97, 114, 199, 201
Munn, Mrs., 62, 69, 83, 85, 94, 108
Murray, Mr. W. R., 80, 134, 172
Museum, The, 239, 243, 285, 286, 289
Musgrave, General A. D., 60-1
Musgrave, Mrs., 63
Musgrove, Mr. John B., 137, 206, 240
Myson, Mrs. Anne, 266, 278, 288
Myson, Mr. J. G., 158, 166, 266, 282, 283, 284, 288

Name, Alteration of Hospital's, 106, 227
Napper, Dr. Albert, 13, 14
National Health Service, 50, 110, 124, 135, 140
National Hospital Plan, 217, 226, 237
Nationalisation, 140
Neely, Mr. J. A. C., 256
New Zealand Government, Gift from, 124
Norfolk, Duke of, 216
Northen, Dr. Mary, 260, 293
Norris, Mr. R. W., 263, 284
Nurses' Accommodation, 18, 87, 93, 95, 99, 104, 109, 112-3, 115, 133-4, 139, 162-3
Nurses, Number employed, 27, 37, 44, 72, 76, 156, 186, 204
Nurses' Training School, 156, 165, 168, 204

Oakleigh, 133-4, 142, 146, 165, 169, 173, 194, 203, 213, 234, 242
Observer, East Grinstead, 269, 281
Occupational Therapy Department, 97, 154, 183, 199, 212, 294
Oliver, Mr. John, 187, 203-4
Opening of Children's Ward, 172
Opening of Holtye Road Hospital, 66
Opening of Lansdowne House, 27
Opening of Queen's Road Hospital, 42
Ophthalmic Department, 135, 282
Orchard, Sister, 283
Orcutt, Dr. Roger, 195, 206, 264
Orr-Ewing, Dr. A., 56, 70, 162
Osborne, Mr. H., 61, 70, 87
Osmond-Clarke, Mr. H., 129

Tuffill, Mr. S. G., 155, 206
Tunbridge Wells Health Authority, 216, 236, 246, 258, 260, 263-4, 268, 270, 277, 278, 279
Turk, Dr. Barbara, 282, 293
Turner, Mr. Peter, 249, 253, 254, 255, 263
Turner, Miss M. E., 37, 38
Tuson, Mr. K. W. R., 240, 256
Tyler, Mr. A., 70, 79, 93

Unit General Manager, 255, 257, 258, 260, 271, 279
Unit Management Committee, 261, 265, 270, 276, 284
Ussher, Dr. C W. J., 240, 242, 247

Venn, Dr. P. J., 275-6, 294
Vevers, Dr. J. J., 245, 293
Viall, Mr. John, 69, 86
Vine, Miss E., 180
Visiting Hours, 29, 153, 201
Voss, Mr. Simon, 186-7

Wagg, Mr. Alfred, 89, 94, 100, 109, 110, 124, 128, 141, 176, 179, 193, 225
Wagg, Miss Elsie, 58, 60, 63, 69, 89
Wagg Ward, 261, 262, 263, 269-70
Wagstaff, Mr. E. A., 150, 152, 154, 172, 181, 203
Waldegrave, Mr. William, 279
Walker, Dr. D. G., 89
Walker, Dr. S. L., 45, 52
Walker, Sister, 97, 132
Wallis, Miss Iris, 63, 69, 120, 141, 184, 204
Wallis, Dr. P. E., 26-8, 43, 47, 75
Wallis, Dr. W. E., 47, 70, 169
Walrus Committee, 292
Ward, Mr. Terence G., 121, 141, 152, 155, 195, 204, 208
Ward, Sir Terence, 227, 234, 274, 277-8
Ward-Booth, Mr. R. P., 293
Waring, Dr., 15
Warrenside, 87, 93, 104, 133-4, 150, 185, 213, 242, 262
Waterson, Mrs., 95, 98
Watson, Mr. John, 131, 151, 192-3, 195, 200, 208, 220, 224, 227, 230, 238, 242, 250, 277

Watson, Dr. W. G., 47-8
Webb, Mr. Geoffrey, 111, 121
Webb, Stephen, 267
Weekes, Dr. C. R. H., 165, 185
Welfare Committee, 94, 97, 100, 106, 112-4, 120, 124, 129, 135, 160, 183-4, 189, 190, 193
Werb, Mr. A. W., 209, 222, 237, 258
Westminster Bank, 143
Wheeler, Flt/Lt., 100, 110, 135
Whitfield, Mr. F. B., 35, 43, 53, 57
Whitley-Hughes, Mr. E. P., 46, 61, 69, 85, 96
Whitley-Hughes & Luscombe, Messrs., 70, 79, 143, 170
Whitworth, Mr. A. E., 137, 141, 151-2, 154, 157-8, 160
Wilde, Miss Frankie, 180, 243
Willard, Miss Barbara, 217
Williams, Dr. I. A., 198, 206
Williams, Mr. Peter, 170, 181, 187, 195, 197, 203, 218, 224-5, 275, 291-2
Willmer, Mr. A., 69, 79
Wilson, Dr. H. F., 74, 87, 121, 133
Winchester, Miss, 293
Wintle, Mr. W. C. (Peter), 166
Wisdom, Mr. Norman, 279
Wise, Miss G. M., 147, 172, 189
Wolfson Foundation, 221, 224
Wood, Sister, 166, 213
Woodland, Rev. C. C., 27-8, 32, 42-3, 45, 57
Wootton, Miss Rosemary, 147, 212, 222, 241, 254, 288
Working Party, 180-3, 232
Worlock, Dr. Michael, 163, 206, 256, 273
Wragg, Mr. E. J., 167, 175
Wright-Edwards, Dr. C., 39
Wynter, Dr. Andrew, 13, 16, 18

X-ray Department, 43, 53-4, 56, 68, 73, 75-6, 78, 93, 112, 125, 129, 130, 211, 233, 254, 264, 266

Yates-Bell, Mr. A. J., 155
Youard, Rev. W. W., 45
Young, Sister, 194
Young, Mr. W., 28, 43, 45